Quizlet 사용법

▶ 온라인 학습사이트
Quizlet 바로가기

스마트폰, 태블릿, 컴퓨터에서 재미있고 효과적인 어휘 공부를 할 수 있는 학습 사이트!
Flash Card와 Spell Check, 게임 등의 서비스를 제공하며, 미국에서는 이미 주요 교육 수단으로 자리잡은 학습 시스템

01 Quizlet 사용방법

Step 1. 네이버 QR 인식기 **또는** 별도의 QR 인식기를 **실행시켜 페이지 상단의 QR코드를 인식합니다.**

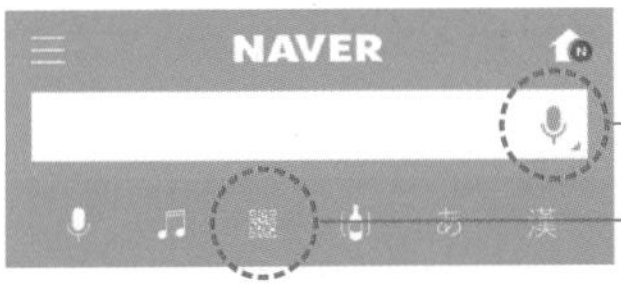

ⓐ 네이버 앱에서 마이크 아이콘 클릭합니다.
ⓑ QR 코드 인식기를 클릭합니다.

Step 2. **원하는 학습 일차를 선택합니다.**

Step 3. 원하는 어휘의 **MP3 음원을 선택하여 듣습니다.**

KB011625

02 Quizlet의 다양한 학습기능

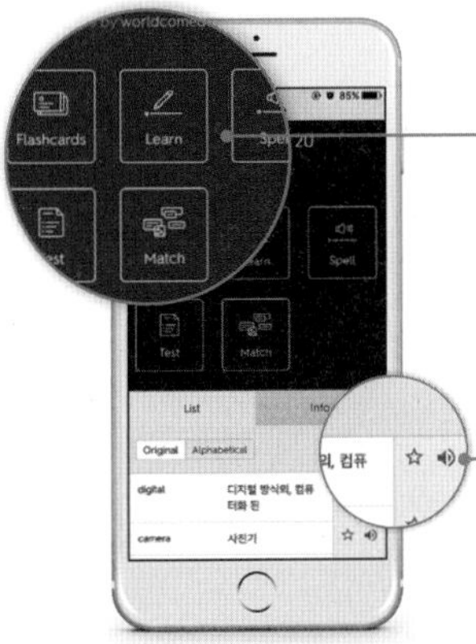

STUDY와 PLAY를 통해 다양한 방식으로 재밌게 학습할 수 있습니다.

- STUDY : Flashcard, Learn, Spell, Test
- PLAY : Match

단어 혹은 스피커 버튼을 누르면 음성을 들을 수 있습니다.

* Google Play에서 Quizlet 어플리케이션 다운로드 및 이용이 가능합니다.

QR 코드 사용법

보다 쉽고 간편하게 접근할 수 있는 학습 방법!
QR코드 인식을 통한 Word Max 6단계 시리즈 음원 바로 듣고 학습하기

01 첫 번째, 네이버 앱을 통해 QR코드 사용하기

Step 1. 네이버 QR 인식기 또는 별도의 QR 인식기를 실행시킵니다.

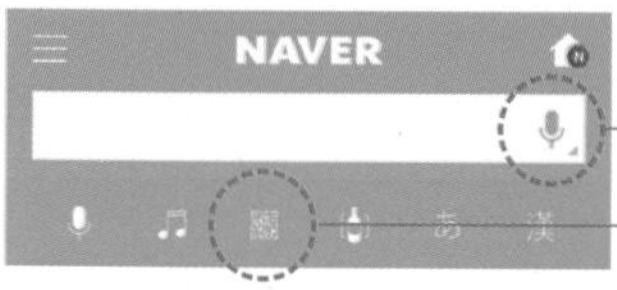

ⓐ 네이버 앱에서 마이크 아이콘 클릭합니다.
ⓑ QR 코드 인식기를 클릭합니다.

Step 2. 내지의 QR 코드를 인식합니다.

Step 3. MP3 음원이 유튜브를 통해 다운로드 없이 이용 가능합니다.

WORD MAX 3 5300

WorldCom Edu

WORD MAX 5300 3

초판	2016년 10월 31일
지은이	김 지 훈, 김 채 원
영문검수	Kenneth Drenen
책임편집	신 은 진
편집팀	월드컴 에듀 편집팀
펴낸이	임 병 업
디자인	임 예 슬, 김 지 현, 차 지 원
펴낸곳	(주)월드컴 에듀
등록	2016년 10월 31일
주소	서울시 강남구 언주로 120, 912호 (도곡동, 인스토피아빌딩)
전화	02)3273-4300 (대표)
팩스	02)3273-4303
홈페이지	www.wcbooks.co.kr
이메일	wc4300@wcbooks.co.kr

WORD MAX 5300 여는 글

언어를 배울 때 어휘 학습은 모든 언어 학습자가 가장 먼저 시작하는 분야이면서 동시에 가장 숙달하기 어려운 분야입니다. 이는 문법이나 읽기, 듣기와는 다른 어휘 학습의 독특한 측면이며 다른 학습 방식이 필요한 이유이기도 합니다. 수능을 비롯한 최근의 영어 시험 경향은 결국 어휘사용능력이 전반적인 문제 해결의 핵심 요소가 되고 있습니다.
WORD MAX 5300은 최신 경향에 맞추어 가장 효율적인 어휘 학습 방식을 제공하고자 합니다.

WORD MAX 5300시리즈는 과학적인 방법으로 최대의 효과를 얻을 수 있도록 어휘를 엄선했습니다.

WORD MAX 5300시리즈는 총 6권의 수준별 구성으로 최신 출제 경향과 엄선된 예문 및 다양하고 풍부한 리뷰 테스트를 통해 어휘 활용 능력을 최대화 할 수 있도록 구성했습니다.
최근 12년의 수능 및 각종 시험 기출 문제와 교과서 자료를 중심으로 자체 데이터베이스를 통해 학습 대상 어휘를 엄선했습니다. 특히 기출 빈도와 출제 예상도를 고려하여 선정한 어휘들은 효율적인 어휘 학습을 도와 줄 것입니다.

단계별로 세분화되고 실용성 있는 어휘 학습 환경을 제공합니다.

Level 1~3은 핵심적인 어휘를 풍부한 예문과 리뷰 테스트를 통해 예비중학 과정부터 중등 내신 대비까지 학생들의 기본적 영어 능력 향상에 도움이 되도록 구성했습니다.
Level 4~6은 최근 12년간의 수학능력시험, 모의고사, 학력평가의 기출문제를 토대로 어휘를 선정하였습니다. 더불어 각 어휘의 출제 맥락을 연구하고 수준별 분류 및 보정과정을 통해 단순 어휘 학습을 넘어 전반적인 영어 활용 능력을 향상 시킬 수 있게 구성했습니다.

다양한 어휘 활용 연습 기회를 제공하여 전반적인 영어 실력의 향상을 목표로 합니다.

WORD MAX 5300시리즈는 일일 테스트를 비롯한 Review Test의 총 8개 섹션의 다양한 테스트를 통해 학습한 어휘를 완전히 이해하고 활용할 수 있도록 했습니다. 쓰임에 따라 다양한 뜻을 가진 어휘들과 이에 대한 실용성 높은 예문들은 영어 사용 능력 향상에 확실한 도움이 될 것입니다.

어휘 학습 방법에 대한 이견은 많지만 어휘 학습 대상 선정의 중요성에 대해서는 연구자와 일선 교육자 모두 공감하고 있습니다. WORD MAX 5300시리즈를 충실히 학습한다면 어휘를 학습하는 재미 뿐만 아니라 영어 전반에서 실력 향상을 성취 할 수 있을 것이라 자부합니다.

WORD MAX 5300시리즈와 함께 어휘 학습에 최고의 결과를 얻을 수 있기를 기원합니다.

- 월드컴 에듀 편집팀 일동

구성 및 활용

1 단계별 30일 구성의 계획적 어휘 학습!

'단어 → 어구 → 예문' 순으로 자연스럽게 확장되는 학습을 통해 어휘력을 향상합니다.

하루 30개
단계별 30일 구성

동사의 3단 변화형과 비교형 제시를 통해
시제별 동사 형태를 연습합니다.

다양한 예문을 통해
표제어를 응용 학습합니다.

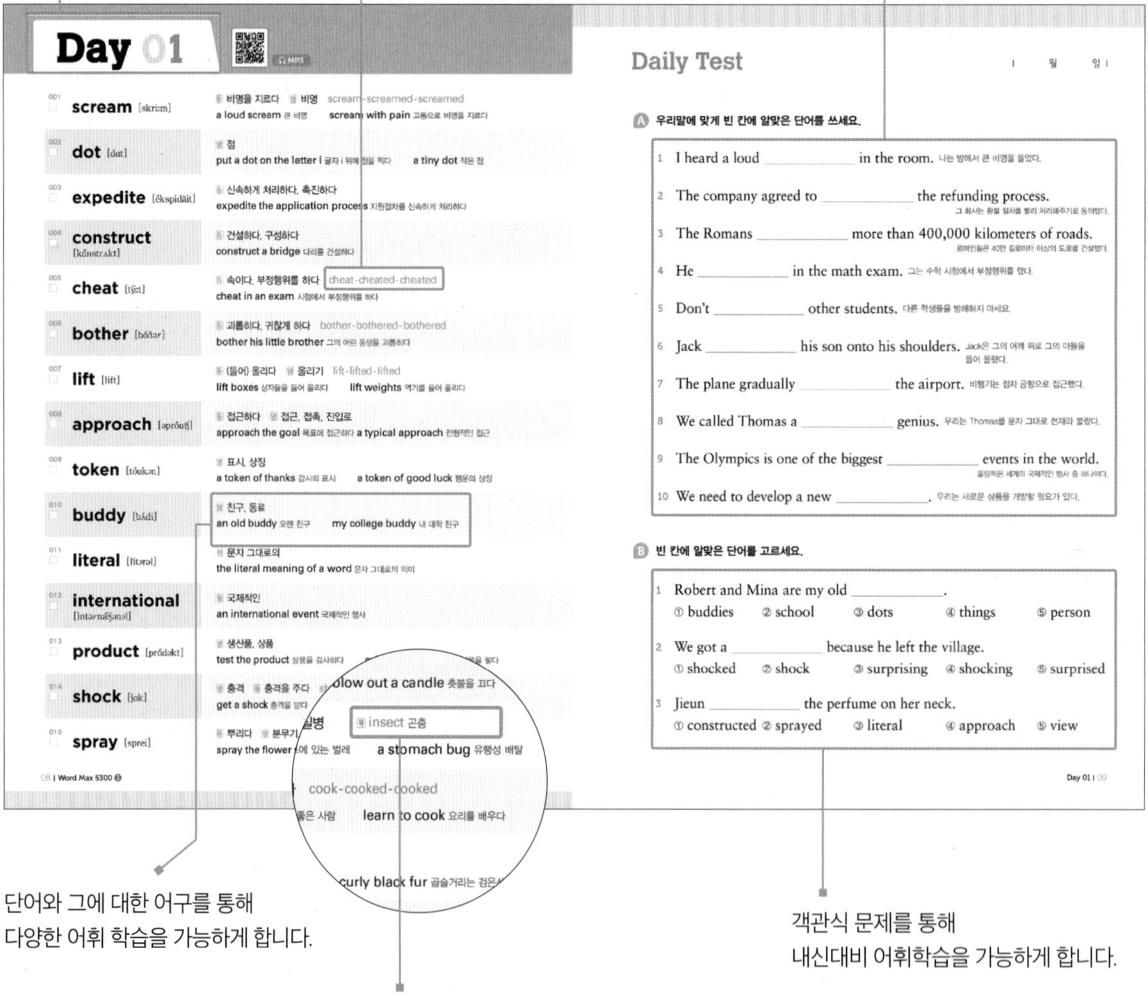
Day 01

001	scream [skriːm]	동 비명을 지르다 명 비명 scream-screamed-screamed a loud scream 큰 비명 scream with pain 고통으로 비명을 지르다
002	dot [dɑt]	명 점 put a dot on the letter i 글자 i 위에 점을 찍다 a tiny dot 작은 점
003	expedite [ékspidàit]	동 신속하게 처리하다, 촉진하다 expedite the application process 지원절차를 신속하게 처리하다
004	construct [kánstrʌkt]	동 건설하다, 구성하다 construct a bridge 다리를 건설하다
005	cheat [tʃiːt]	동 속이다, 부정행위를 하다 cheat-cheated-cheated cheat in an exam 시험에서 부정행위를 하다
006	bother [bɑ́ðər]	동 괴롭히다, 귀찮게 하다 bother-bothered-bothered bother his little brother 그의 어린 동생을 괴롭히다
007	lift [lift]	동 (들어) 올리다 명 올리기 lift-lifted-lifted lift boxes 상자들을 들어 올리다 lift weights 역기를 들어 올리다
008	approach [əpróutʃ]	동 접근하다 명 접근, 접촉, 진입로 approach the goal 목표에 접근하다 a typical approach 전형적인 접근
009	token [tóukən]	명 표시, 상징 a token of thanks 감사의 표시 a token of good luck 행운의 상징
010	buddy [bʌ́di]	명 친구, 동료 an old buddy 오랜 친구 my college buddy 내 대학 친구
011	literal [lítərəl]	형 문자 그대로의 the literal meaning of a word 문자 그대로의 의미
012	international [ìntərnǽʃənəl]	형 국제적인 an international event 국제적인 행사
013	product [prɑ́dəkt]	명 생산품, 상품 test the product 상품을 검사하다
014	shock [ʃɑk]	명 충격 동 충격을 주다 get a shock 충격을 받다
015	spray [sprei]	동 뿌리다 명 분무기 spray the flower

blow out a candle 촛불을 끄다
유 insect 곤충
a stomach bug 유행성 배탈
cook-cooked-cooked
learn to cook 요리를 배우다
curly black fur 곱슬거리는 검은

08 | Word Max 5300 ❸

Daily Test | 월 일 |

A 우리말에 맞게 빈 칸에 알맞은 단어를 쓰세요.

1 I heard a loud ________ in the room. 나는 방에서 큰 비명을 들었다.
2 The company agreed to ________ the refunding process. 그 회사는 환불 절차를 빨리 처리해주기로 동의했다.
3 The Romans ________ more than 400,000 kilometers of roads. 로마인들은 40만 킬로미터 이상의 도로를 건설했다.
4 He ________ in the math exam. 그는 수학 시험에서 부정행위를 했다.
5 Don't ________ other students. 다른 학생들을 방해하지 마세요.
6 Jack ________ his son onto his shoulders. Jack은 그의 어깨 위로 그의 아들을 들어 올렸다.
7 The plane gradually ________ the airport. 비행기는 점차 공항으로 접근했다.
8 We called Thomas a ________ genius. 우리는 Thomas를 문자 그대로 천재라 불렀다.
9 The Olympics is one of the biggest ________ events in the world. 올림픽은 세계의 국제적인 행사 중 하나이다.
10 We need to develop a new ________. 우리는 새로운 상품을 개발할 필요가 있다.

B 빈 칸에 알맞은 단어를 고르세요.

1 Robert and Mina are my old ________.
① buddies ② school ③ dots ④ things ⑤ person
2 We got a ________ because he left the village.
① shocked ② shock ③ surprising ④ shocking ⑤ surprised
3 Jieun ________ the perfume on her neck.
① constructed ② sprayed ③ literal ④ approach ⑤ view

Day 01 | 09

단어와 그에 대한 어구를 통해
다양한 어휘 학습을 가능하게 합니다.

객관식 문제를 통해
내신대비 어휘학습을 가능하게 합니다.

유의어, 반의어, 연관 단어 등의
제시를 통해 어휘력을 확장합니다.

2 Review Test 7가지 유형으로 학습 점검하기!

2일마다 학습한 어휘를 다양한 유형의 문제를 통해 반복 학습합니다.

어구 빈칸 완성
우리말에 따라 어구를 완성합니다

영영 풀이
보기에서 영영 풀이에 해당하는 단어를 찾아 봅니다.

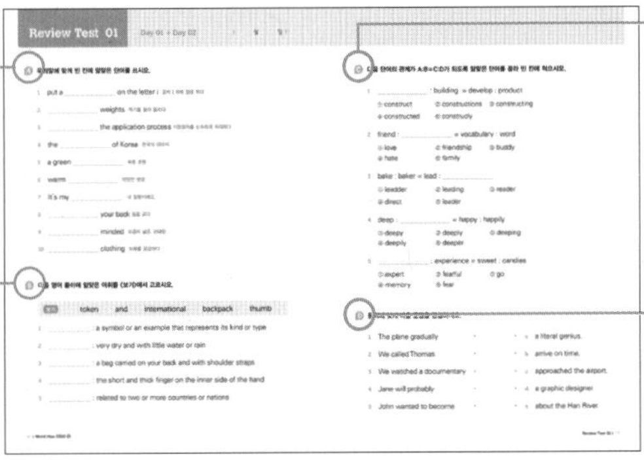

어휘 관계 파악
단어 간의 관계를 파악하여 알맞은 단어를 찾아봅니다.

문장 완성
문맥상 알맞은 문장끼리 연결하여 완성된 문장을 학습합니다.

영영 어휘활용
문장에서 문맥상 알맞은 단어를 선택합니다.

문장 완성
우리말에 따라 보기에서 알맞은 단어를 골라 문장을 완성합니다.

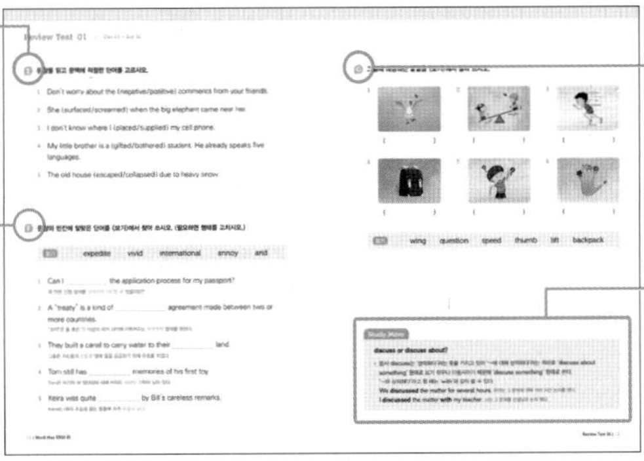

그림-단어 연결
각 그림에 알맞은 단어를 찾아봅니다.

Study More
표제어에 대한 확장된 개념을 제시함으로써 다양한 관점에서 어휘력을 향상 시킬 수 있습니다.

3 Work Book

워크북을 활용하여 단어의 철자와 뜻을 한번 더 반복 학습합니다.

쓰기 노트

일일 테스트

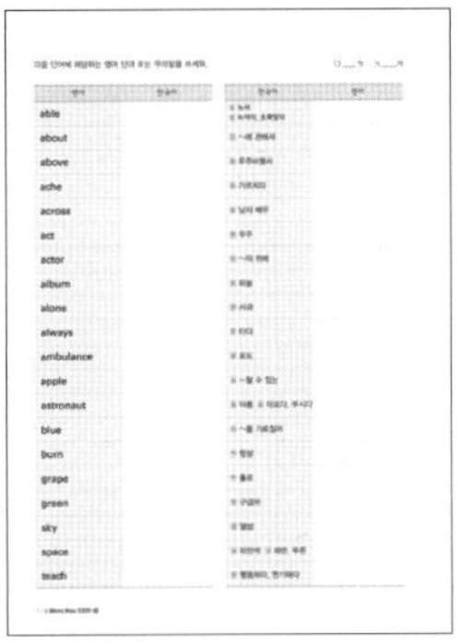

목차

Day 1 08
Day 2 12
Review Test 01 16

Day 3 20
Day 4 24
Review Test 02 28

Day 5 32
Day 6 36
Review Test 03 40

Day 7 44
Day 8 48
Review Test 04 52

Day 9 56
Day 10 60
Review Test 05 64

Day 11 68
Day 12 72
Review Test 06 76

Day 13 80
Day 14 84
Review Test 07 88

Day 15 92
Day 16 96
Review Test 08 100

Day 17 104
Day 18 108
Review Test 09 112

Day 19 116
Day 20 120
Review Test 10 124

Day 21 128
Day 22 132
Review Test 11 136

Day 23 140
Day 24 144
Review Test 12 148

Day 25 152
Day 26 156
Review Test 13 160

Day 27 164
Day 28 168
Review Test 14 172

Day 29 176
Day 30 180
Review Test 15 184

Index 188
Answer Key 195

★ 책 속의 책 Workbook 제공

WORD MAX 3 5300

Day 01

MP3

001 ☐ **scream** [skriːm]
동 비명을 지르다 명 비명 scream-screamed-screamed
a loud scream 큰 비명 scream with pain 고통으로 비명을 지르다

002 ☐ **dot** [dɑt]
명 점
put a dot on the letter i 글자 i 위에 점을 찍다 a tiny dot 작은 점

003 ☐ **expedite** [ékspidàit]
동 신속하게 처리하다, 촉진하다
expedite the application process 지원절차를 신속하게 처리하다

004 ☐ **construct** [kánstrʌkt]
동 건설하다, 구성하다
construct a bridge 다리를 건설하다

005 ☐ **cheat** [tʃiːt]
동 속이다, 부정행위를 하다 cheat-cheated-cheated
cheat in an exam 시험에서 부정행위를 하다

006 ☐ **bother** [báðər]
동 괴롭히다, 귀찮게 하다 bother-bothered-bothered
bother his little brother 그의 어린 동생을 괴롭히다

007 ☐ **lift** [lift]
동 (들어) 올리다 명 올리기 lift-lifted-lifted
lift boxes 상자들을 들어 올리다 lift weights 역기를 들어 올리다

008 ☐ **approach** [əpróutʃ]
동 접근하다 명 접근, 접촉, 진입로
approach the goal 목표에 접근하다 a typical approach 전형적인 접근

009 ☐ **token** [tóukən]
명 표시, 상징
a token of thanks 감사의 표시 a token of good luck 행운의 상징

010 ☐ **buddy** [bʌ́di]
명 친구, 동료
an old buddy 오랜 친구 my college buddy 내 대학 친구

011 ☐ **literal** [lítərəl]
형 문자 그대로의
the literal meaning of a word 문자 그대로의 의미

012 ☐ **international** [ìntərnǽʃənəl]
형 국제적인
an international event 국제적인 행사

013 ☐ **product** [prádəkt]
명 생산품, 상품
test the product 상품을 검사하다 sell a new product 신상품을 팔다

014 ☐ **shock** [ʃɑk]
명 충격 동 충격을 주다 shock-shocked-shocked
get a shock 충격을 받다 a state of shock 충격을 받은 상태

015 ☐ **spray** [sprei]
동 뿌리다 명 분무기, 스프레이 spray-sprayed-sprayed
spray the flower with water 꽃에 물을 뿌리다

Daily Test

| 월 일 |

A 우리말에 맞게 빈 칸에 알맞은 단어를 쓰세요.

1 I heard a loud ______________ in the room. 나는 방에서 큰 비명을 들었다.

2 The company agreed to ______________ the refunding process.
그 회사는 환불 절차를 빨리 처리해주기로 동의했다.

3 The Romans ______________ more than 400,000 kilometers of roads.
로마인들은 40만 킬로미터 이상의 도로를 건설했다.

4 He ______________ in the math exam. 그는 수학 시험에서 부정행위를 했다.

5 Don't ______________ other students. 다른 학생들을 방해하지 마세요.

6 Jack ______________ his son onto his shoulders.
Jack은 그의 어깨 위로 그의 아들을 들어 올렸다.

7 The plane gradually ______________ the airport. 비행기는 점차 공항으로 접근했다.

8 We called Thomas a ______________ genius. 우리는 Thomas를 문자 그대로 천재라 불렀다.

9 The Olympics is one of the biggest ______________ events in the world.
올림픽은 세계의 국제적인 행사 중 하나이다.

10 We need to develop a new ______________. 우리는 새로운 상품을 개발할 필요가 있다.

B 빈 칸에 알맞은 단어를 고르세요.

1 Robert and Mina are my old ______________.
① buddies ② school ③ dots ④ things ⑤ person

2 We got a ______________ because he left the village.
① shocked ② shock ③ surprising ④ shocking ⑤ surprised

3 Jieun ______________ the perfume on her neck.
① constructed ② sprayed ③ literal ④ approach ⑤ view

Day 01

MP3

016 **gifted** [gíftid]
형 재능이 있는 유 talented 재능 있는
a gifted musician 재능 있는 음악가 highly gifted 재능이 아주 뛰어난

017 **sunlight** [sʌ́nlàit]
명 햇빛, 햇살 유 sunshine 햇살
a ray of sunlight 한 줄기 햇살

018 **theme** [θiːm]
명 주제, 테마
the main theme 중심 테마 a theme song 주제가

019 **image** [ímidʒ]
명 이미지, 인상
a visual image 시각 이미지 an image of Korea 한국의 이미지

020 **speed** [spiːd]
명 속도
speed limit 제한 속도 a speed of 70 km/h 시속 70km의 속도

021 **leader** [líːdər]
명 지도자, 대표
become a leader 지도자가 되다 a great leader 훌륭한 지도자

022 **deeply** [díːpli]
부 깊게
bow deeply 머리를 깊이 숙여 인사하다 sink deeply 깊게 가라앉다

023 **elbow** [élbou]
명 팔꿈치
stretch out my elbow 팔꿈치를 뻗다

024 **fearful** [fíərfəl]
형 무서운, 걱정하는
a fearful dog 무서운 개 be fearful of ~을 두려워하다

025 **route** [ruːt]
명 길, 경로, 노선
the shortest route to Suwon 수원까지 가장 짧은 경로

026 **meadow** [médou]
명 목초지, 초원
a green meadow 푸른 초원

027 **negative** [négətiv]
형 부정적인 부 negatively 부정적으로
show a negative attitude 부정적인 태도를 보이다

028 **reporter** [ripɔ́ːrtər]
명 기자
a sports reporter 스포츠 기자 a news reporter 뉴스 보도 기자

029 **gate** [geit]
명 문, 입구, 탑승구
open the gate 문을 열다 meet at Gate 8 8번 탑승구에서 만나다

030 **rhythm** [ríðəm]
명 리듬, 율동
a song with a fast rhythm 빠른 리듬의 노래

Daily Test

| 월 일 |

A 우리말에 맞게 빈 칸에 알맞은 단어를 쓰세요.

1 I've never seen such a ______________ student like Amy.
나는 Amy처럼 재능 있는 학생을 보지 못했다.

2 Plants need enough ______________ to grow. 식물은 성장하기에 충분한 햇살이 필요하다.

3 What's the main ______________ of this passage? 이 글의 주제는 무엇인가요?

4 Stricter ______________ limits will be announced next week.
다음 주에 더 강화된 제한 속도가 발표될 것이다.

5 He was a powerful ______________. 그는 강력한 지도자였다.

6 Keep your ______________ inside the vehicle. 팔꿈치를 차 밖으로 내지 마세요.

7 Staying home alone at night was a very ______________ experience.
밤에 홀로 집에 있는 것은 매우 무서운 경험이었다.

8 Cows were peacefully grazing in the ______________.
소들이 목초지에서 평화롭게 풀을 뜯고 있다.

9 People expressed ______________ opinions about the performance.
사람들은 그 공연에 대해 부정적인 의견을 보였다.

10 The ______________ to the gym is locked. 체육관으로 가는 입구가 잠겨있다.

B 빈 칸에 알맞은 단어를 고르세요.

1 The ship was starting to sink ______________.
① fearful ② fastly ③ deeply ④ around ⑤ slight

2 Which is the quickest ______________ from Busan to Masan?
① route ② street ③ speed ④ vehicle ⑤ gate

3 The ______________ of the Salsa music is fast.
① gifted ② arms ③ rhythm ④ meadow ⑤ sunlight

Day 02

MP3

031 **sunshine** [sʌ́nʃàin]
명 햇빛, 햇살
warm sunshine 따뜻한 햇살　enjoy the sunshine 햇살을 즐기다

032 **scratch** [skrætʃ]
동 긁다, 할퀴다　명 긁힌 자국, 상처
scratch your back 등을 긁다　a scratched CD 긁힌 CD

033 **documentary** [dɑ̀kjəméntəri]
명 다큐멘터리, 기록물
watch a documentary 다큐멘터리를 보다

034 **fault** [fɔːlt]
명 잘못, 결함, 결점　형 faulty 결함이 있는
It's my fault. 내 잘못이에요　his only fault 그의 유일한 결점

035 **shame** [ʃeim]
명 수치심, 부끄러움
feel shame 수치심을 느끼다　blush with shame 부끄러워 얼굴이 빨개지다

036 **accent** [ǽksènt]
명 억양, 말투
a strong accent 강한 억양　a foreign accent 외국인 같은 말투

037 **wing** [wiŋ]
명 날개
an eagle's wing 독수리의 날개　spread the wings 날개를 펴다

038 **easily** [íːzəli]
부 쉽게
get tired easily 쉽게 피곤해하다　cut easily 쉽게 잘리다

039 **boss** [bɑs]
명 상사, 사장
the new boss in the company 회사의 새로운 사장

040 **arid** [ærid]
형 매우 건조한, 무미 건조한
an arid region 건조한 지역　an arid speech 무미 건조한 연설

041 **discuss** [diskʌ́s]
동 의논하다, 상의하다　discuss-discussed-discussed
discuss a problem with friends 친구들과 문제에 대해 상의하다

042 **liberal** [líbərəl]
형 자유로운, 진보적인
liberal minded 마음이 넓은, 관대한　a liberal politician 진보적 정치인

043 **hierarchy** [háiərɑ̀ːrki]
명 계급(제), 계층　형 hierarchical 계층적인
a ruling hierarchy 지배 계급　rise in the hierarchy 계층이 올라가다

044 **cash** [kæʃ]
명 현금
pay in cash 현금으로 지불하다　spare cash 여분의 현금

045 **finally** [fáinəli]
부 마침내
finally finish the homework 마침내 숙제를 마치다

Daily Test

| 월 일 |

A 우리말에 맞게 빈 칸에 알맞은 단어를 쓰세요.

1 People are enjoying the warm ____________. 사람들이 따뜻한 햇살을 즐기는 중이다.

2 The chimpanzee used a small stick to ____________ his own back.
그 침팬지는 등을 긁기 위해 작은 막대기를 사용했다.

3 We watched a ____________ about the Han River.
우리는 한강에 대한 다큐멘터리를 보았다.

4 I felt ____________ at hearing the news. 그 소식을 듣고 난 수치심을 느꼈다.

5 Youngjin spoke with a strong British ____________.
영진은 강한 영국 억양으로 말했다.

6 Nick is the new ____________ in our company. Nick은 우리 회사의 새로운 사장이다.

7 This is an extremely ____________ land. 이 지역은 극심하게 건조한 지역이다.

8 You should ____________ the problem with your parents.
너는 이 문제를 부모님과 상의해야 한다.

9 People in this country have a ____________ view on foreign cultures.
이 나라 사람들은 외국 문화에 대해 관대한 관점을 가지고 있다.

10 The young general quickly rose in the ____________.
그 젊은 장군은 빠르게 높은 계급에 도달했다.

B 빈 칸에 알맞은 단어를 고르세요.

1 It's not your ____________.
① fault ② liberal ③ shame ④ kind ⑤ wrong

2 John solved the problem ____________.
① easy ② hardly ③ difficult ④ easily ⑤ final

3 You can pay in ____________ or by credit card.
① arid ② cash ③ wallet ④ fault ⑤ liberal

Day 02

MP3

046 novel [nάvəl]
명 소설
write a novel 소설을 쓰다　read a detective novel 추리소설을 읽다

047 knowledge [nάlidʒ]
명 지식
medical knowledge 의학적 지식

048 shower [ʃáuər]
명 소나기, 샤워　동 샤워하다
have a shower 샤워를 하다　a heavy shower 심한 소나기

049 place [pleis]
동 두다, 놓다　place-placed-placed
place the book on the table 그 책을 탁자 위에 두다

050 coupon [kjúːpɑn]
명 쿠폰, 할인권
have a coupon for the movie 영화 쿠폰을 갖고 있다

051 probably [prάbəbli]
부 아마(도)
probably true 아마도 사실인　probably be late 아마도 늦다

052 supply [səplái]
동 공급하다　명 공급　supply-supplied-supplied
supply clothing 의류를 공급하다　food supply 식량 공급

053 graphic [grǽfik]
형 생생한, 사실적인
a graphic description of the butterfly 나비에 대한 생생한 묘사

054 backpack [bǽkpæ̀k]
명 배낭　동 배낭을 지고 걷다
a black backpack 검은색 배낭　wear a backpack 배낭을 매다

055 vivid [vívid]
형 생생한, 선명한
a vivid blue 선명한 파란색　vivid memories 선명한 기억

056 thumb [θʌm]
명 엄지
thumbs up 승인, 찬성　thumbs down 거절, 불찬성

057 closely [klóusli]
부 가까이, 밀접하게
look closely 가까이서 보다　follow closely 바짝 따라가다

058 question [kwéstʃən]
동 질문하다　question-questioned-questioned
question about Jeju Island 제주도에 대해 질문하다

059 annoy [ənɔ́i]
동 짜증나게 하다
annoy me 나를 짜증나게 하다　annoy very much 매우 짜증나게 하다

060 collapse [kəlǽps]
동 (건물 등이)무너지다, 쓰러지다　명 붕괴, 쓰러짐
The old bridge collapsed. 오래된 다리가 무너졌다.

Daily Test

| 월 일 |

Ⓐ 우리말에 맞게 빈 칸에 알맞은 단어를 쓰세요.

1 He is writing a detective ______________. 그는 추리 소설을 쓰고 있다.

2 Kate has a wide ______________ of American history.
Kate는 미국 역사에 대해 방대한 지식을 갖고 있다.

3 She ______________ some dolls on the bed. 그녀는 침대 위에 인형 몇 개를 놓았다.

4 Jane will ______________ arrive on time. Jane은 아마 제시간에 도착할 것이다.

5 They decided to stop the ______________ of water.
그들은 물의 공급을 중단하기로 결정했다.

6 John wanted to become a ______________ designer.
John은 그래픽 디자이너가 되고 싶었다.

7 I'd like to wear the white ______________. 나는 저 하얀색 배낭을 매고 싶어요.

8 She wears a ______________ red dress. 그녀는 선명한 빨간색 드레스를 입고 있다.

9 He ______________ his teacher about the history of America.
그는 선생님께 미국의 역사에 대해 질문했다.

10 His joke ______________ me. 그의 농담은 나를 짜증나게 했다.

Ⓑ 빈 칸에 알맞은 단어를 고르세요.

1 He gave the idea the ______________ up.
① thumbs ② elbows ③ head ④ shower ⑤ place

2 Look ______________ at the center of the photo.
① place ② supply ③ closely ④ annoy ⑤ close

3 He suddenly ______________ on stage and was carried to the hospital.
① burn ② probably ③ possible ④ collapsed ⑤ novel

Review Test 01

Day 01 + Day 02 | 월 일 |

A 우리말에 맞게 빈 칸에 알맞은 단어를 쓰시오.

1 put a ________________ on the letter i 글자 i 위에 점을 찍다

2 ________________ weights 역기를 들어 올리다

3 ________________ the application process 지원절차를 신속하게 처리하다

4 the ________________ of Korea 한국의 이미지

5 a green ________________ 푸른 초원

6 warm ________________ 따뜻한 햇살

7 It's my ________________. 내 잘못이에요.

8 ________________ your back 등을 긁다

9 ________________ minded 마음이 넓은, 관대한

10 ________________ clothing 의류를 공급하다

B 다음 영어 풀이에 알맞은 어휘를 〈보기〉에서 고르시오.

보기	token	arid	international	backpack	thumb

1 ______________ : a symbol or an example that represents its kind or type

2 ______________ : very dry and with little water or rain

3 ______________ : a bag carried on your back and with shoulder straps

4 ______________ : the short and thick finger on the inner side of the hand

5 ______________ : related to two or more countries or nations

C 다음 단어의 관계가 A:B=C:D가 되도록 알맞은 단어를 골라 빈 칸에 적으시오.

1 ______________ : building = develop : product

① construct ② constructions ③ constructing

④ constructed ⑤ construcly

2 friend : ______________ = vocabulary : word

① love ② friendship ③ buddy

④ hate ⑤ family

3 bake : baker = lead : ______________

① leadder ② leading ③ reader

④ direct ⑤ leader

4 deep : ______________ = happy : happily

① deepy ② deeply ③ deeping

④ deepily ⑤ deeper

5 ______________ : experience = sweet : candies

① expert ② fearful ③ go

④ memory ⑤ fear

D 문맥에 맞게 다음 문장을 완성하시오.

1	The plane gradually •	• a	a literal genius.
2	We called Thomas •	• b	arrive on time.
3	We watched a documentary •	• c	approached the airport.
4	Jane will probably •	• d	a graphic designer.
5	John wanted to become •	• e	about the Han River.

E 문장을 읽고 문맥에 적절한 단어를 고르시오.

1 Don't worry about the (negative/positive) comments from your friends.

2 She (surfaced/screamed) when the big elephant came near her.

3 I don't know where I (placed/supplied) my cell phone.

4 My little brother is a (gifted/bothered) student. He already speaks five languages.

5 The old house (escaped/collapsed) due to heavy snow.

F 문장의 빈칸에 알맞은 단어를 〈보기〉에서 찾아 쓰시오. (필요하면 형태를 고치시오.)

보기	expedite	vivid	international	annoy	arid

1 Can I ____________ the application process for my passport?
제 여권 신청 절차를 신속하게 처리할 수 있을까요?

2 A "treaty" is a kind of ______________ agreement made between two or more countries.
"조약"은 둘 혹은 그 이상의 국가 사이에 이루어지는 국제적인 합의를 뜻한다.

3 They built a canal to carry water to their ____________ land.
그들은 자신들의 건조한 땅에 물을 공급하기 위해 수로를 지었다.

4 Tom still has ____________ memories of his first toy.
Tom은 자기의 첫 장난감에 대해 아직도 생생한 기억이 남아 있다.

5 Keira was quite ____________ by Bill's careless remarks.
Keira는 Bill의 조심성 없는 말들에 아주 짜증이 났다.

G 그림에 해당하는 낱말을 〈보기〉에서 골라 쓰시오.

1 

(   )

2 

(   )

3 

(   )

4 

(   )

5 

(   )

6 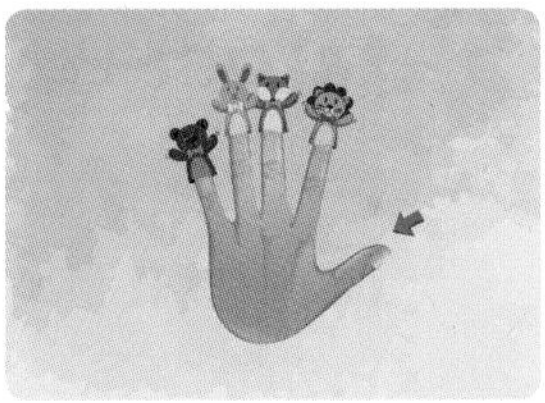

(   )

보기 wing   question   speed   thumb   lift   backpack

Study More

discuss or discuss about?

- 동사 discuss는 '상의하다'라는 뜻을 가지고 있어 '~에 대해 상의하다'라는 의미로 'discuss about something' 형태로 쓰기 쉬우나 타동사이기 때문에 'discuss something' 형태로 쓴다.
  '~와 상의하다'라고 할 때는 'with'와 같이 쓸 수 있다.
  We **discussed** the matter for several hours. 우리는 그 문제에 대해 여러 시간 논의를 했다.
  I **discussed** the matter **with** my teacher. 나는 그 문제를 선생님과 논의 했다.

Day 03

MP3

061 **accept** [əksépt]
동 받아들이다 accept-accepted-accepted
accept the apology 사과를 받아들이다

062 **former** [fɔ́ːrmə(r)]
형 이전의, 전임의
a former president 전임 대통령

063 **rainfall** [réinfɔ̀ːl]
명 강우(량)
normal rainfall 평균 강우량 monthly rainfall 월간 강우량

064 **mass media** [mæs míːdiə]
명 대중 매체
live in an age of mass media 대중 매체의 시대에 살다

065 **target** [tάːrgit]
명 목표, 과녁
achieve a target 목표를 달성하다 hit the target 과녁에 명중하다

066 **leisure** [líːʒər]
명 여가 형 한가한
enjoy your leisure time 여가 시간을 즐기다

067 **kindness** [káindnis]
명 친절, 다정함 형 kind 친절한
Thank you for your kindness. 당신의 친절에 감사합니다.

068 **plant** [plænt]
명 공장 유 factory 공장
work at a chemical plant 화학 공장에서 일하다

069 **admiral** [ǽdmərəl]
명 해군 장성, 제독
a Full Admiral 해군 대장 Admiral Yi Sun-sin 이순신 장군

070 **decorate** [dékərèit]
동 장식하다 decorate-decorated-decorated
decorate a room with balloons 풍선으로 방을 꾸미다

071 **natural** [nǽtʃərəl]
형 자연의, 자연스러운
natural disaster 자연 재해 natural resources 천연 자원

072 **unhappy** [ʌnhǽpi]
형 불행한
his unhappy childhood 그의 불행한 어린 시절

073 **compete** [kəmpíːt]
동 경쟁하다 compete-competed-competed
compete with each other 서로 경쟁하다

074 **break out** [breik aut]
(부정적인 사건이) 발생하다 명 outbreak 발생, 발발
A fire broke out. 화재가 발생했다.

075 **stressful** [strésfəl]
형 스트레스가 많은
a stressful job 스트레스가 많은 직장

Daily Test

| 월 일 |

A 우리말에 맞게 빈 칸에 알맞은 단어를 쓰세요.

1 She ______________ my apology. 그녀는 내 사과를 받아들였다.

2 This month's ______________ is below average. 이번 달 강우량은 평균 이하이다.

3 The ______________ audience of our program is teenagers. 우리 프로그램의 주 목표 관객은 10대이다.

4 In summer, there are lots of ______________ activities to enjoy. 여름에는 즐길만한 다양한 여가 활동들이 많다.

5 The company will build a new ______________ in this area. 그 회사는 이 지역에서 공장을 지을 것이다.

6 ______________ Mullen has never been defeated in a sea battle. Mullen제독은 해전에서 패한 적이 없다.

7 Mom ______________ the house with flowers. 엄마는 꽃들로 집을 꾸미셨다.

8 A flood is a common ______________ disaster in this region. 홍수는 이 지방에서 흔히 일어나는 자연 재해이다.

9 I don't like to ______________ with other people. 나는 다른 사람들과 경쟁하는 것을 좋아하지 않는다.

10 Suddenly, a fight between players ______________. 갑자기 선수들 사이에 싸움이 일어났다.

B 빈 칸에 알맞은 단어를 고르세요.

1 Treat tourists with ______________.

① kind ② rainfall ③ kindness ④ acceptance ⑤ natural

2 The bad news ______________ people to be surprised.

① leisure ② caused ③ unhappy ④ stressful ⑤ make

3 Studying math is ______________ for me.

① accepted ② stressful ③ target ④ graphic ⑤ compete

Day 03

MP3

076 **keep track of** [ki:p træk əv]
~을 파악하다, 기억하다
keep track of new movies 새로 나온 영화를 파악하다

077 **studio** [stjú:diòu]
명 스튜디오, 촬영소
visit a recording studio 녹음 스튜디오를 방문하다

078 **creative** [kriéitiv]
형 창조적인, 창의력이 있는
a creative idea 창의적인 생각 creative students 창의력이 있는 학생들

079 **combine** [kəmbáin]
동 결합하다, 혼합하다 combine-combined-combined
combine two classes 두 반을 합치다 combine ideas 생각을 결합하다

080 **individual** [ìndəvídʒuəl]
형 각각의, 개인의, 개성 있는
individual views 개인적인 견해 an individual style 개성 있는 스타일

081 **physical** [fízikəl]
형 신체적인 +physique 명 체격
check your physical condition 몸 상태를 확인하다

082 **slice** [slais]
명 (얇은) 조각
cut meat into slices 고기를 얇은 조각으로 자르다

083 **layer** [léiər]
명 층, 겹
a layer of rock 암석 층 the ozone layer 오존층

084 **silver** [sílvər]
명 은
a silver ring 은반지 silver coins 은화

085 **match** [mætʃ]
동 어울리다, 복잡하다 match-matched-matched
match the room 그 방과 어울리다 match your needs 필요에 부합하다

086 **weaken** [wí:kən]
동 약화시키다
weaken the will of the members 회원들의 동기를 약화시키다

087 **still** [stil]
형 조용한, 고요한, 가만히 있는
sit still 가만히 앉아있다 a still lake 고요한 호수

088 **case** [keis]
명 경우, 사건
in many cases 많은 경우에는 a murder case 살인 사건

089 **boost** [bu:st]
동 신장시키다, 북돋우다
boost exports 수출을 신장시키다 boost confidence 자신감을 북돋우다

090 **bottom** [bátəm]
명 밑, 바닥 반 top 꼭대기
at the bottom of the page 페이지 아래쪽

Daily Test

| 월 일 |

A **우리말에 맞게 빈 칸에 알맞은 단어를 쓰세요.**

1 Can you ____________ all the sites we've visited?
우리가 방문한 곳들을 다 기억할 수 있니?

2 I think Tim's idea is very ____________. 나는 Tim의 생각이 매우 창의적이라 생각한다.

3 ____________ flour and eggs in the bowl. 밀가루와 달걀을 그릇에 넣고 섞으세요.

4 We should respect the basic rights of ____________.
우리는 개개인의 기본적인 권리를 존중해야 한다.

5 This exercise is good for your ____________ health.
이 운동은 당신의 신체 건강에 좋다.

6 A thick ____________ of dust covered the chair. 두터운 먼지가 의자를 뒤덮었다.

7 I painted the door red to ____________ the wall.
나는 벽과 어울리도록 문을 빨간색으로 칠했다.

8 A long illness ____________ his will to travel.
오랜 병이 여행에 대한 그의 의지를 약화시켰다.

9 The classroom was very ____________. 교실은 매우 조용했다.

10 In this ____________, you should apologize to Mina.
이 경우에는 네가 미나에게 사과를 해야 한다.

B **빈 칸에 알맞은 단어를 고르세요.**

1 I ate a ____________ of bread and two cookies.
① slice ② sheets ③ bottle ④ layer ⑤ still

2 There are some coins at the ____________ of the stairs.
① bottom ② high ③ graphic ④ studio ⑤ case

3 The teacher's praise ____________ Tim's confidence greatly.
① broke out ② boosted ③ creative ④ time ⑤ combine

Day 04

MP3

091 ☐ **wisely** [wáizli]
부 현명하게
talk wisely 현명하게 말하다   act wisely 현명하게 행동하다

092 ☐ **treasure** [tréʒər]
명 보물
bury the treasure 보물을 묻다   hide the treasure 보물을 숨기다

093 ☐ **ceramic** [sərǽmik]
명 도자기, 질그릇 형 도자기의, 요업의
ceramic products 요업 제품   ceramic tiles 세라믹 타일

094 ☐ **influential** [ìnfluénʃəl]
형 영향력 있는
a highly influential leader 꽤 영향력 있는 지도자

095 ☐ **adventurous** [ədvéntʃərəs]
형 모험심이 강한
adventurous tourists 모험심이 강한 여행자들

096 ☐ **wallpaper** [wɔ́:lpèipər]
명 벽지
hang wallpaper 벽지를 바르다   black wallpaper 검은색 벽지

097 ☐ **channel** [tʃǽnəl]
명 (TV) 채널
a drama channel 드라마 채널   change channels 채널을 바꾸다

098 ☐ **keep up with** [ki:p ʌp wið]
~와 연락하고 지내다, ~을 잘 파악하다
keep up with old friends 오랜 친구들과 연락하고 지내다

099 ☐ **heritage** [héritidʒ]
명 유산
the cultural heritage 문화 유산   world heritage sites 세계 유적지

100 ☐ **pipe** [paip]
명 관, 배관
a cold water pipe 냉수로   a gas pipe 가스관

101 ☐ **be up to** [bi ʌp tu:]
~에 달려 있다.
It's up to you whether you go or not. 갈지 말지 네게 달렸다.

102 ☐ **uncomfortable** [ʌnkʌ́mfərtəbl]
형 불편한
wear an uncomfortable dress 불편한 드레스를 입다

103 ☐ **universe** [jú:nəvə̀:rs]
명 우주   형 universal 일반적인, 전세계적인
the magnitude of the universe 우주의 거대함

104 ☐ **rubber** [rʌ́bər]
명 고무 형 고무의
a rubber tree 고무 나무   a pair of rubber boots 고무 장화 한 쌍

105 ☐ **original** [ərídʒənəl]
형 원래의
the original meaning of the word 그 단어의 원래 뜻

Daily Test

| 월 일 |

Ⓐ 우리말에 맞게 빈 칸에 알맞은 단어를 쓰세요.

1 She hid the ______________ under the closet. 그녀는 옷장 밑에 보물을 숨겼다.

2 These ______________ cups are all handmade. 이 세라믹 컵들은 모두 수작업으로 만들어졌다.

3 He was an ______________ actor among teenagers.
그는 10대 사이에서 영향력 있는 배우였다.

4 Ben was an ______________ captain. Ben은 모험심이 강한 선장이었다.

5 There will be a horror movie on ______________ 7 at 10 o'clock.
7번 채널에서 10시에 공포영화를 방영할 것이다.

6 James ______________ his old school friends.
James는 그의 오랜 학창시절 친구들과 연락하고 지낸다.

7 It ______________ you whether or not you join the race.
경주에 참여할 지 말지는 네게 달렸다.

8 This chair is quite ______________. 이 의자는 꽤 불편하군요.

9 The magnitude of the ______________ is incredible. 우주의 거대함은 믿기 힘들 정도다.

10 Wendy is playing with a ______________ ball. Wendy는 고무공을 가지고 놀고 있다.

Ⓑ 빈 칸에 알맞은 단어를 고르세요.

1 Linda always talks ______________.
① wise ② influential ③ originally ④ wisely ⑤ uncomfortable

2 We should preserve our cultural ______________.
① adventure ② heritages ③ layer ④ original ⑤ match

3 His ______________ design was really creative.
① treasure ② kindness ③ physical ④ weaken ⑤ original

Day 04

MP3

106 **breathtaking** [bréθtèikiŋ]
형 놀랄만한, 아슬아슬한
a breathtaking view 놀랄만한 전경

107 **inherent** [inhí(:)ərənt]
형 고유의, 내재된
the dolphin's inherent feature 돌고래 고유의 특징

108 **score** [skɔːr]
명 점수 동 득점하다 score-scored-scored
a high score 높은 득점 score again 다시 득점하다

109 **delete** [dilíːt]
동 삭제하다 delete-deleted-deleted
delete her name from the list 목록에서 그녀의 이름을 지우다

110 **present** [prézənt]
동 주다, 수여하다 present-presented-presented
present Peter with a black tie Peter에게 검은 넥타이를 주다

111 **silly** [síli]
형 어리석은, 바보 같은
make a silly mistake 어리석은 실수를 하다 a silly answer 바보 같은 답

112 **underground** [ʌ̀ndərgráund]
형 지하의
walk through an underground passage 지하도를 걷다

113 **sketch** [sketʃ]
명 밑그림 동 스케치를 하다 sketch-sketched-sketched
make a sketch 스케치를 하다 sketch a portrait 초상화를 그리다

114 **delivery** [dilívəri]
명 배달
delivery service 배달 서비스 special delivery 속달(빠른 우편)

115 **scold** [skould]
동 꾸짖다 scold-scolded-scolded
scold mildly 가볍게 꾸짖다 scold a child 아이를 야단치다

116 **prey** [prei]
명 먹이, 사냥감
catch its prey 사냥감을 잡다 become prey to ~의 먹이감이 되다

117 **weird** [wiərd]
형 기이한, 기묘한 유 odd 이상한, 특이한
have a weird dream 기이한 꿈을 꾸다 a weird sound 기묘한 소리

118 **officer** [ɔ́(:)fisər]
명 장교, 경찰관
a military officer 육군 장교 a police officer 경찰관

119 **calm** [kaːm]
형 차분한, 침착한
keep calm 침착함을 유지하다 a calm voice 차분한 목소리

120 **decision** [disíʒən]
명 결정 동 decide 결정하다
make a decision 결정을 내리다 a big decision 중요한 결정

Daily Test

| 월 일 |

Ⓐ 우리말에 맞게 빈 칸에 알맞은 단어를 쓰세요.

1 We enjoyed a ______________ view of Hong Kong from this hotel.
우리는 이 호텔에서 홍콩의 놀랄만한 전경을 경험했다.

2 Curiosity is an ______________ trait of the human being.
호기심은 인간의 내재된 특징이다.

3 Once you ______________ a computer file, it is difficult to restore it.
일단 컴퓨터 파일을 한 번 지우면 그것을 복구하기는 어렵다.

4 The teacher ______________ Maggie with a dictionary as a prize.
선생님은 Maggie에게 상으로 사전을 주었다.

5 There is a big ______________ cave in the city. 그 도시에는 큰 지하 동굴이 있다.

6 Her ______________ of the tower is very lifelike. 그녀의 그 탑 스케치는 실물과 똑같다.

7 I sent the package by special ______________. 나는 빠른 우편으로 그 소포를 보냈다.

8 He ______________ Lisa because she didn't finish her homework.
Lisa가 숙제를 다 하지 않아서 그는 그녀를 꾸짖었다.

9 The man was wearing a ______________ hat. 그 남자는 이상한 모자를 쓰고 있었다.

10 My brother wants to become a military ______________.
내 남동생은 육군 장교가 되고 싶어한다.

Ⓑ 빈 칸에 알맞은 단어를 고르세요.

1 The final ______________ was 3-4.
① case ② calm ③ score ④ inherent ⑤ prey

2 It's difficult to make a ______________ about the job.
① decide ② result ③ weird ④ officer ⑤ decision

3 Stay ______________ and sit down.
① present ② delivery ③ calmly ④ scoldly ⑤ calm

Review Test 02

Day 03 + Day 04 | 월 일 |

A 우리말에 맞게 빈 칸에 알맞은 단어를 쓰시오.

1 hit the ______________ 과녁에 명중하다

2 natural ______________ 자연 재해

3 A fire ______________. 화재가 발생했다.

4 ______________ new movies 새로 나온 영화를 파악하다

5 a ______________ lake 고요한 호수

6 ______________ tourists 모험심이 강한 여행자들

7 the cultural ______________ 문화 유산

8 ______________ again 다시 득점하다

9 ______________ a child 아이를 야단치다

10 have a ______________ dream 기이한 꿈을 꾸다

B 다음 영어 풀이에 알맞은 어휘를 〈보기〉에서 고르시오.

보기	former	weird	leisure	break out	original

1 ____________ : something or someone that existed in the past

2 ____________ : free time you can spend as you wish, e.g., away from work or study

3 ____________ : something unpleasant such as war or disease that happens suddenly

4 ____________ : being the first or earliest form of something

5 ____________ : unusual or strange

C 다음 단어의 관계가 A:B=C:D가 되도록 알맞은 단어를 골라 빈 칸에 적으시오.

1 ______________ : acceptance = combine : combination

① accept ② accepted ③ accepting
④ acceptly ⑤ accepts

2 top : ______________ = thick : thin

① up ② tower ③ ground
④ bottom ⑤ high

3 lock : unlock = comfortable : ______________

① uncomfortable ② incomfortable ③ comfort
④ comforty ⑤ uncomfort

4 ______________ : mental = light : dark

① psychological ② head ③ body
④ physical ⑤ problem

5 work : ______________ = thick : thin

① difficult ② same ③ leisure
④ match ⑤ stressful

D 문맥에 맞게 다음 문장을 완성하시오.

1 This month's rainfall is • • a in the bowl.

2 I don't like to compete • • b below average.

3 Combine flour and eggs • • c is very lifelike.

4 There is a horror movie • • d with other people.

5 Her sketch of the tower • • e on Channel 7.

E 문장을 읽고 문맥에 적절한 단어를 고르시오.

1 It is (up to you/silly) whether or not you join our book club.

2 It is (creative/natural) that you are worried about speaking before the audience.

3 The incident (caused/scolded) him to fear wild animals.

4 Jamie reads newspapers regularly to (keep up with/keep away from) new technologies.

5 Mr.Johnson (presented/prevented) new afterschool programs to the parents.

F 문장의 빈칸에 알맞은 단어를 〈보기〉에서 찾아 쓰시오. (필요하면 형태를 고치시오.)

보기	weird	influential	plant	weaken	decorate

1 The defeat in the match ____________ the team's confidence.
그 시합에서의 패배가 팀의 자신감을 약화시켰다.

2 The little girl ____________ the living room with colorful balloons.
어린 소녀는 거실을 다양한 색깔의 풍선들로 장식했다.

3 He was the most ____________ figure in the field.
그는 그 분야에서 가장 영향력있는 인물이었다.

4 A ____________ smell is coming from the kitchen.
부엌에서 이상한 냄새가 나고 있다.

5 Many kinds of plastic products are produced in this ____________.
많은 종류의 플라스틱 제품이 이 공장에서 생산된다.

G 그림과 낱말이 잘못 짝지어진 것을 고르시오. ·· (   )

ⓐ

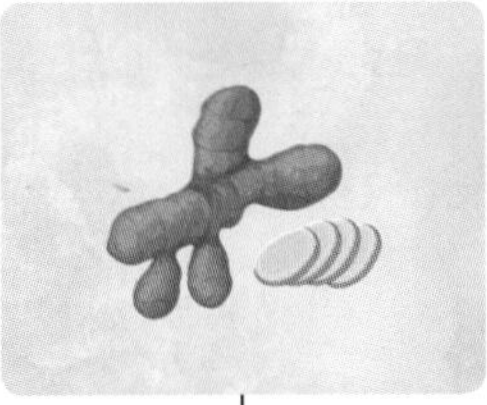

slice

ⓑ

stressful

ⓒ

scold

ⓓ

delivery

H 낱말과 어울리는 그림을 연결하시오.

1 treasure •   • ⓐ 

2 target •   • ⓑ 

Study More

present의 다양한 의미

- [명사] : '선물, 현재'
- [동사] : '제시하다, 발표하다'

  present a report to the committee 보고서를 위원회에 발표하다

  *'제시하다, 발표하다'라는 의미로 쓰일 때 명사형은 presentation이다.

  give a **presentation** at a meeting 모임에서 발표를 하다
- [형용사] : '현재의(=current), ~에 참석한'

  at the **present** time 현재로서는, 요즈음

Day 05

MP3

121 **clue** [kluː]
명 단서
a key clue 중요한 단서 leave an important clue 중요한 단서를 남기다

122 **gladly** [glǽdli]
부 기쁘게, 고맙게
welcome gladly 기쁘게 환영하다 accept gladly 기쁘게 받아들이다

123 **territory** [téritɔ̀ːri]
명 지역, 영토
foreign territory 외국 영토 mountainous territory 산간 지역

124 **legendary** [lédʒəndèri]
형 전설적인
become the legendary author 전설적인 작가가 되다

125 **publish** [pʌ́bliʃ]
동 출판하다 publish-published-published
publish a book 책을 출판하다 publish a journal 잡지를 발행하다

126 **method** [méθəd]
명 방법 유 way 방법
an effective method of losing weight 살을 빼는 효과적인 방법

127 **audience** [ɔ́ːdiəns]
명 관중, 청중
draw a large audience 많은 관중을 끌다

128 **include** [inklúːd]
동 포함하다, 포함시키다 include-included-included
include the important examples 중요한 예시를 포함하다

129 **period** [pí(ː)əriəd]
명 기간, 시대
a short period 짧은 기간 a period of 6 years 6년의 시간

130 **soda** [sóudə]
명 소다, 탄산음료
drink some soda 탄산음료를 마시다 a glass of soda 소다 한 잔

131 **in charge of** [in tʃɑːrdʒ əv]
책임이 있는, 담당하는
be in charge of the school basketball team 교내 농구팀을 담당하다

132 **embarrass** [imbǽrəs]
동 당황스럽게 만들다
embarrass everybody 모두를 당황시키다

133 **fantasy** [fǽntəsi]
명 공상, 상상
have fantasies about ~에 대한 환상을 갖다

134 **filter** [fíltər]
동 여과하다, 거르다 명 필터, 여과장치 filter-filtered-filtered
filter water 물을 여과하다 an air filter 공기 필터

135 **wetland** [wetlənd]
명 습지
wetlands in Africa 아프리카의 습지대

Daily Test

| 월 일 |

A 우리말에 맞게 빈 칸에 알맞은 단어를 쓰세요.

1 The thief left a key ____________ in the room. 도둑은 방 안에 중요한 단서를 남겼다.

2 We should do something to protect our ____________.
우리의 영토를 보호하기 위해 다 함께 무엇이라도 해야한다.

3 The company ____________ the novel in over twenty languages.
회사는 그 소설을 20여 개의 언어로 출판하였다.

4 There are many effective ____________ of studying math.
수학을 연구하는 많은 효과적인 방법들이 있다.

5 The ____________ was moved by his performance.
그의 공연에 많은 청중들이 감동받았다.

6 This ticket ____________ lunch and admission to the show.
이 티켓은 점심식사와 공연 관람이 포함되어 있다.

7 The novel is set in the Roman ____________. 그 소설은 로마시대를 배경으로 한다.

8 There is a glass of ____________ on the table. 탁자 위에 소다 한 잔이 있다.

9 The rumor ____________ many people. 그 소문은 많은 사람들을 당황하게 했다.

10 This ____________ removes dirt from water. 이 여과장치는 물에서 불순물을 제거시킨다.

B 빈 칸에 알맞은 단어를 고르세요.

1 Peter asked Jane to marry him, and she ____________ accepted.
① glad ② happy ③ gladly ④ excitement ⑤ cry

2 Many people want to see the ____________ monster.
① legendary ② audience ③ leisure ④ period ⑤ filter

3 They are living in a ____________.
① clue ② sketch ③ wetland ④ include ⑤ filter

Day 05

MP3

136 **regular** [régjələr]
형 규칙적인 　 부 regularly 규칙적으로
regular size 보통 사이즈 　 regular readers 정기 독자들

137 **amaze** [əméiz]
동 놀라게 하다 　 amaze-amazed-amazed
amaze the crowd 관중들을 놀라게 하다

138 **wire** [waiər]
명 철사, 선
a thin wire 얇은 철사 　 a wire fence 철조망 울타리

139 **indoor** [índɔ̀:r]
형 실내의 　 반 outdoor 실외의
indoor games 실내 경기 　 indoor tennis court 실내 테니스 코트

140 **replay** [rí:plèi]
명 재경기, 재연 　 동 다시 하다, ~을 재연하다 　 replay-replayed-replayed
replay the accident 그 사고를 재연하다

141 **cotton** [kátən]
명 면, 면직물
a cotton shirt 면 티셔츠 　 cotton fields 목화 밭

142 **confidence** [kánfidəns]
명 신뢰, 자신감 　 형 confident 자신감 있는
lose confidence 자신감을 잃다 　 build confidence 신뢰를 쌓다

143 **enemy** [énəmi]
명 적
a natural enemy 천적 　 fight an enemy 적과 싸우다

144 **incredible** [inkrédəbl]
형 믿을 수 없는, 믿기 힘든
an incredible story 믿을 수 없는 이야기

145 **vital** [váitəl]
형 필수적인 　 유 crucial 결정적인, 중대한
vital roles 필수적인 역할 　 vital to/for ~에 필수적인

146 **landmark** [lǽndmà:rk]
명 랜드마크, 주요 지형지물
a historical Korean landmark 한국의 역사적인 랜드마크

147 **precious** [préʃəs]
형 귀중한, 값비싼
precious time 귀중한 시간 　 precious memories 귀중한 기억

148 **wear** [wɛər]
동 닳다, 낡다 　 wear-wore-worn
wear a hole in my sock 양말이 낡아서 구멍이 뚫리다

149 **successful** [səksésfəl]
형 성공적인
live a successful life 성공적인 삶을 살다

150 **commodity** [kəmádəti]
명 상품, 물품, 원자재 　 유 goods 상품, 제품
commodity prices 물가 　 staple commodities 중요 물품

Daily Test

A 우리말에 맞게 빈 칸에 알맞은 단어를 쓰세요.

1 ______________ meetings will be held on Friday afternoons.
정규 회의는 금요일 오후에 있을 예정이다.

2 Everyone was ______________ at the size of the event.
모두가 그 행사의 규모에 놀랐다.

3 I often swim in the ______________ swimming pool.
나는 종종 실내 수영장에서 수영을 한다.

4 Harry ______________ the scene in his mind. Harry는 그 장면을 마음속에서 계속 떠올렸다.

5 Mom bought a ______________ dress for me. 엄마는 날 위해 면 드레스를 사오셨다.

6 He lost ______________ because he failed the test.
그가 시험에 떨어졌기 때문에 자신감을 잃었다.

7 I heard an ______________ story last night. 나는 어젯밤에 믿을 수 없는 이야기를 들었다.

8 Water is ______________ to human life. 물은 인간 생존에 필수적이다.

9 Every moment with my family is ______________.
내 가족과 함께하는 모든 시간은 귀중하다.

10 The new shoes have almost ______________ out. 새로 산 신발이 거의 다 닳았다.

B 빈 칸에 알맞은 단어를 고르세요.

1 The frog is a natural ______________ of the bee.
① enemy ② environment ③ amaze ④ vital ⑤ landmark

2 ______________ prices have fallen a little this year.
① Community ② Indoor ③ Commodity ④ Universe ⑤ Precious

3 She was one of the most ______________ writers in Japan.
① indoor ② successful ③ regular ④ amaze ⑤ cotton

Day 06

MP3

151 **separate** [sépərit]
형 분리된, 따로 떨어진 동 분리하다 separate-separated-separated
two separate closets 두 개의 분리된 옷장

152 **totally** [tóutəli]
부 완전히, 전적으로
totally lost 완전히 잃은 totally different 전적으로 다른

153 **immigrant** [íməgrənt]
명 이민자, 이주민
an immigrant worker 이주 노동자

154 **private** [práivit]
형 사적인
private story 사적인 이야기 private life 사적인 생활

155 **survey** [sə́:rvei]
동 살피다 명 (설문) 조사
do a survey 설문조사를 하다

156 **animation** [ænəméiʃən]
명 만화 영화, 애니메이션
animation series 만화영화 시리즈

157 **youth** [ju:θ]
명 젊음, 젊은이
the passion of youth 젊은이의 열정 eternal youth 영원한 젊음

158 **exclude** [iksklú:d]
동 제외하다, 배제하다 명 exclusion 제외, 배제
exclude a possibility 가능성을 배제하다

159 **handle** [hǽndl]
동 다루다 명 손잡이 handle-handled-handled
handle a computer 컴퓨터를 다루다 turn the handle 손잡이를 돌리다

160 **carrot** [kǽrət]
명 당근
make a carrot cake 당근 케이크를 만들다

161 **disadvantage** [dìsədvǽntidʒ]
명 약점, 불리한 점
a serious disadvantage 심각한 약점

162 **head** [hed]
동 ~로 향하다 head-headed-headed
head south 남쪽으로 향하다 head out of town 마을을 떠나다

163 **charge** [tʃɑ:rdʒ]
명 요금 동 청구하다
delivery charge 배달 요금 charge for the repair 수리비를 청구하다

164 **rough** [rʌf]
형 거친, 고르지 못한
hard and rough 단단하고 거친 rough hands 거친 손

165 **historic** [histɔ́(:)rik]
형 역사적인 *historical 형 역사에 관련된
visit historic sites 역사적 장소를 방문하다

Daily Test

| 월 일 |

A 우리말에 맞게 빈 칸에 알맞은 단어를 쓰세요.

1 The cook ______________ the seeds. 요리사가 씨를 분리했다.

2 Harry solved the problem in a ______________ different way.
Harry는 전혀 다른 방법으로 그 문제를 해결했다.

3 The media looked into their ______________ lives.
대중매체는 그들의 사적인 생활을 주의깊게 살폈다.

4 Only five students responded to the ______________ yesterday.
어제 다섯 명의 학생만이 설문조사에 답했다.

5 Everyone wants to keep their ______________.
모든 사람들이 그들의 젊음을 유지하고 싶어한다.

6 He can't ______________ the machine by himself. 그는 혼자서 저 기계를 다루지 못해요.

7 One ______________ of this computer is its price. 이 컴퓨터의 한가지 단점은 가격이다.

8 Students ______________ for the door. 학생들이 문 쪽으로 향했다.

9 The company ______________ 300 dollars for repairs.
회사는 수리비로 300달러를 청구하였다.

10 The two countries made a ______________ decision.
그 두 나라는 역사적인 결정을 내렸다.

B 빈 칸에 알맞은 단어를 고르세요.

1 Mom ______________ the game CD from our shopping list.
① excluded ② separation ③ animation ④ rough ⑤ incredible

2 ______________ from many countries settled in this town.
① Surveys ② Immigrants ③ Handles ④ Territories ⑤ Cottons

3 My skin is too ______________ these days.
① totally ② roughly ③ youth ④ rough ⑤ handle

Day 06

MP3

166 **wedding** [wédiŋ]
명 결혼식, 혼례 *marriage 명 결혼
the wedding anniversary 결혼 기념일

167 **odd** [ɑd]
형 이상한
odd people 이상한 사람들 an odd expression 이상한 표현

168 **ginseng** [dʒínseŋ]
명 인삼
dig up ginseng 인삼을 캐다 ginseng tea 인삼차

169 **income** [ínkʌm]
명 수입, 소득
high income 높은 소득 a fixed income 고정 수입

170 **official** [əfíʃəl]
형 공식적인
official visit 공식적인 방문 an official announcement 공식 발표

171 **organization** [ɔ̀ːrgənizéiʃən]
명 조직, 단체, 기구
work for an international organization 국제 단체에서 일하다

172 **fancy** [fǽnsi]
형 장식이 많은, 화려한 명 공상, 환상
wear a fancy hat 화려한 모자를 쓰다 a strange fancy 이상한 공상

173 **dust** [dʌst]
명 먼지 형 dusty 먼지투성이인
a cloud of dust 흙먼지 a dust fog 자욱한 먼지

174 **crawl** [krɔːl]
동 (엎드려) 기다 crawl-crawled-crawled
start to crawl 기어 다니기 시작하다 crawl into ~에 기어 들어가다

175 **maker** [méikər]
명 ~을 만드는 사람, 제조사
a car maker 자동차 제조 회사 a trouble maker 사고 뭉치

176 **despite** [dispáit]
전 ~에도 불구하고 유 in spite of ~에도 불구하고
despite the bad weather 나쁜 날씨에도 불구하고

177 **provide** [prəváid]
동 제공하다 provide-provided-provided
provide the best service 최상의 서비스를 제공하다

178 **proper** [prápər]
형 적절한
proper words 적절한 말 at a proper time 적당한 때에

179 **tremble** [trémbl]
동 떨다, 흔들리다 유 shake 흔들다, 흔들리다
tremble with fear 공포에 몸을 떨다

180 **expect** [ikspékt]
동 기대하다 expect-expected-expected
expect a good score 좋은 점수를 기대하다

Daily Test

| 월 일 |

A 우리말에 맞게 빈 칸에 알맞은 단어를 쓰세요.

1 They look so ______________. 그들은 좀 이상해 보인다.

2 ______________ is the specialty of the city. 인삼은 이 도시의 특산품이다.

3 Her yearly ______________ is higher than mine. 그녀의 연간 소득은 내 것 보다 높다.

4 This is my second ______________ visit to Korea. 이번이 나의 두 번째 공식 한국 방문이다.

5 Max wants to work for an international volunteer ______________.
Max는 국제 봉사 단체에서 일하길 원한다.

6 The truck raised a cloud of ______________ when it passed by.
트럭이 지나갈 때 흙먼지를 일으켰다.

7 My daughter started to ______________. 내 딸은 기어 다니기 시작했다.

8 ______________ the doctor's warning, he played in the match.
의사의 경고에도 불구하고 그는 경기에 나갔다.

9 We will ______________ the best possible service to our customers.
우리는 고객들에게 최상의 서비스를 제공할 것입니다.

10 The speaker's voice began to ______________. 그 발표자의 목소리가 떨리기 시작했다.

B 빈 칸에 알맞은 단어를 고르세요.

1 Annie is a trouble ______________!
① maker ② person ③ odd ④ problem ⑤ fancy

2 Let's discuss this issue again at a ______________ time.
① despite ② proper ③ property ④ income ⑤ youth

3 They ______________ Sarah to come to the party.
① expectation ② expected ③ official ④ odd ⑤ crawl

Review Test 03

Day 05 + Day 06 | 월 일 |

A 우리말에 맞게 빈 칸에 알맞은 단어를 쓰시오.

1 accept ________________ 기쁘게 받아들이다

2 draw a large ________________ 많은 관중을 끌다

3 ________________ everybody 모두를 당황시키다

4 an ________________ story 믿을 수 없는 이야기

5 a ________________ role 필수적인 역할

6 an ________________ worker 이주 노동자

7 eternal ________________ 영원한 젊음

8 a serious ________________ 심각한 약점

9 an ________________ announcement 공식 발표

10 ________________ the bad weather 나쁜 날씨에도 불구하고

B 다음 영어 풀이에 알맞은 어휘를 〈보기〉에서 고르시오.

보기 territory method tremble income commodity

1 ______________ : a product that can be sold or bought

2 ______________ : land that is owned by a particular country

3 ______________ : a way of doing something

4 ______________ : the money you make from work, service, or business

5 ______________ : to shake because you are nervous or afraid

C 다음 단어의 관계가 A:B=C:D가 되도록 알맞은 단어를 골라 빈 칸에 적으시오.

1 legend : ______________ = youth : young

① legendary ② myth ③ legending
④ tale ⑤ story

2 include : ______________ = advantage : disadvantage

① outclude ② disclude ③ imclude
④ unclude ⑤ exclude

3 ______________ : exercise = high : income

① regular ② health ③ regularly
④ take ⑤ sports

4 write : novel = ______________ : food

① delicious ② provide ③ Korean
④ play ⑤ home

5 success : ______________ = sorrow : sorrowful

① succeed ② succesly ③ successing
④ successful ⑤ successfully

D 문맥에 맞게 다음 문장을 완성하시오.

1	The novel is set •	• a	because he failed the test.
2	Harry replayed •	• b	in the Roman period.
3	He lost confidence •	• c	began to tremble.
4	He can't handle •	• d	the machine by himself.
5	The speaker's voice •	• e	the scene in his mind.

E 문장을 읽고 문맥에 적절한 단어를 고르시오.

1 Tom is (in charge of/in terms of) the sales department.

2 The kids were (charged/amazed) by the sight of the rainbow.

3 The entrance fee (includes/replays) a free lunch for four people.

4 Your help was (vital/rough) to the success of the musical.

5 She is wearing a (fancy/rough) hat with soft feathers.

F 문장의 빈칸에 알맞은 단어를 〈보기〉에서 찾아 쓰시오. (필요하면 형태를 고치시오.)

보기	commodity	clue	publish	despite	survey

1 Last year, the company ____________ a number of books on popular science.
그 회사는 지난 해에 대중 과학에 대한 책들을 여러 권 출판했다.

2 ____________ unexpected difficulties, they finally finished the project on time.
예상치 못한 어려움에도 불구하고 그들은 마침내 제 시간에 프로젝트를 끝마쳤다.

3 According to the ____________, students want more science classes.
학교의 설문 조사에 의하면 학생들은 더 많은 과학 수업을 원한다.

4 After years of enduring effort, researchers found a ____________ to the disease.
수년 동안의 지속적인 노력 끝에 연구자들은 그 질병에 대한 실마리를 찾았다.

5 Recently the prices of staple ____________ have risen sharply.
최근에 중요 물품들의 가격이 급격히 올랐다.

G 그림에 해당하는 낱말을 〈보기〉에서 골라 쓰시오.

1 

(　　　　　　)

2 

(　　　　　　)

3 

(　　　　　　)

4 

(　　　　　　)

5 

(　　　　　　)

6 

(　　　　　　)

보기 soda crawl wedding dust cotton carrot

Study More

weird 비슷한 의미를 가진 단어들

- strange '이상한, 낯선', odd '이상한,특이한', unusual '특이한, 흔치 않은', mysterious '이해하기 힘든, 특이한', eerie '괴상한, 으스스한', peculiar '이상한, ~에 특유한', eccentric '괴짜의, 특이한'
  a **mysterious** phenomenon 특이한 현상　an **eerie** sound 으스스한 소리
  a custom **peculiar** to Asia 아시아에 특유한 풍속　**eccentric** behavior 별난 행동

Day 07

MP3

181 **mixture** [míkstʃər]
명 혼합물
a mixture of chocolate and butter 초콜릿과 버터의 혼합물

182 **bloody** [blʌ́di]
형 유혈의, 피의
a bloody war 피비린내 나는 전쟁 have a bloody nose 코피가 나다

183 **maple** [méipl]
명 단풍나무
a maple leaf 단풍잎 plant a maple tree 단풍나무를 심다

184 **starfish** [stɑ́ːrfiʃ]
명 불가사리
find a starfish 불가사리를 발견하다

185 **backward** [bǽkwərd]
형 뒤의 전 뒤로
count backward from fifty 50에서부터 거꾸로 세다

186 **tomb** [tuːm]
명 무덤 유 grave 무덤, 묘
a royal tomb 왕릉 an ancient tomb 고대 무덤

187 **investigate** [invéstəgèit]
동 조사하다, 수사하다 명 investigation 조사, 수사
investigate the cause of the accident 그 사건의 원인을 조사하다

188 **mascot** [mǽskət]
명 마스코트
our team's mascot 우리 팀의 마스코트

189 **reply** [riplái]
동 답하다 명 대답 reply-replied-replied
reply to a letter 편지에 답하다 a late reply 늦은 답장

190 **research** [risə́ːrtʃ]
동 조사하다, 연구하다 명 조사, 연구
historical research 역사적 연구 do research 연구를 하다

191 **monthly** [mʌ́nθli]
형 매월의, 한 달에 한 번의
a monthly magazine 월간지 a monthly salary 월급

192 **suffer** [sʌ́fər]
동 고통받다, 시달리다 suffer-suffered-suffered
suffer from ~로부터 고통받다 suffer from a disease 질병을 앓다

193 **condiment** [kɑ́ndəmənt]
명 양념, 조미료
minced condiment 다진 양념 a spicy condiment 매운 양념

194 **kin** [kin]
명 친족, 친척
be kin to ~와 친척인 be kin to the president 대통령과 친척인

195 **used to** [juːst tuː]
~하곤 했다 , (한때는) ~이었다
used to+동사원형 ~하곤 했었다 used to swim 수영을 하곤 했었다

Daily Test

| 월 일 |

A 우리말에 맞게 빈 칸에 알맞은 단어를 쓰세요.

1 They stopped the ______________ battle. 그들은 피비린내 나는 전투를 멈추었다.

2 There are many ______________ leaves on the street. 거리에 단풍잎이 많이 있다.

3 She stepped ______________ when she saw the dog. 그녀는 그 개를 보자 뒤로 물러섰다.

4 People found some treasure in the ancient ______________.
사람들은 그 고대무덤에서 약간의 보물들을 발견했다.

5 Police officers are ______________ the crime. 경찰들이 그 범죄에 대해서 조사하고 있다.

6 Can you ______________ to the letter as soon as possible?
가능한 빨리 편지에 답을 줄 수 있나요?

7 I started to do ______________ about dinosaurs. 나는 공룡에 대한 연구를 시작했다.

8 She is reading a ______________ fashion magazine. 그녀는 월간 패션지를 읽고 있다.

9 The cook uses special ______________ for his dishes.
그 요리사는 자신의 요리에 특별한 양념을 쓴다.

10 Yuri is ______________ to Jane. 유리는 Jane과 친척이다.

B 빈 칸에 알맞은 단어를 고르세요.

1 Put the egg ______________ into the cup.
① monthly ② backward ③ research ④ kin ⑤ mixture

2 He has ______________ from stress for a long time.
① suffered ② tomb ③ made ④ mascot ⑤ reply

3 We ______________ play badminton in this park.
① using to ② used to ③ be used to ④ use to ⑤ using

Day 07

MP3

196 **high-tech** [hai tek]
형 첨단 기술의
high-tech industries 첨단 기술 산업

197 **recover** [rikʌ́vər]
동 회복하다 recover-recovered-recovered
recover his health 그의 건강을 회복하다

198 **root** [ru(:)t]
명 뿌리, 근원
the roots of the apple tree 사과나무의 뿌리

199 **intelligent** [intélidʒənt]
형 영리한, 똑똑한
an intelligent child 똑똑한 아이 look intelligent 영리해 보이다

200 **refund** [ríːfʌnd]
명 환불 동 환불하다 refund-refunded-refunded
receive a refund 환불을 받다 refund money 돈을 환불받다

201 **scientist** [sáiəntist]
명 과학자
become a scientist 과학자가 되다 a nuclear scientist 핵 과학자

202 **shut** [ʃʌt]
동 (문을) 닫다, (눈을) 감다 shut-shut-shut
shut the door 문을 닫다 shut his eyes 눈을 감다

203 **wheel** [hwiːl]
명 바퀴
a front wheel 앞 바퀴 a bike wheel 오토바이 바퀴

204 **envy** [énvi]
동 부러워하다 형 envious 부러워하는
envy his success 그의 성공을 부러워하다 feel no envy 부러워하지 않다

205 **anger** [ǽŋgər]
명 화, 분노
control his anger 그의 분노를 억제하다 in anger 화가 나서

206 **jewel** [dʒúːəl]
명 보석
a jewel thief 보석 도둑 a jewel case 보석 상자

207 **gap** [gæp]
명 갈라진 틈, 격차
generation gap 세대 차이 make a gap 차이를 만들다

208 **effective** [iféktiv]
형 효과적인 유 efficient 능률적인, 효율적인
an effective way to lose weight 살을 빼는 효과적인 방법

209 **wooden** [wúdən]
형 나무로 된, 목재의
a wooden chair 나무로 된 의자

210 **bowl** [boul]
명 그릇, 한 그릇(의 양)
a salad bowl 샐러드 그릇 a bowl of rice 밥 한 공기

Daily Test

| 월 일 |

A 우리말에 맞게 빈 칸에 알맞은 단어를 쓰세요.

1 We live in the ______________ age. 우리는 첨단 기술 시대를 살고 있다.

2 Harry is ______________ from the operation. Harry는 수술에서 회복하는 중이다.

3 He pulled up the tree by its ______________. 그는 뿌리째 그 나무를 뽑았다.

4 Thomas is an ______________ student. Thomas는 현명한 학생이다.

5 He received a tax ______________ this month. 이번 달에 그는 세금 환불을 받았다.

6 He ______________ the door loudly and went out. 그는 문을 세게 닫고 밖으로 나갔다.

7 Helen changed the ______________ of the bicycle. Helen은 자전거의 바퀴를 교체했다.

8 All of our classmates ______________ Sam's success.
우리 반 학생들 모두 Sam의 성공을 부러워한다

9 By relaxing and meditating, you can get rid of ______________.
휴식과 명상을 함으로써 당신은 화를 없앨 수 있습니다.

10 We found an ______________ solution to this problem.
우리는 이 문제에 대한 효과적인 해결책을 찾았다.

B 빈 칸에 알맞은 단어를 고르세요.

1 Jieun ate two ______________ of soup.
① bowls ② roots ③ pieces ④ wheels ⑤ angers

2 Do you feel any generation ______________ in your family?
① refund ② gap ③ envy ④ emotion ⑤ bloody

3 Some people are moving ______________ boxes.
① tree ② wooden ③ wood ④ monthly ⑤ tremble

Day 08

MP3

211 **wheelchair** [hwíːltʃὲər]
명 휠체어
wheelchair users 휠체어 사용자들　push a wheelchair 휠체어를 밀다

212 **improve** [imprúːv]
동 향상시키다　improve-improved-improved
improve your health 너의 건강을 증진시키다

213 **camp** [kæmp]
명 야영지, 텐트
make camp 텐트를 세우다　go camping 야영하러 가다

214 **contact** [kάntækt]
명 연락, 접촉　동 접촉하다　contact-contacted-contacted
get in contact with ~와 접촉, 연락하다

215 **overseas** [óuvərsìːz]
형 해외의　부 해외로
overseas trade 해외 무역　go overseas 해외로 가다

216 **since** [sins]
전 ~이래 줄곧
since 1998 1998년 이래로　since graduation 졸업 이후로

217 **issue** [íʃuː]
명 주제, 쟁점, 사안
a sensitive issue 민감한 주제　educational issues 교육 쟁점들

218 **lecture** [léktʃər]
명 강의　동 강의하다
a lecture on English literature 영문학에 대한 강의

219 **online** [aːnǀlain;ɔːn-]
형 온라인의
use an online bookstore 인터넷 서점을 이용하다

220 **detail** [ditéil]
명 세부사항　형 detailed 상세한
the details of the event 그 행사의 세부사항

221 **perform** [pərfɔ́ːrm]
동 수행하다, 공연하다　perform-performed-performed
perform a ceremony 의식을 행하다　perform a task 일을 수행하다

222 **plenty** [plénti]
명 많음, 충분
plenty of money 충분한 돈　have plenty of food 많은 음식이 있다

223 **comparable** [kάmpərəbl]
형 비교할 만한, 비슷한
remotely comparable 간접적으로 비교할만한

224 **theory** [θí(ː)əri]
명 이론　형 theoretical 이론적인
in theory 이론상으로는　scientific theory 과학 이론

225 **gradually** [grǽdʒəwəli]
부 서서히, 점차적으로
improve gradually 서서히 발전하다

Daily Test

| 월 일 |

A 우리말에 맞게 빈 칸에 알맞은 단어를 쓰세요.

1 Fresh vegetables help to ______________ your health.
신선한 채소는 당신의 건강을 증진시키는 걸 도와준다.

2 Once you arrive at the party, ______________ us.
일단 파티에 도착하면 우리에게 연락하세요.

3 They've lived in Seoul ______________ 2005. 그들은 2005년 이래로 서울에 살고 있다.

4 The election was a big ______________ last week. 선거가 지난 주에는 큰 쟁점이었다.

5 Eric will give a ______________ on the future of education.
Eric은 다음 달에 교육의 미래에 대해 강의를 할 것이다.

6 I usually buy clothes through ______________ shopping.
나는 대개 온라인 쇼핑으로 옷들을 산다.

7 Students ______________ a play for the school festival.
학교 축제에서 학생들은 연극을 공연했다.

8 Don't worry. We have ______________ of time. 걱정하지마. 우리는 시간이 많이 있어.

9 The two cities are ______________ to each other in terms of population.
인구 면에서 그 두 도시는 서로 비교할 만하다.

10 According to John's ______________, life exists on Mars.
John의 이론에 따르면, 화성에는 생명체가 살고 있다.

B 빈 칸에 알맞은 단어를 고르세요.

1 The number of people going ______________ for travel is increasing.
① country ② overseas ③ since ④ contact ⑤ high-tech

2 The police provided some ______________ of the accident.
① camp ② wooden ③ details ④ plenty ⑤ online

3 The weather is changing ______________.
① since ② gradually ③ intelligent ④ anger ⑤ wisely

Day 08

MP3

226 **orchestra** [ɔ́ːrkistrə]
명 오케스트라, 관현악단
the school orchestra 학교 관현악단　a jazz orchestra 재즈 오케스트라

227 **result** [rizʌ́lt]
명 결과
get a good result 좋은 결과를 얻다　as a result 결과적으로

228 **system** [sístəm]
명 제도, 체계, 조직
the Korean education system 한국의 교육 시스템

229 **sentence** [séntəns]
명 문장　+paragraph 명 문단
a correct sentence 올바른 문장　write a sentence 문장을 쓰다

230 **magical** [mǽdʒikəl]
형 마법의, 마법적인　명 magic 마법
magical powers 마법적인 힘　magical effect 마법의 효과

231 **thunder** [θʌ́ndər]
명 천둥(소리), 우레
a crash of thunder 우르르 쾅 하는 천둥소리

232 **aim** [eim]
명 목표　유 goal 목표
achieve the aim 목표를 달성하다　the final aim 최종 목표

233 **command** [kəmǽnd]
동 명령하다　명 명령　command-commanded-commanded
give a command to the soldiers 군인들에게 명령을 내리다

234 **presentation** [prìːzəntéiʃən]
명 수여, 발표
the presentation ceremony 수여식　give a presentation 발표 하다

235 **drum** [drʌm]
명 북, 드럼　동 두드리다　drum-drummed-drummed
beat a drum 북을 치다　drum on the door 문을 두드리다

236 **sheet** [ʃiːt]
명 (종이) 한 장, (침대) 시트
a sheet of paper 종이 한 장　change the sheet 침대 시트를 갈다

237 **crosswalk** [krɔ́(ː)swɔ̀ːk]
명 횡단보도
take a crosswalk 횡단보도를 건너다

238 **pollution** [pəljúːʃən]
명 오염, 공해
water pollution 수질 오염　noise pollution 소음 공해

239 **ignore** [ignɔ́ːr]
동 무시하다　ignore-ignored-ignored
ignore the safety rules 안전 규칙을 무시하다

240 **reflect** [riflékt]
동 반영하다, 반사하다　reflected-reflected-reflected
reflect the light 빛을 반사하다　reflect Tim's idea 팀의 생각을 반영하다

Daily Test

| 월 일 |

A 우리말에 맞게 빈 칸에 알맞은 단어를 쓰세요.

1 Jinju is a member of the school ______________. 진주는 학교 관현악단의 일원이다.

2 He was satisfied with the wonderful ______________. 그는 훌륭한 결과에 만족했다.

3 We need a new computer ______________. 우리는 새로운 컴퓨터 시스템이 필요하다.

4 The witch has strong ______________ powers. 그 마녀는 강력한 마법의 힘을 가졌다.

5 Our final ______________ is to win the race. 우리의 최종 목표는 경주에서 이기는 것이다.

6 The general ______________ the soldiers to cross the river.
장군은 병사들에게 강을 건너라고 명령했다.

7 I will give a ______________ in science class tomorrow.
나는 내일 과학 시간에 발표를 할 것이다.

8 Take extra care when you approach a ______________.
횡단보도에 접근할 때는 특별한 주의를 기울여라.

9 Air ______________ is a very serious problem in Seoul.
공기 오염은 서울의 매우 심각한 문제이다.

10 She ______________ the warning and went to the forest.
그녀는 경고를 무시하고 숲으로 향했다.

B 빈 칸에 알맞은 단어를 고르세요.

1 Lightning usually comes with loud ______________.
① sentence ② thunder ③ weather ④ aim ⑤ power

2 I need some ______________ of paper to write the report.
① packs ② cans ③ loaves ④ bottles ⑤ sheets

3 The window ______________ light into the room.
① system ② reflected ③ online ④ result ⑤ command

Review Test 04 Day 07 + Day 08

| 월 일 |

A 우리말에 맞게 빈 칸에 알맞은 단어를 쓰시오.

1 count ______________ from fifty 50에서부터 거꾸로 세다

2 ______________ to a letter 편지에 답하다

3 be ______________ to the president 대통령과 친척인

4 ______________ one's health 건강을 회복하다

5 a front ______________ 앞 바퀴

6 get in ______________ with ~와 접촉하다

7 ______________ graduation 졸업 이후로

8 ______________ a task 일을 수행하다

9 a ______________ of paper 종이 한 장

10 ______________ Tim's idea 팀의 생각을 반영하다

B 다음 영어 풀이에 알맞은 어휘를 〈보기〉에서 고르시오.

보기	condiment	gap	ignore	refund	orchestra

1 ____________ : something used to add flavor to food such as ketchup or mustard

2 ____________ : the money given back to a buyer who returns a product

3 ____________ : a space between two things, people, or events

4 ____________ : a group of people playing different musical instruments together

5 ____________ : to not care about something or someone that you see or hear

C 다음 단어의 관계가 A:B=C:D가 되도록 알맞은 단어를 골라 빈 칸에 적으시오.

1 mix : ______________ = recover : recovery

① mixed ② mixture ③ mixing
④ mixery ⑤ mixful

2 ______________ : table = tall : tree

① wooden ② desk ③ chair
④ plenty ⑤ circle

3 month : ______________ = day : daily

① monthly ② monthed ③ monthily
④ months ⑤ monthful

4 compare : ______________ = avoid : avoidable

① compared ② comparrable ③ comparing
④ comparible ⑤ comparable

5 maple : leaf = college : ______________

① historical ② bike ③ lecture
④ historian ⑤ weather

D 문맥에 맞게 다음 문장을 완성하시오.

1 They stopped •	• a the bloody battle.
2 The cook uses special •	• b and went to the forest.
3 Fresh vegetables help •	• c to improve your health.
4 Our final aim •	• d is to win the race.
5 She ignored the warning •	• e condiments for his dishes.

E 문장을 읽고 문맥에 적절한 단어를 고르시오.

1 I think this essay (reflects/regrets) Tom's view on social issues.

2 My little sister can now count (forward/backward) from 10 to 1.

3 Because the toy he bought was faulty, Sam asked for a (refund/recover).

4 They felt a wide (gap/mixture) between their opinions.

5 Scientists (investigated/invested) the cause of the flood in the region.

F 문장의 빈칸에 알맞은 단어를 〈보기〉에서 찾아 쓰시오. (필요하면 형태를 고치시오.)

보기 research theory envy overseas pollution

1 The company closed some of its ____________ branches.
그 회사는 해외 지사 중 몇 곳을 철수시켰다.

2 In ____________, the idea could be turned into a real product.
이론 상으로는 그 아이디어는 실제 제품이 될 수도 있을 것이다.

3 Recently, many countries agreed to reduce environmental ____________.
최근에 많은 국가들이 환경 오염을 줄이자는 데 동의했다.

4 His task at the new company is to do market ____________.
그가 새로운 회사에서 맡은 첫 업무는 시장 조사를 하는 것이다.

5 John ____________ Ron's wide knowledge of natural science.
John은 자연 과학에 대한 Ron의 방대한 지식을 부러워한다.

G 그림과 낱말이 잘못 짝지어진 것을 고르시오. .... (   )

ⓐ

maple

ⓑ

root

ⓒ

scientist

ⓓ

tomb

H 낱말과 어울리는 그림을 연결하시오.

1 drum •

2 presentation •

• ⓐ

• ⓑ

Study More

despite와 비슷한 의미를 가진 단어와 용법

- [in spite of] : '에도 불구하고'　[regardless of] : '~에 상관없이'
- despite와 in spite of는 거의 같은 의미로 쓰인다.
  Despite / In spite of financial difficulties, she managed to finish her studies.
  경제적 어려움에도 불구하고 그녀는 학업을 마칠 수 있었다.
- despite는 전치사이다. 따라서 despite of처럼 쓰지 않도록 주의한다.
  despite of financial difficulties (X)

Day 09

MP3

241 **organism** [ɔ́:rgənìzəm]
명 생물, 유기체 | 형 organic 유기농의, 유기체의
the social organism 사회적 유기체 | the living organism 생물체

242 **encourage** [inkə́:ridʒ]
동 격려하다, 북돋아주다 encourage-encouraged-encouraged
encourage each other 서로를 격려하다

243 **fear** [fiər]
명 공포, 두려움 동 ~을 두려워하다 fear-feared-feared
a fear of bugs 벌레에 대한 공포 | fear death 죽음을 두려워하다

244 **champion** [tʃǽmpiən]
명 우승자, 챔피언
the world baseball champion 세계 야구대회 우승자

245 **highway** [háiwèi]
명 고속도로
along the coastal highway 해안 도로를 따라서

246 **galaxy** [gǽləksi]
명 은하계
the mystery of our galaxy 우리 은하의 미스터리

247 **distance** [dístəns]
명 거리 | 형 distant 먼
a short distance 짧은 거리

248 **rich** [ritʃ]
형 다채로운, 풍부한
be rich in ~이 풍부한 | a country rich in oil 기름이 풍부한 나라

249 **sensor** [sénsər]
명 센서, 감지기
a heat sensor 화재 경보기

250 **vision** [víʒən]
명 시력, 시야 | 형 visual 시각의, 눈으로 보는
have poor vision 시력이 나쁘다 | vision loss 시력 손상

251 **manage** [mǽnidʒ]
동 간신히 ~하다, ~을 잘 해내다 manage-managed-managed
manage to arrive on time 간신히 제 시간에 도착하다

252 **appetite** [ǽpətàit]
명 식욕
loss of appetite 식욕 감퇴 | have a big appetite 식욕이 왕성하다

253 **wealthy** [wélθi]
형 부유한 | 명 wealth 부, (많은) 재산
a wealthy family 부유한 가족

254 **prove** [pru:v]
동 증명하다, 입증하다 prove-proved-proved
prove the theory 이론을 입증하다 | prove a fact 사실을 증명하다

255 **disabled** [diséibld]
형 장애가 있는
physically disabled 신체적인 장애가 있는

Daily Test

| 월 일 |

A 우리말에 맞게 빈 칸에 알맞은 단어를 쓰세요.

1 The human body is the best example of a complex living ___________.
인간의 몸은 복잡한 생물체의 가장 좋은 예이다.

2 James ___________ his daughter to finish the project.
James는 그의 딸이 프로젝트를 마칠 수 있도록 격려했다.

3 There are countless numbers of stars in the ___________.
은하계에는 셀 수 없이 많은 별들이 있다.

4 Watch the tree from a ___________. 거리를 두고 나무를 보세요.

5 Korea is a country ___________ in history and culture.
한국은 역사와 문화가 다채로운 나라이다.

6 There is a heat ___________ on the wall. 벽에 화재 경보기가 달려있다.

7 Playing too many computer games can cause ___________ loss.
컴퓨터 게임을 많이 하는 것은 시력 손상을 일으킬 수 있다.

8 I ___________ to stop him crying. 나는 그가 우는 것을 겨우 멈추게 했다.

9 Lisa's family was ___________ and kind. Lisa의 가족은 부유하고 친절했다.

10 He needs to ___________ that he paid for the book.
그는 책 값을 지불했다는 것을 증명해야 한다.

B 빈 칸에 알맞은 단어를 고르세요.

1 We drove the car along the coastal ___________.
① highway ② storm ③ champion ④ disabled ⑤ pollution

2 Going for a walk helps build a(n) ___________.
① food ② encourage ③ appetite ④ distance ⑤ manager

3 He is physically ___________ because of an accident.
① able ② disabled ③ enable ④ sensor ⑤ rich

Day 09

MP3

256 **confuse** [kənfjúːz]
동 (사람을) 혼란 시키다, 혼동시키다 confuse-confused-confused
confuse your family 가족을 혼란 시키다

257 **spare** [spɛər]
형 예비의, 따로 떼어놓는
spare time 여가 시간 spare rooms 남는 방

258 **grand** [grænd]
형 웅장한, 화려한
live in a grand castle 웅장한 성에서 살다

259 **carpenter** [kάːrpəntər]
명 목수
carpenter's shop 목공소 a clever carpenter 솜씨 좋은 목수

260 **lifetime** [láiftàim]
명 일생, 생애
once in a lifetime 생애 한 번 during his lifetime 그의 일생 동안

261 **windmill** [wíndmìl]
명 풍차 *mill 명 방앗간, 제분소
a large windmill 큰 풍차 operate a windmill 풍차를 가동하다

262 **awful** [ɔ́ːfəl]
형 끔찍한
an awful experience 끔찍한 경험 an awful smell 지독한 냄새

263 **earthquake** [ə́ːrθkwèik]
명 지진
a strong earthquake 강한 지진 feel an earthquake 지진을 느끼다

264 **thanks to** [θæŋks tuː]
~덕분에 *owing to ~때문에
thanks to his effort 그의 노력 덕분에

265 **string** [striŋ]
명 끈, 줄
a piece of string 끈 한 가닥 tie strings 끈을 묶다

266 **author** [ɔ́ːθər]
명 작가
her favorite author 그녀의 좋아하는 작가

267 **sculpture** [skʌ́lptʃər]
명 조각품
ancient Greek sculptures 고대 그리스 조각품들

268 **absorb** [əbsɔ́ːrb]
동 흡수하다, 빨아들이다 absorb-absorbed-absorbed
absorb water 물을 흡수하다, 빨아들이다 absorb heat 열을 흡수하다

269 **enable** [inéibl]
동 가능하게 하다
enable students to watch the movie 학생들이 그 영화를 보게 하다

270 **think over** [θiŋk óuvər]
~을 심사 숙고하다
think over the matter 그 일에 대해 심사 숙고하다

Daily Test

| 월 일 |

A 우리말에 맞게 빈 칸에 알맞은 단어를 쓰세요.

1 The news ______________ every student. 그 소식은 모든 학생들을 혼란스럽게 했다.

2 The mountain was beautiful and ______________. 그 산은 아름답고 웅장했다.

3 The kind ______________ repaired my chair. 친절한 목수가 내 의자를 고쳐주었다.

4 A single ______________ can power many homes.
풍차 한 개는 많은 가정에 에너지를 공급할 수 있다.

5 The ______________ destroyed most buildings in the town.
지진이 마을의 대부분의 건물들을 파괴했다.

6 Tie the box up with black ______________. 검은 끈으로 그 상자를 묶으세요.

7 J.K.Rowling is the ______________ of the Harry Potter series.
J.k.Rowling은 해리포터 시리즈의 작가다.

8 James collects ______________ of animals. James는 동물 조각품들을 수집한다.

9 This shirt ______________ sweat very well. 이 셔츠는 땀을 잘 흡수한다.

10 Confidence has ______________ him to try many different things.
자신감이 그에게 여러 가지를 시도해 볼 수 있게 했다.

B 빈 칸에 알맞은 단어를 고르세요.

1 Don't worry, I have a(n) ______________ key.
① spare ② circle ③ grand ④ enable ⑤ sense

2 ______________ Billy's help, we could solve the problem.
① Although ② Thanks to ③ Despite ④ Anyway ⑤ However

3 We will ______________ your offer.
① organism ② think over ③ confuse ④ keep up with ⑤ make

Day 10

MP3

271 **proportion** [prəpɔ́ːrʃən]
명 비율,부분
equal proportion 동등한 비율

272 **giraffe** [dʒərǽf]
명 기린
a giraffe's long neck 기린의 긴 목

273 **deal** [diːl]
동 다루다
deal with ~을 다루다, 처리하다　deal with a problem 문제를 처리하다

274 **role** [roul]
명 역할
a major role 주된 역할　play an important role 중요한 역할을 하다

275 **humanism** [hjúːmənìzəm]
명 인본주의, 휴머니즘
the ideas of humanism 인본주의의 신념

276 **surround** [səráund]
동 둘러싸다, 에워싸다　surround-surrounded-surrounded
surround the house 집을 둘러싸다

277 **deceive** [disíːv]
동 속이다, 기만하다　deceive-deceived-deceived
deceive her parents 그녀의 부모님을 속이다

278 **symptom** [símptəm]
명 증상
flu symptoms 감기 증상　a specific symptom 특정한 증상

279 **pass away** [pæs əwéi]
동 사망하다, 돌아가시다
pass away five years ago 5년 전에 돌아가시다

280 **unlike** [ʌnláik]
전 ~와 다른
unlike other people 다른 사람들과 다른

281 **figurative** [fígjərətiv]
형 비유적인
a figurative expression 비유적인 표현

282 **maintain** [meintéin]
동 유지하다　maintain-maintained-maintained
maintain balance 균형을 유지하다　maintain silence 침묵을 유지하다

283 **preserve** [prizə́ːrv]
동 보호하다, 보존하다　preserve-preserved-preserved
preserve the environment 자연을 보존하다

284 **book** [buk]
동 예약하다　유 reserve 예약하다
book a restaurant 식당을 예약하다　book a flight 항공편을 예약하다

285 **chest** [tʃest]
명 가슴, 흉부
chest pains 가슴 통증　beat her chest 그녀의 가슴을 치며 슬퍼하다

Daily Test

| 월 일 |

A 우리말에 맞게 빈 칸에 알맞은 단어를 쓰세요.

1 A large ______________ of the country is taken up by the desert.
그 나라의 대부분은 사막으로 덮여 있다.

2 She played an important ______________ in solving the problem.
그녀는 그 문제를 해결하는 데 중요한 역할을 했다.

3 The house is ______________ by a big forest. 그 집은 커다란 숲으로 둘러싸여 있다.

4 Don't ______________ yourself. 자기 자신을 속이지 마세요.

5 Flu ______________ include headache and fever. 감기 증상은 두통과 열을 포함한다.

6 My grandmother ______________ five years ago. 할머니께서는 5년 전에 돌아가셨다.

7 ______________ other people, Lily didn't like the performance.
대부분의 사람들과 달리, Lily는 그 공연을 좋아하지 않았다.

8 Don't use too many ______________ expressions in formal documents.
공식적인 문서에 비유적인 표현은 너무 많이 쓰지 마세요.

9 He exercises everyday to ______________ his health.
그는 건강을 지키기 위해 매일 운동한다.

10 Can I ______________ a flight to London? 런던 행 비행기를 예약할 수 있나요?

B 빈 칸에 알맞은 단어를 고르세요.

1 ______________ order is very important.
① Maintaining ② proportion ③ role ④ surround ⑤ lifetime

2 The movie ______________ with the accident.
① humanism ② symptoms ③ awful ④ figurative ⑤ deals

3 Put your left hand on the right side of your ______________.
① role ② chest ③ proportion ④ absorb ⑤ grand

Day 10

MP3

286 bind [baind]

동 묶다 bind-bound-bound

bind your hair 머리를 묶다 bind up a wound 부상을 붕대로 묶다

287 weapon [wépən]

명 무기

nuclear weapons 핵무기 a secret weapon 비밀 무기

288 enlarge [inlɑ́ːrdʒ]

동 확대하다, 확장하다 enlarge-enlarged-enlarged

enlarge a photo 사진을 확대하다 enlarge a park 공원을 확장하다

289 diverse [divə́ːrs]

형 다양한

diverse cultures 다양한 문화들 diverse ideas 다양한 견해

290 folk [fouk]

명 (복수취급) 사람들 형 민속의

country folk 시골 사람들 folk culture 민속 문화

291 valid [vǽlid]

형 유효한, 타당한 반 invalid 무효한, 근거없는

a valid concert ticket 유효한 콘서트 표 a valid reason 타당한 이유

292 emphasize [émfəsàiz]

동 강조하다 emphasize-emphasized-emphasized

emphasize the importance of exercise 운동의 중요성을 강조하다

293 quantity [kwɑ́ntəti]

명 양, 수량, 분량

a small quantity of food 적은 양의 음식

294 obtain [əbtéin]

동 얻다 obtain-obtained-obtained

obtain useful advice 유용한 조언을 얻다

295 involve [inválv]

동 수반하다, 포함하다 involve-involved-involved

involve a dangerous task 위험한 일을 수반하다

296 appropriate [əpróupriət]

형 적절한 반 inappropriate 부적절한

an appropriate method 적절한 방법 appropriate words 적절한 말

297 absolute [ǽbsəlùːt]

형 절대의, 절대적인 부 absolutely 전적으로

absolute truth 절대 진리 have absolute power 절대 권력을 가지다

298 status [stéitəs]

명 신분, 지위, 자격

social status 사회적 지위 equal status 동일한 자격

299 impressive [imprésiv]

형 인상적인, 감명 깊은

an impressive movie 감명 깊은 영화

300 rescue [réskjuː]

명 구조 동 구하다, 구조하다 rescue-rescued-rescued

hope of rescue 구조의 희망

Daily Test

| 월 일 |

Ⓐ 우리말에 맞게 빈 칸에 알맞은 단어를 쓰세요.

1 They began to ______________ a prisoner to a tree. 그들은 나무에 죄수를 묶기 시작했다.

2 We'd like to ______________ this photo. 우리는 이 사진을 확대하고 싶어요.

3 There are ______________ views about the cause of the accident. 그 사고의 이유에 대해 다양한 견해가 있다.

4 I know some interesting ______________ tales about the tree. 나는 저 나무에 관한 재미있는 민화를 몇 개 알고 있다.

5 The teacher ______________ the importance of exercise. 선생님은 운동의 중요성을 강조하셨다.

6 There is a large ______________ of food on the table. 탁자 위에는 많은 양의 음식이 있었다.

7 I ______________ some useful information from the book. 나는 그 책에서 유용한 정보들을 얻었다.

8 Don't ______________ us in that matter. 우리를 그 일에 포함시키지 말아요.

9 His example is ______________. 그의 예시는 적절했다.

10 Her new movie was very ______________. 그녀의 새 영화는 매우 인상적이었다.

Ⓑ 빈 칸에 알맞은 단어를 고르세요.

1 Your reason is not ______________.

① valid ② weapon ③ tale ④ deceive ⑤ rescue

2 Many people want to have a high social ______________.

① folk ② village ③ status ④ reason ⑤ preview

3 People ______________ a child from drowning.

① went ② rescued ③ bound ④ passed away ⑤ unlike

Review Test 05

Day 09 + Day 10 | 월 일 |

A 우리말에 맞게 빈 칸에 알맞은 단어를 쓰시오.

1 the social ________________ 사회적 유기체

2 ________________ each other 서로를 격려하다

3 a heat ________________ 화재 경보기

4 ________________ your family 가족을 혼란시키다

5 an ________________ experience 끔찍한 경험

6 ________________ the house 집을 둘러싸다

7 ________________ her parents 그녀의 부모님을 속이다

8 a ________________ expression 비유적인 표현

9 ________________ cultures 다양한 문화들

10 an ________________ method 적절한 방법

B 다음 영어 풀이에 알맞은 어휘를 〈보기〉에서 고르시오.

보기 highway encourage proportion giraffe organism

1 ______________ : a very tall animal with a long neck and thin legs

2 ______________ : to give someone confidence or hope to do something

3 ______________ : the relationship between one thing and another in terms of size or number

4 ______________ : any living thing that can act on its own

5 ______________ : a large road where people drive fast

C 다음 단어의 관계가 A:B=C:D가 되도록 알맞은 단어를 골라 빈 칸에 적으시오.

1 ________________ : distant = diversity : diverse

① distance ② far ③ distancity
④ distantly ⑤ away

2 famous : ________________ = skilled : carpenter

① popular ② author ③ unfamous
④ pretty ⑤ cloud

3 animal : ________________ = flower : rose

① land ② plants ③ zoo
④ lifetime ⑤ giraffe

4 ________________ : wildlife = give : present

① animal ② looking ③ preserve
④ make ⑤ forest

5 watch : documentary = ________________ : hotel

① great ② Korean ③ East
④ book ⑤ taste

D 문맥에 맞게 다음 문장을 완성하시오.

1	Lisa's family was •	• a	most buildings in the town.
2	The earthquake destroyed •	• b	information from the book.
3	She played an important role •	• c	wealthy and kind.
4	I know some interesting •	• d	folk tales about the tree.
5	I obtained some useful •	• e	in solving the problem.

E 문장을 읽고 문맥에 적절한 단어를 고르시오.

1 The scientist successfully (proved/deceived) his theory.

2 The new principal (emphasized/rescued) the importance of helping each other.

3 (Despite/Thanks to) the development of computer graphics, we can make a movie about anything.

4 The scholarship (enabled/absorbed) him to go to college.

5 When you travel overseas, you need a (vital/valid) passport.

F 문장의 빈칸에 알맞은 단어를 〈보기〉에서 찾아 쓰시오. (필요하면 형태를 고치시오.)

보기	manage	absolute	proportion	diverse	appropriate

1 Although she was extremely tired, she ____________ to walk home.
그녀는 아주 피곤했지만 집까지 간신히 걸어왔다.

2 The students in this school come from ____________ countries.
이 학교의 학생들은 다양한 국가에서 왔다.

3 It is not ____________ to eat or drink in the public library.
공공 도서관에서 먹거나 마시는 것은 적절하지 않다.

4 Toys make up a large ____________ of the company's sales.
장난감이 그 회사의 판매에서 큰 비율을 차지하고 있다.

5 The Romans did not want to give ____________ power to one person.
로마인들은 한 개인에게 절대적인 권력을 주는 것을 원치 않았다.

G 그림에 해당하는 낱말을 〈보기〉에서 골라 쓰시오.

1

(　　　　　　　)

2
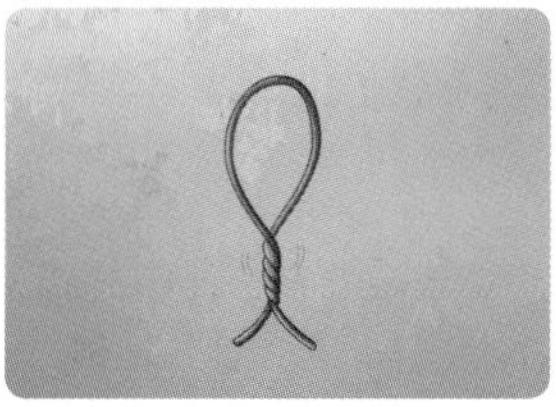
(　　　　　　　)

3

(　　　　　　　)

4

(　　　　　　　)

5

(　　　　　　　)

6

(　　　　　　　)

보기 champion appetite weapon string windmill bind

Study More

manage의 용법

- '(단체, 일정, 감정 등을) 운영하다, 관리하다, 감당하다'

  manage a sales department 영업 부서를 관리하다

  manage anger and stress 분노와 스트레스를 감당하다

  Can you **manage** dinner next week? 다음 주에 식사를 한 번 더 할 수 있니?

- '~에 성공하다/~을 해내다' *[manage to+동사] 형태로 자주 쓰인다.

  My mother **managed to pass** her driving test. 어머니는 용케 운전 시험에 합격했다.

Day 11

MP3

301 **declare** [diklέər]
동 선언하다, 표명하다 명 declaration 선언
declare independence 독립을 선언하다

302 **blackboard** [blǽkbɔ̀:rd]
명 칠판
write on the blackboard 칠판 위에 쓰다

303 **refuse** [réfju:s]
동 거절하다 refuse-refused-refused
refuse her request 그녀의 요청을 거절하다

304 **tap** [tæp]
동 (가볍게) 톡톡 두드리다 tap-tapped-tapped
tap on the window 창문을 두드리다

305 **maximum** [mǽksəməm]
형 최고의, 최대의
the maximum speed 최고 속도

306 **minimum** [mínəməm]
형 최저의, 최소한의
a minimum price 최저가 a minimum wage 최저 임금

307 **actually** [ǽktʃuəli]
부 실제로, 실은
actually happen 실제로 일어나다 actually difficult 실제로 어려운

308 **classmate** [klǽsmèit]
명 반 친구
meet my classmate 내 반 친구를 만나다

309 **signal** [sígnəl]
명 신호 동 신호를 보내다
a stop signal 정지 신호 traffic signals 교통 신호

310 **highlight** [háilàit]
동 강조하다 명 가장 흥미로운 부분, 하이라이트
highlight the benefits of language study 언어 학습의 이점을 강조하다

311 **sincere** [sinsíər]
형 진실된, 온후한 부 sincerely 진실되게
sincere love 진실된 사랑 sincere thanks 진실된 감사

312 **bet** [bet]
동 내기하다 명 내기 bet-bet-bet
bet 10 dollars on the team 그 팀에 10달러를 걸다

313 **chore** [tʃɔ:r]
명 허드렛일, 하기 싫은 일
do a chore 집안일을 하다 a boring chore 지루한 허드렛일

314 **chilly** [[tʃíli]
형 쌀쌀한, 추운
a chilly weather 쌀쌀한 날씨

315 **concentrate** [kάnsəntrèit]
동 집중하다 concentrate-concentrated-concentrated
concentrate on studying 공부에 집중하다

Daily Test

| 월 일 |

A 우리말에 맞게 빈 칸에 알맞은 단어를 쓰세요.

1 The referees ______________ the game a draw. 심판진은 경기를 무승부로 선언했다.

2 Peter ______________ to help the poor. Peter는 가난한 사람들을 돕기를 거절했다.

3 Don't ______________ at the door. 문을 두드리지 마세요.

4 The ______________ speed of the train is about 250km per hour.
기차의 최고 속도는 약 시속 250km이다.

5 We traveled all around the world at ______________ expense.
우리는 최소한의 비용으로 전 세계를 여행했다.

6 He ______________ doesn't like the car. 그는 실은 그 차를 좋아하지 않는다.

7 I will play soccer with my ______________ tomorrow.
나는 내일 우리 반 친구들과 축구를 할 것이다.

8 The police officer gave us a ______________ to stop.
경찰관은 우리에게 정지 신호를 보냈다.

9 I didn't watch the game, just the ______________ later on.
나는 그 게임을 보지는 않았고, 나중에 하이라이트를 봤다.

10 I have many ______________ friends. 나는 진실된 친구들이 많이 있다.

B 빈 칸에 알맞은 단어를 고르세요.

1 It's ______________ outside. Put on your gloves.
① sincere ② chilly ③ maximum ④ minimum ⑤ chore

2 I want to ______________ on watching the movie.
① maximum ② tap ③ concentrate ④ concentrating ⑤ concentration

3 The father ______________ on his son's shoulder.
① refused ② highlighted ③ declared ④ confused ⑤ tapped

Day 11

MP3

316 **satellite** [sǽtəlàit]
명 인공위성
a weather satellite 기상 위성 a satellite picture 위성 사진

317 **shuttle** [ʃʌ́tl]
명 정기 왕복 항공기(버스, 열차)
a shuttle train 정기 왕복 버스 a space shuttle 우주 왕복선

318 **delay** [diléi]
명 지연, 지체 동 미루다, 연기하다
a long delay 긴 지연 a two-hour delay 2시간의 지연

319 **solution** [səljúːʃən]
명 해결책, 해법
a unique solution 독특한 해법 a simple solution 간단한 해결책

320 **fully** [fúli]
부 완전히, 충분히
fully understand 완전히 이해하다

321 **department** [dipáːrtmənt]
명 부서, 학과
the marketing department 마케팅 부서 the art department 예술부

322 **generous** [dʒénərəs]
형 인심좋은, 관대한
a generous teacher 관대한 선생님 a generous woman 인자한 여성

323 **population** [pàpjəléiʃən]
명 인구
the population of Seoul 서울의 인구 population growth 인구 성장

324 **frame** [freim]
명 뼈대, 틀, 액자
the frame of a house 집의 틀 a picture frame 사진 액자

325 **lyrics** [líriks]
명 (복수형태) (노래의) 가사, 서정시
a song with poetic lyrics 시적인 가사의 노래

326 **industry** [índəstri]
명 산업, 업계
a chemical industry 화학 산업 the film industry 영화계

327 **opposite** [ápəzit]
전 건너편에 형 반대의
opposite the opera house 오페라 하우스 맞은 편

328 **understanding** [ʌ̀ndərstǽndiŋ]
명 이해, 이해력
understanding of the problem 문제에 대한 이해

329 **dizzy** [dízi]
형 어지러운, 아찔한
feel dizzy 현기증이 나다 a dizzy height 아찔한 높이

330 **even though** [íːvən ðou]
비록 ~일지라도
even though I didn't study hard 비록 열심히 공부하지 않았을지라도

Daily Test

| 월 일 |

A 우리말에 맞게 빈 칸에 알맞은 단어를 쓰세요.

1 NASA controls various ______________. NASA는 다양한 위성들을 제어한다.

2 We don't have time to ______________. 우리는 지체할 시간이 없어요.

3 Lily has a clever ______________ to global warming.
Lily는 지구 온난화에 대해 기발한 해결책을 갖고 있다.

4 We ______________ understand Sally's condition.
우리는 Sally의 상태에 대해 충분히 이해한다.

5 Peter worked at the sales ______________. Peter는 영업부에서 일했다.

6 Our Korean history teacher is really ______________.
우리 한국사 선생님은 정말 너그러우시다.

7 The singer writes ______________ for most of his songs.
그 가수는 자기 곡 대부분의 가사를 쓴다.

8 My father worked in the advertisement ______________.
우리 아빠는 광고계에서 일하셨다.

9 Yujin's car is on the ______________ side of the road. 도로 맞은 편에 유진의 차가 있다.

10 Linda has a great ______________ of modern art.
Linda는 현대 미술에 높은 이해력을 갖고 있다.

B 빈 칸에 알맞은 단어를 고르세요.

1 We are in a space ______________!
① universe ② shuttle ③ solution ④ cover ⑤ frame

2 The ______________ of the village is increasing rapidly.
① popular ② delay ③ department ④ population ⑤ dizzy

3 ______________ it may seem difficult at first, you will like it.
① Generally ② Highlight ③ Actually ④ Even though ⑤ Lovely

Day 12

MP3

331 **journey** [dʒə́ːrni]
명 여행
a weekend journey 주말 여행

332 **shelter** [ʃéltər]
명 피난처
a storm shelter 태풍으로부터의 피난처

333 **hurricane** [hə́ːrəkèin]
명 허리케인
the path of a hurricane 허리케인의 진로

334 **ruler** [rúːlər]
명 통치자, 지배자
a strong ruler 강력한 통치자

335 **tax** [tæks]
명 세금
raise taxes 세금을 올리다 pay a tax 세금을 납부하다

336 **fingerprint** [fíŋgərprìnt]
명 지문
leave her fingerprints 그녀의 지문을 남기다

337 **slip** [slip]
동 미끄러지다 slip-slipped-slipped
slip on the ice 얼음 위에서 미끄러지다

338 **budget** [bʌ́dʒit]
명 예산 동 예산을 세우다
a monthly budget 월간 예산 the education budget 교육 예산

339 **electricity** [ilektrísəti]
명 전기 형 electric 전기의, 전기에 의한
save electricity 전기를 절약하다 produce electricity 전기를 생산하다

340 **insult** [insʌ́lt]
명 모욕 동 모욕하다 insult-insulted-insulted
a personal insult 인신 공격 insult other people 다른 사람을 모욕하다

341 **summarize** [sʌməraiz]
동 요약하다 명 summary 요약
summarize the report 보고서를 요약하다

342 **scrape** [skreip]
동 긁어내다, 벗겨내다 scrape-scraped-scraped
scrape the ice 얼음을 긁어내다 scrape paint off 페인트를 긁어내다

343 **reveal** [rivíːl]
동 드러내다, 밝히다 reveal-revealed-revealed
reveal a secret 비밀을 밝히다 reveal the truth 진실을 밝히다

344 **below** [bilóu]
부 아래에 전 ~아래에
below average 평균 이하 below the knee 무릎 아래에

345 **brick** [brik]
명 벽돌
a brick wall 벽돌담 a brick house 벽돌집

Daily Test

| 월 일 |

A 우리말에 맞게 빈 칸에 알맞은 단어를 쓰세요.

1 Our ______________ to Osaka took about 3 hours.
우리의 오사카로의 여행은 약 3시간이 걸렸다.

2 There are two storm ______________ in our city.
우리 도시에는 두 개의 태풍 피난처가 있다.

3 Peter was the ______________ of our village, in name only.
Peter는 우리 마을의 이름뿐인 지도자였다.

4 The government will raise ______________ this year. 정부는 올해 세금을 올릴 계획이다.

5 These days many devices use ______________ instead of passwords.
요즘에는 많은 장치들이 비밀번호 대신 지문을 사용한다.

6 You should be careful not to ______________ on the ice.
얼음 위에서 넘어지지 않도록 조심해야 한다.

7 We should save ______________. 우리는 전기를 절약해야 한다.

8 Don't ______________ my friends. 내 친구들을 모욕하지 마세요.

9 She ______________ long reports concisely. 그녀는 긴 보고서들을 간결한 말로 요약했다.

10 Let's ______________ mud off the door. 문에 진흙을 긁어냅시다.

B 빈 칸에 알맞은 단어를 고르세요.

1 You should learn to make a monthly ______________.
① budget ② money ③ fingerprint ④ electricity ⑤ slip

2 Answer the questions ______________.
① under ② below ③ high ④ spirit ⑤ down

3 It is important to ______________ the truth.
① generous ② insulted ③ chore ④ reveal ⑤ obtaining

Day 12

MP3

346 **space** [speis]
명 우주
the first man in space 우주로 간 최초의 남자

347 **passion** [pǽʃən]
명 열정 형 passionate 열정적인
have a passion for ~에 대한 열정이 있다

348 **as long as** [əz lɔ(:)ŋ əz]
~하는 한
as long as the weather is good 날씨가 좋기만 한다면

349 **national** [nǽʃənəl]
형 국가의, 전국적인
a national holiday 국경일 a national park 국립공원

350 **display** [displéi]
동 전시하다 명 전시 display-displayed-displayed
display electric goods 전자 제품을 전시하다

351 **billion** [bíljən]
명 10억
earn a billion dollars 10억 달러를 벌다 billions of 수십억의

352 **perspective** [pərspéktiv]
명 관점, 시각 +aspect 명 전망, 양상
see an issue from a different perspective 쟁점을 다른 관점에서 바라 보다

353 **optical** [áptikəl]
형 시각적인
optical effects 시각 효과 an optical illusion 착시현상

354 **rush** [rʌʃ]
동 서두르다 rush-rushed-rushed
need to rush 서두를 필요가 있다 rush around 분주하게 돌아다니다

355 **trait** [treit]
명 특성 유 characteristic 특징, 특질
personality traits 성격적 특성 a genetic trait 유전적 특성

356 **compass** [kʌ́mpəs]
명 나침반
read a compass 나침반을 읽다 a map and compass 지도와 나침반

357 **pole** [poul]
명 막대기, (지구의) 극
the North Pole 북극 the South Pole 남극

358 **rely on** [rilái ən]
~에 의존하다, ~에 의지하다 유 count on ~에 기대다
rely on his parents 그의 부모님께 의존하다

359 **lid** [lid]
명 뚜껑
take off a lid 뚜껑을 열다 a disposable lid 일회용 뚜껑

360 **impossible** [impásəbl]
형 불가능한, 믿기 어려운
an impossible plan 실현 불가능한 계획

Daily Test

| 월 일 |

A 우리말에 맞게 빈 칸에 알맞은 단어를 쓰세요.

1 His ______________ for dancing is amazing. 그의 춤에 대한 열정은 놀랍다.

2 Let's go to Seoraksan ______________ Park next week.
다음 주에 설악산 국립공원에 가자.

3 He will ______________ his paintings in the gallery next week.
그는 다음 주에 갤러리에서 그의 그림들을 전시할 것이다.

4 ______________ of people use the software. 수십억의 사람들이 그 소프트웨어를 사용한다.

5 We need to handle this issue from a student's ______________.
우리는 이 문제를 학생의 관점에서 처리해야 합니다.

6 The ______________ effects of this movie are awesome.
그 영화의 시각효과는 놀라웠다.

7 We don't need to ______________. 우리는 서두를 필요가 없어요.

8 Empathy is a human ______________. 공감력은 인간의 특성 중의 하나이다.

9 Nowadays most people ______________ Smartphones for Internet access.
요즈음에는 대부분의 사람들이 인터넷 사용을 위해 스마트폰에 의존한다.

10 Amber opened the ______________ of the jar and looked inside it.
Amber는 항아리의 뚜껑을 열고 안쪽을 살펴보았다.

B 빈 칸에 알맞은 단어를 고르세요.

1 I'll keep dancing ______________ I am physically capable.
① although ② in spite of ③ as long as ④ national ⑤ rely on

2 Mr. Kim wants to explore the North ______________.
① Pole ② Fall ③ Pull ④ Shelter ⑤ Side

3 It's ______________ to arrive on time.
① billions ② possibly ③ perspective ④ impossible ⑤ trait

Review Test 06

A 우리말에 맞게 빈 칸에 알맞은 단어를 쓰시오.

1 ______________ her request 그녀의 요청을 거절하다

2 a stop ______________ 정지 신호

3 a boring ______________ 지루한 허드렛일

4 the marketing ______________ 마케팅 부서

5 ______________ of the problem 문제에 대한 이해

6 a storm ______________ 태풍으로부터의 피난처

7 ______________ on the ice 얼음 위에서 미끄러지다

8 ______________ a secret 비밀을 밝히다

9 ______________ the weather is good 날씨가 좋기만 한다면

10 a genetic ______________ 유전적 특성

B 다음 영어 풀이에 알맞은 어휘를 〈보기〉에서 고르시오.

보기	perspective	bet	lid	pole	budget

1 ____________ : a particular way of seeing or handling something

2 ____________ : a movable cover for a container such as a box, jar, or can

3 ____________ : a long and thin piece of wood that can be placed in the ground

4 ____________ : a particular amount of money set aside for spending

5 ____________ : to agree to pay something for one's guess

C 다음 단어의 관계가 A:B=C:D가 되도록 알맞은 단어를 골라 빈 칸에 적으시오.

1 ______________ : passion = generous : generosity

① passionate ② passionous ③ passions
④ passionally ⑤ passioning

2 protect : protection = solve : ______________

① difficult ② solution ③ problem
④ answer ⑤ solvution

3 actual : ______________ = easy : easily

① actualty ② act ③ acting
④ actually ⑤ actor

4 ______________ : minimum = high : low

① miniature ② large ③ max
④ minimal ⑤ maximum

5 magic : magical = nation : ______________

① nations ② America ③ national
④ country ⑤ nationally

D 문맥에 맞게 다음 문장을 완성하시오.

1 The police officer gave us •	• a	a signal to stop.
2 My father worked in •	• b	mud off the door.
3 These days many devices use •	• c	of this movie are awesome.
4 Let's scrape •	• d	fingerprints instead of passwords.
5 The optical effects •	• e	the advertisement industry.

E 문장을 읽고 문맥에 적절한 단어를 고르시오.

1 We need to see the problem from a different (perspective/trait).

2 She (scraped/declared) that what she said was true.

3 The man (refused/referred) to talk with me.

4 Because of a headache she can't (concentrate/rely) on her homework.

5 The (opposite/proportion) of the beginning is the end.

F 문장의 빈칸에 알맞은 단어를 〈보기〉에서 찾아 쓰시오. (필요하면 형태를 고치시오.)

보기	scrape	reveal	delay	trait	highlight

1 The bus was ____________ for 30 minutes.
버스는 30분이나 지연되었다.

2 She ____________ old paint off the wall.
그녀는 오래된 페인트를 벽에서 긁어냈다.

3 The newspaper article ____________ the importance of developing children's creativity.
그 신문 기사는 어린이들의 창의력을 발달 시키는 것의 중요성을 강조했다.

4 The data collected so far ____________ an interesting fact.
지금까지 수집된 자료는 흥미로운 사실 한 가지를 드러내 보인다.

5 Boldness is one of many ____________ of good leaders.
대담함은 훌륭한 지도자에게 요구되는 여러 특성 중의 하나다.

G 그림과 낱말이 잘못 짝지어진 것을 고르시오. .... (   )

ⓐ

blackboard

ⓑ

lyrics

ⓒ

satellite

ⓓ

classmate

H 낱말과 어울리는 그림을 연결하시오.

1 bricks •

2 compass •

• ⓐ

• ⓑ

Study More

'태풍, 폭풍'에 대한 단어들

- cyclone, hurricane, typhoon 은 모두 '(열대성) 폭풍/태풍'이라는 의미를 가지고 있다. 그러나 hurricane과 typhoon은 실제로는 tropical cyclone '열대성 폭풍'의 한 종류로서 발생 지역에 따라 다르게 불린다.
- cyclone 인도양에서 발생하는 폭풍, typhoon 북태평양에서 발생하는 폭풍
  hurricane 서인도 제도와 대서양에서 발생하는 폭풍

Day 13

MP3

361 **liquid** [líkwid]
명 액체 형 액체의
liquid soup 액체 비누 liquid medicine 물약

362 **campaign** [kæmpéin]
명 (사회적) 운동, 캠페인
conduct an environmental campaign 환경 캠페인을 벌이다

363 **make-up** [meik ʌp]
명 화장품, 화장
lip make-up 입술 화장 a make-up artist 메이크업 아티스트

364 **draw** [drɔː]
동 끌어당기다, 잡아 당기다 명 무승부 draw-drew-drawn
draw a cart 수레를 끌다 draw curtains 커튼을 치다

365 **conduct** [kάndʌ̀kt]
동 (특정 행동을) 하다, 실시하다
conduct an experiment 실험을 하다

366 **impression** [impréʃən]
명 인상, 느낌
the first impression 첫인상

367 **exhibit** [igzíbit]
동 전시하다 exhibit-exhibited-exhibited 명 exhibition 전시, 전시회
exhibit photos 사진들을 전시하다

368 **starve** [stɑːrv]
동 굶주리다, 굶어 죽다 starve-starved-starved
starving people 굶주린 사람들 be starving 배가 많이 고픈

369 **post** [poust]
명 우편 동 우편을 발송하다 post-posted-posted
the post office 우체국 by post 우편으로

370 **notice** [nóutis]
명 주의, 공고 동 알아차리다, 인지하다 notice-noticed-noticed
put up a notice 공고를 내다 notice a mistake 실수를 알아차리다

371 **erupt** [irʌ́pt]
동 폭발하다, 터지다 erupt-erupted-erupted 명 eruption 폭발
the volcano began to erupt 화산이 폭발하기 시작하다

372 **stay up** [stei ʌp]
안 자다, 깨어 있다
stay up late studying 밤새 공부하다

373 **remain** [riméin]
동 여전히 ~이다, 남다 remain-remained-remained
remain silent 여전히 침묵을 지키다 remain friends 친구로 남다

374 **press** [pres]
동 누르다, 바짝 대다
press a button 버튼을 누르다

375 **intellectual** [ìntəléktʃuəl]
형 지능의, 지적인
intellectual capacity 지적 능력 intellectual property 지적 재산

Daily Test

| 월 일 |

A 우리말에 맞게 빈 칸에 알맞은 단어를 쓰세요.

1 The ____________ medicine is for the baby. 그 물약은 아기 거에요.

2 This store sells a variety of eye ____________ products.
이 가게는 다양한 종류의 눈 화장 제품을 판다.

3 The university ____________ an online survey. 그 대학은 온라인 설문 조사를 했다.

4 Making a good first ____________ is very important.
좋은 첫인상을 만드는 것은 매우 중요하다.

5 The gallery ____________ some Van Gogh paintings.
그 갤러리에서는 반 고흐의 그림들 일부를 전시했다.

6 Students are raising money to help ____________ children.
학생들은 굶주린 아이들을 돕기 위해 모금을 하고 있다.

7 She didn't ____________ my mistake. 그녀는 내 실수를 알아차리지 못했다.

8 The bomb could ____________ at any time. 그 폭탄은 언제든지 터질 수 있다.

9 Minhyuk ____________ silent. 민혁은 여전히 침묵을 지키고 있다.

10 If you want to open the box, ____________ number "2".
상자를 열고 싶다면, 2번을 누르세요.

B 빈 칸에 알맞은 단어를 고르세요.

1 We ____________ all night studying for final exams.
① exhibited ② make-up ③ barbecue ④ stayed up ⑤ rushing

2 The horse is ____________ a wagon.
① drew ② drawing ③ conducting ④ displaying ⑤ posting

3 A high ____________ capacity is required for the work.
① exhibit ② erupt ③ intellectual ④ press ⑤ tax

Day 13

MP3

376 **talented** [tǽləntid]
형 재능 있는 　 유 gifted 재능이 있는
a talented player 재능있는 선수 　 a talented artist 재능있는 예술가

377 **occur** [əkə́:r]
동 발생하다, 일어나다 　 occur-occurred-occurred
A natural disaster occurred. 자연 재해가 일어났다.

378 **experiment** [ikspérəmənt]
명 실험 　 동 실험하다 　 experiment-experimented-experimented
the result of an experiment 실험의 결과

379 **hatch** [hætʃ]
동 부화하다 　 hatch-hatched-hatched
hatch eggs 알을 부화하다 　 be about to hatch 막 부화하려고 하다

380 **code** [koud]
명 암호, 부호
break a code 암호를 풀다

381 **durable** [djú(:)ərəbl]
형 견고한, 오래가는
be durable 지속성이 있다 　 durable plastic 오래가는 플라스틱

382 **rent** [rent]
명 집세, 방세 　 동 세를 내다, 빌리다
rent an apartment 아파트를 임대하다 　 rent a car 차를 빌리다

383 **grassland** [grǽslæ̀nd]
명 풀밭, 초원 　 유 meadow 목초지
a rough grassland 거친 초원

384 **expense** [ikspéns]
명 비용, 돈
living expenses 생활비 　 free of expense 무료로

385 **connection** [kənékʃən]
명 연결, 관련성
a connection between health and exercise 건강과 운동간의 관련성

386 **achieve** [ətʃí:v]
동 성취하다, 달성하다 　 achieve-achieved-achieved
achieve his goal 그의 목표를 달성하다

387 **metal** [métəl]
명 금속
a metal pipe 금속 파이프 　 made of metal 금속으로 만든

388 **adviser** [ədváizər]
명 조언자, 상담가
a legal adviser 법적 조언자 　 a careers adviser 진로 상담가

389 **harm** [hɑ:rm]
동 해를 끼치다 　 명 손해, 피해 　 harm-harmed-harmed
harm the environment 환경에 해를 끼치다

390 **log** [lɔ(:)g]
명 통나무
a log cabin 통나무 오두막 　 hollow out a log 통나무를 도려내다

Daily Test

| 월 일 |

A 우리말에 맞게 빈 칸에 알맞은 단어를 쓰세요.

1 Many accidents ______________ last week. 많은 사고가 지난 주에 일어났다.

2 We need hot water to do the ______________.
우리는 실험을 하기 위해 뜨거운 물이 필요합니다.

3 The duckling is about to ______________. 오리 새끼가 막 부화하려고 한다.

4 The building is strong and ______________. 그 건물은 튼튼하고 견고하다.

5 We will ______________ a room from Mr. Brown.
우리는 Brown씨에게서 방 하나를 빌릴거에요.

6 There is a ______________ between the two accidents. 두 사고는 관련성이 있다.

7 Nick ______________ his dream of buying his own car.
Nick은 차를 사겠다는 그의 꿈을 이뤘다.

8 The box is made of ______________. 저 상자는 금속으로 만들어졌다.

9 She is a perfect careers ______________. 그녀는 완벽한 진로 상담가이다.

10 Eating junk food does ______________ to your health.
인스턴트 음식을 먹는 것은 당신의 건강을 해친다.

B 빈 칸에 알맞은 단어를 고르세요.

1 The house was built at great ______________.
① expense ② experiment ③ code ④ grassland ⑤ posting

2 Yuna Kim is a ______________ figure skater.
① talent ② connection ③ talented ④ achieve ⑤ notice

3 The lake was surrounded by beautiful ______________ cabins.
① hatch ② log ③ tree ④ leaves ⑤ harm

Day 14

MP3

391 **congratulation** [kəngrætʃəléiʃən]
명 축하 동 congratulate 축하하다
a letter of congratulations 축하 편지

392 **genius** [dʒíːnjəs]
명 천재, 천재성
a hidden genius 숨겨진 천재 a scientific genius 과학적 천재성

393 **lunar** [lúːnər]
형 달의
the lunar surface 달의 표면 a lunar month 음력 달

394 **allowance** [əláuəns]
명 용돈, 수당
receive an allowance 용돈을 받다 a traveling allowance 여행비

395 **make up for** [meik ʌp fər]
만회하다, 보상하다
make up for a mistake 실수를 만회하다

396 **form** [fɔːrm]
명 유형, 형태, 서식 동 형성하다
various forms of energy 다양한 형태의 에너지

397 **appearance** [əpí(ː)ərəns]
명 겉모습, 외모
a smart appearance 멋진 모습 physical appearance 신체 외모

398 **illusion** [iljúːʒən]
명 환상, 오해, 착각
an optical illusion 착시(현상) an illusion about ~에 대한 환상

399 **empire** [émpaiər]
명 제국
the fall of the empire 제국의 멸망 rule an empire 제국을 통치하다

400 **examine** [igzǽmin]
동 조사하다, 검토하다 examine-examined-examined
examine the report 보고서를 검토하다

401 **offer** [ɔ́(ː)fər]
동 제공하다, 권하다 offer-offered-offered
offer him a new position 그에게 새 직책을 제안하다

402 **certain** [sə́ːrtən]
형 확실한
a certain fact 확실한 사실 look certain 확실해 보이다

403 **protect** [prətékt]
동 보호하다 명 protection 보호
protect wild animals 야생 동물을 보호하다

404 **work** [wəːrk]
동 효과가 있다 work-worked-worked
This medicine works. 이 약이 효과가 있다.

405 **mop** [mɑp]
명 대걸레 동 대걸레로 닦다
a mop and bucket 대걸레와 양동이

Daily Test

| 월 일 |

A 우리말에 맞게 빈 칸에 알맞은 단어를 쓰세요.

1 There is a big crater on the ______________ surface. 달의 표면에는 큰 분화구가 있다.

2 She used up her ______________ in three days. 그녀는 3일만에 용돈을 다 써버렸다.

3 She is practicing hard to ______________ her mistake.
그녀는 자신의 실수를 만회하기 위해 더 열심히 연습하고 있다.

4 My brother ______________ a rock band in school.
우리 오빠는 학교에서 락 밴드를 결성했다.

5 Nancy came to the seminar with a neat ______________.
Nancy는 세미나에 단정한 모습으로 왔다.

6 Rainbow is an example of optical ______________. 무지개는 착시 현상의 한 예이다.

7 I want to learn more about the Roman ______________ more.
나는 로마 제국에 대해서 더 배우고 싶다.

8 He ______________ Sue's report. 그는 Sue의 보고서를 검토했다.

9 He ______________ us a great dinner. 그는 우리에게 훌륭한 저녁식사를 제공하였다.

10 This medicine doesn't ______________ well. 이 약은 효과가 좋지 않다.

B 빈 칸에 알맞은 단어를 고르세요.

1 The most important mission for us is to ______________ the environment.
① protect ② lunar ③ protection ④ allowance ⑤ metal

2 He is a hidden ______________.
① certain ② genius ③ mop ④ empire ⑤ work

3 Sohyun is ______________ the floor.
① form ② lunar ③ renting ④ mopping ⑤ offering

Day 14

MP3

406 **jar** [dʒɑːr]
명 병, 항아리
a jar of jam 잼 한 병　a honey jar 꿀단지

407 **jury** [dʒú(ː)əri]
명 배심원
jury system 배심원 제도　serve on a jury 배심원 역할을 하다

408 **proverb** [právəːrb]
명 속담
an old proverb 오래된 속담　a famous proverb 유명한 속담

409 **state** [steit]
명 상태 , (미국의) 주
a state of mind 정신 상태　a western state 서부 주

410 **flavor** [fléivər]
명 풍미, 맛
cherry flavor 체리 맛　a strong flavor 강한 맛

411 **worse** [wəːrs]
형 더 나쁜
get worse 더 나빠지다　feel worse 기분이 더 나빠지다

412 **accidentally** [æksidéntəli]
부 우연히, 뜻하지않게
meet accidentally 우연히 만나다

413 **raw** [rɔː]
형 날것의, 익히지 않은
raw meat 생고기　eat a raw onion 생양파를 먹다

414 **chemical** [kémikəl]
형 화학의
chemical process 화학 과정　chemical reaction 화학 반응

415 **pedal** [pédəl]
명 (자전거, 자동차의) 페달
reach the pedal 페달에 발이 닿다　bicycle pedals 자전거 페달

416 **migrate** [máigreit]
동 이주하다　migrate-migrated-migrated
migrate from A to B A에서 B로 이주하다

417 **stress** [stres]
동 강조하다　stress-stressed-stressed
stress the importance of education 교육의 중요성을 강조하다

418 **last** [læst]
동 지속되다
last about an hour 한 시간 동안 지속되다

419 **suck** [sʌk]
동 빨다　suck-sucked-sucked
A baby sucks its thumb. 아기가 자기 엄지 손가락을 빨고 있다.

420 **loss** [lɔ(ː)s]
명 손실　동 lose 잃어버리다, 분실하다
a partial loss 부분적 손실　loss of appetite 식욕 부진

Daily Test

| 월 일 |

A 우리말에 맞게 빈 칸에 알맞은 단어를 쓰세요.

1 In the U.S, a ______________ consists of ordinary citizens. 미국에서 배심원은 평범한 시민들로 구성되어 있다.

2 There are fifty-two ______________ in America. 미국에는 52개의 주가 있다.

3 The weather is getting ______________. 날씨는 더 나빠지고 있다.

4 We met Jackson ______________ at the park. 우리는 공원에서 Jackson을 우연히 만났다.

5 I can't eat ______________ meat. 저는 생고기를 못 먹어요.

6 We will learn about ______________ reactions. 우리는 화학적 반응에 대해 배울 것이다.

7 Jinju will ______________ from Norway to Italy. 진주는 노르웨이에서 이탈리아로 이주 할 것이다.

8 Mary ______________ the importance of exercising. Mary는 운동의 중요성을 강조했다.

9 The meeting ______________ for five hours. 그 회의는 5시간째 계속되었다.

10 He is suffering from ______________ of appetite. 그는 식욕 부진으로 고생하고 있다.

B 빈 칸에 알맞은 단어를 고르세요.

1 Remember the ______________: "Easy come, easy go."
① proverb ② jar ③ chemical ④ appearance ⑤ reaction

2 Which ______________ of ice cream do you want?
① raw ② flavor ③ tasty ④ fever ⑤ loss

3 Katie always ______________ juice up noisily through her straw.
① jury ② sucking ③ sucks ④ stress ⑤ loss

Review Test 07 Day 13 + Day 14 | 월 일 |

A 우리말에 맞게 빈 칸에 알맞은 단어를 쓰시오.

1 the first ______________ 첫인상

2 ______________ late studying 밤새 공부하다

3 a ______________ artist 재능있는 예술가

4 break a ______________ 암호를 풀다

5 free of ______________ 무료로

6 receive an ______________ 용돈을 받다

7 ______________ the report 보고서를 검토하다

8 a ______________ and bucket 대걸레와 양동이

9 ______________ system 배심원 제도

10 meet ______________ 우연히 만나다

B 다음 영어 풀이에 알맞은 어휘를 〈보기〉에서 고르시오.

보기	jar	illusion	appearance	empire	expense

1 ______________ : the way something looks

2 ______________ : a group of countries or a region ruled by one ruler

3 ______________ : something that looks different from what it really is

4 ______________ : the money that you need to pay for or buy something

5 ______________ : a glass container with a round body and a lid

C 다음 단어의 관계가 A:B=C:D가 되도록 알맞은 단어를 골라 빈 칸에 적으시오.

1 connect : ______________ = appear : appearance

① connection ② collection ③ connected
④ corruption ⑤ connectly

2 ______________ : experiment = host : party

① science ② special ③ play
④ conduct ⑤ program

3 ______________ : wildlife = care : children

① protect ② caring ③ certain
④ cared ⑤ stay up

4 offer : ______________ = invent : invented

① offering ② solution ③ offered
④ propose ⑤ unoffer

5 rule : ______________ = boil : water

① safety ② empire ③ ruler
④ school ⑤ century

D 문맥에 맞게 다음 문장을 완성하시오.

1	If you want to open the box, •	• a	work well.
2	Rainbow is an example •	• b	press number "2."
3	This medicine doesn't •	• c	of optical illusion.
4	Mary stressed •	• d	loss of appetite.
5	He is suffering from •	• e	the importance of exercising.

E 문장을 읽고 문맥에 적절한 단어를 고르시오.

1 She is a genius. I have never seen such a (talented/durable) painter.

2 On this mountain, avalanches usually (occur/migrate) in spring.

3 The doctor carefully (examined/hatched) the patient's hand.

4 Susan worked hard to (make room for/make up for) the lost time.

5 We are (certain/involved) that he will win the game.

F 문장의 빈칸에 알맞은 단어를 〈보기〉에서 찾아 쓰시오. (필요하면 형태를 고치시오.)

보기	impression	chemical	exhibit	raw	achieve

1 She ____________ the goal of being a biologist.
그녀는 생물학자가 되겠다는 목표를 성취했다.

2 Chloe's painting left a good ____________ on us.
Chloe의 그림은 우리에게 좋은 인상을 남겼다.

3 The painter's work is ____________ only in this gallery.
그 작가의 작품은 이 갤러리에서만 전시된다.

4 My family prefers ____________ carrots to cooked carrots.
우리 가족은 익힌 당근 보다는 익히지 않은 당근을 더 좋아한다.

5 Some ____________ elements found in minerals are also found in living things.
광물에 있는 어떤 화학 원소들은 살아있는 생명체들에게도 존재한다.

G 그림에 해당하는 낱말을 〈보기〉에서 골라 쓰시오.

1 

( )

2 

( )

3 

( )

4 

( )

5 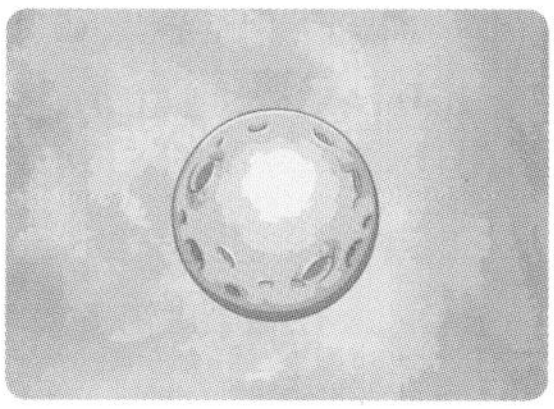

( )

6 

( )

보기 hatch eruption bike pedal lunar liquid draw

Study More

혼동하기 쉬운 단어 emigrants vs. immigrants

- [emigrants] : '다른 나라로 나가는 이주자' [immigrants] : '다른 나라에서 들어오는 이주자'
- 영어는 라틴어와 그리스어 어휘를 많이 받아들였으며 라틴어 접두사 -e, -ex는 주로 'out'이라는 의미를 가지며 -in, -im등은 주로 'in'의 뜻을 가진다.
  export 수출 vs. import 수입

Day 15

MP3

421 **argument** [ɑ́ːrgjumənt]
명 논쟁, 말다툼 　동 argue 논쟁하다
a big argument 큰 말다툼 　win an argument 논쟁에서 이기다

422 **drugstore** [drʌ́gstɔ̀ːr]
명 약국 　유 pharmacy 약국
go to the drugstore 약국에 가다 　at a drugstore 약국에서

423 **repetition** [rèpətíʃən]
명 반복 　동 repeat 반복하다
learn by repetition 반복을 통해 배우다

424 **spin** [spin]
동 돌다, 회전시키다 　spin-spun-spun
spin a top 팽이를 돌리다 　The fan spins. 선풍기가 돌다.

425 **director** [diréktər]
명 지도자, 책임자
board of directors 이사회 　a regional director 지역 책임자

426 **dialect** [dáiəlèkt]
명 사투리, 방언
speak in a dialect 사투리로 얘기하다 　a regional dialect 지역 방언

427 **rate** [reit]
명 비율
the birth rate 출생률 　the discount rate 할인율

428 **project** [prádʒekt]
명 계획, 연구과제, 사업계획
complete a project 연구 과제를 완료하다

429 **personality** [pərsənǽləti]
명 성격, 인격
a cheerful personality 활기찬 성격

430 **available** [əvéiləbl]
형 구할 수 있는, 여유가 있는
freely available 자유롭게 이용할 수 있는

431 **bump** [bʌmp]
동 ~에 부딪치다
bump against the wall 벽에 부딪치다

432 **well-known** [wel noun]
형 유명한, 잘 알려진
a well-known restaurant 잘 알려진 식당

433 **flow** [flou]
명 흐름 　동 흐르다 　flow-flowed-flowed
the flow of history 역사의 흐름 　flow rapidly 빠르게 흐르다

434 **waterproof** [wɔ́ːtərprùːf]
형 방수의
wear a waterproof hat 방수 모자를 쓰다

435 **restore** [ristɔ́ːr]
동 복구하다
difficult to restore 복구하기 어려운

Daily Test

| 월 일 |

A 우리말에 맞게 빈 칸에 알맞은 단어를 쓰세요.

1 I had a big ______________ with my sister. 나는 여동생과 크게 다투었다.

2 Students can learn English effectively by ______________.
학생들은 반복을 통해 효과적으로 영어를 배울 수 있다.

3 The boys are ______________ tops. 소년들이 팽이를 돌리고 있다.

4 Nick is the new regional ______________. Nick이 새로운 지역 책임자이다.

5 I'm interested in a variety of regional ______________.
나는 다양한 지역 방언에 대해 관심이 있다.

6 They will complete the ______________ by the end of this year.
그들은 그 연구 과제를 이번 연말까지 완료할 것이다.

7 This ticket is ______________ for a week. 이 표는 일주일 동안 사용 가능하다.

8 She ______________ into a door and hurt her head. 그녀는 문에 부딪혀 머리를 다쳤다.

9 The pianist composed a number of ______________ piano sonatas.
그 피아니스트는 잘 알려진 피아노 소나타 여러 곡을 작곡했다.

10 The river ______________ to the ocean. 강은 바다로 흐른다.

B 빈 칸에 알맞은 단어를 고르세요.

1 The birth ______________ is decreasing sharply.
① rate ② spin ③ life ④ flow ⑤ worse

2 Cindy has a gentle and kind ______________.
① dialect ② pedal ③ stress ④ personality ⑤ bump

3 Mr. Anderson is ______________ old pictures.
① bumping ② argument ③ restoring ④ restore ⑤ available

Day 15

MP3

436 **secondary** [sékəndèri]
형 제 2의, 중등 교육의
a secondary infection 2차 감염 a secondary school 중학교

437 **relative** [rélətiv]
명 친척
my friends and relatives 내 친구들과 친척들

438 **slippery** [slípəri]
형 미끄러운, 미끈거리는
a slippery floor 미끄러운 바닥

439 **fix** [fiks]
동 고정하다 fix-fixed-fixed
fix a picture to the wall 벽에 그림을 고정시키다

440 **get rid of** [get rid əv]
~을 제거하다, 없애다
get rid of viruses 바이러스를 제거하다

441 **mention** [ménʃən]
동 언급하다 mention-mentioned-mentioned
mention the rumor again 다시 그 소문을 언급하다

442 **announcement** [ənáunsmənt]
명 발표, 소식 동 announce 발표하다
make an announcement 발표 하다

443 **chop** [tʃɑp]
동 (음식을) 다지다, 썰다 chop-chopped-chopped
chop the meat 고기를 다지다 chop up 잘게 썰다

444 **peasant** [pézənt]
명 농부, 소작농
a peasant in the country 시골의 농부 a peasant farmer 소작농

445 **portable** [pɔ́ːrtəbl]
형 휴대하기 쉬운, 휴대용의
a portable computer 휴대용 컴퓨터 a portable TV 휴대용 TV

446 **survive** [sərváiv]
동 살아남다 survive-survived-survived 명 survival 생존
Only three survived. 세 명만이 살아남았다.

447 **erase** [iréis]
동 지우다 erase-erased-erased +eraser 명 지우개
erase the wrong answer 틀린 답을 지우다

448 **migrant** [máigrənt]
명 이주자
migrant workers 이주 노동자 migrant birds 철새

449 **mince** [mins]
동 (고기 등을) 갈다, 잘게 썰다
mince meat 고기를 잘게 썰다 mince garlic 마늘을 다지다

450 **pandemic** [pændémik]
명 (전국적인) 유행병 형 유행성의
a global pandemic 세계적인 유행병 pandemic bird flu 유행성 조류 독감

Daily Test

| 월 일 |

A 우리말에 맞게 빈 칸에 알맞은 단어를 쓰세요.

1 Be careful! The floor is very ______________. 조심해 바닥이 아주 미끄러워.

2 Linda ______________ a shelf to the wall. Linda는 선반을 벽에 고정시켰다.

3 Regular exercise will ______________ stress. 규칙적인 운동이 스트레스를 없애 줄 것입니다.

4 The author of the book ______________ her childhood in the preface.
그 책의 저자는 서문에 자신의 어린 시절에 대해 언급했다.

5 There will be an important ______________ tomorrow.
내일 중요한 발표가 있을 예정이다.

6 ______________ the carrots and onions. 당근과 양파를 잘게 써세요.

7 My grandfather was a ______________ in the countryside.
우리 할아버지는 시골의 소작농이셨다.

8 Jack was the only one who ______________ in the desert.
Jack은 사막에서 유일하게 살아남은 사람이었다.

9 Sam ______________ the wrong answer. Sam은 틀린 답을 지웠다.

10 She peeled the onion and ______________ it. 그녀는 양파를 껍질을 벗기고 난 다음 잘게 썰었다.

B 빈 칸에 알맞은 단어를 고르세요.

1 We need a new ______________ computer.
① portable ② restore ③ secondary ④ argument ⑤ fix

2 There are various ______________ birds in the world.
① complete ② get rid of ③ migrant ④ fly ⑤ peasant

3 The government is trying to stop the spread of ______________ bird flu.
① project ② pandemic ③ mention ④ chop ⑤ erase

Day 16

MP3

451 **catch up with** [kætʃ ʌp wið]
따라잡다
catch up with him in a minute 곧 그를 따라 잡다

452 **lung** [lʌŋ]
명 폐
lung cancer 폐암 lung damage 폐 손상

453 **realistic** [rì(:)əlístik]
형 현실적인
set a realistic goal 현실적인 목표를 세우다

454 **Antarctic** [ænta:rktik]
형 남극의
Antarctic climate 남극 기후 The Antarctic 남극 대륙

455 **postpone** [pous*t*póun]
동 연기하다 postpone-postponed-postponed
postpone a meeting 회의를 연기하다

456 **leap** [li:p]
동 뛰다, 뛰어오르다 leap-leaped/leapt-leaped/leapt
leap over a fence 울타리를 뛰어 넘다

457 **take ~ into account** [teik íntə əkáunt]
~을 고려하다 유 consider 고려하다
take all variables into account 모든 변수를 고려하다

458 **ideal** [aidí(:)əl]
형 이상적인, 가장 알맞은
ideal beauty 이상적인 아름다움 ideal for ~에 이상적인

459 **bank** [bæŋk]
명 둑
the river bank 강둑 run along the bank 강둑을 따라 뛰다

460 **stick** [stik]
동 붙이다
stick the stamp on the envelope 엽서에 우표를 붙이다

461 **vertical** [vә́:*r*tik*ə*l]
형 수직의 반 horizontal 수평의, 수평선의
use vertical blinds 수직형 블라인드를 사용하다

462 **worth** [wə:*r*θ]
형 가치가 있는 명 가치, 값어치
of little worth 가치가 없는 worth ~ing ~할 가치가 있다

463 **extreme** [ikstrí:m]
형 극도의, 극심한
extreme sports 극한의 운동 extreme cold 매서운 추위

464 **rare** [rεə*r*]
형 드문, 희귀한
a rare plant 희귀한 식물 a rare disease 희귀병

465 **concrete** [kɑ̀nkrí:t]
형 구체적인
concrete evidence 구체적인 증거 a concrete example 구체적인 예시

Daily Test

| 월 일 |

A 우리말에 맞게 빈 칸에 알맞은 단어를 쓰세요.

1 I ran fast to ______________ him. 나는 그를 따라 잡기 위해 빨리 뛰었다.

2 Korea built a research base in the ______________.
한국은 남극에 연구 기지를 건설하였다.

3 The journey was ______________ three times. 여행은 세 번이나 연기되었다.

4 Most basketball players can ______________ very high.
대부분의 농구 선수들은 아주 높이 뛸 수 있다.

5 You should ______________ his physical condition ______________.
너는 그의 몸 상태를 고려해야 한다.

6 Today is ______________ for the picnic. 오늘은 소풍 가기에 이상적이다.

7 Tim and I walked along the ______________. Tim과 나는 강둑을 따라 걸었다.

8 We need glue to ______________ the broken pieces together.
부서진 조각을 함께 붙이기 위해서 풀이 필요하다.

9 The teacher is drawing a ______________ line on the black board.
선생님께서 칠판에 수직선을 그리고 있다.

10 Making a ______________ plan is very important.
구체적인 계획을 세우는 것은 매우 중요하다.

B 빈 칸에 알맞은 단어를 고르세요.

1 Setting a ______________ goal is important.
① realed ② reality ③ really ④ realism ⑤ realistic

2 It's ______________ a try.
① time ② worth ③ fame ④ worthy ⑤ chop

3 Some animals can survive in ______________ cold.
① stick ② extreme ③ so ④ leap ⑤ vertical

Day 16

MP3

466 **meet** [miːt]
동 충족시키다
meet her needs 그녀의 요구를 충족시키다

467 **faucet** [fɔ́ːsit]
명 수도꼭지
turn a faucet off 수도꼭지를 잠그다 the kitchen faucet 주방 수도꼭지

468 **consider** [kənsídər]
동 잘 생각하다, ~로 여기다 consider-considered-considered
consider what to do 무엇을 할지 생각하다

469 **surprising** [sərpráiziŋ]
형 놀라운, 놀랄
a surprising result 놀라운 결과

470 **fountain** [fáuntən]
명 분수, 원천
a fountain in the garden 정원 안에 있는 분수

471 **challenge** [tʃǽlindʒ]
명 도전 동 도전하다
a tough challenge 힘든 도전 accept a challenge 도전을 받아들이다

472 **track** [træk]
명 길, 트랙 동 추적하다 track-tracked-tracked
a running track 경주로 track the train 기차를 추적하다

473 **sight** [sait]
명 시력, 보기, 시야
have good sight 시력이 좋다 come into sight 시야에 들어오다

474 **risk** [risk]
명 위험
the risk of heart disease 심장병의 위험 take a risk 위험을 감수하다

475 **extinct** [ikstíŋkt]
형 멸종된 명 extinction 멸종
become extinct 멸종되다 extinct animal 멸종 동물

476 **infect** [infékt]
동 감염시키다 infect-infected-infected
infect many people 많은 사람을 감염시키다 be infected with ~에 감염된

477 **engine** [éndʒən]
명 엔진, 기관차
a new engine 새 엔진 engine trouble 엔진 고장

478 **constantly** [kánstəntli]
부 끊임없이, 계속
constantly change colors 색을 끊임없이 바꾸다

479 **urge** [əːrdʒ]
동 촉구하다, 요구하다 urge-urged-urged
urge A to B A에게 B하도록 촉구하다

480 **parallel** [pǽrəlèl]
형 평행한
parallel to each other 서로 평행인 parallel lines 평행선

Daily Test

| 월 일 |

A 우리말에 맞게 빈 칸에 알맞은 단어를 쓰세요.

1 It's difficult to ____________ Joe's needs. Joe의 요구를 충족시키는 건 어렵다.

2 Wash your hands and turn the ____________ off. 손을 씻고 수도꼭지를 잠가라.

3 We need some time to ____________ where to go.
우리는 어디로 갈지 생각할 시간이 좀 필요하다.

4 There is a beautiful ____________ in the park. 공원 안에 아름다운 분수가 있다.

5 The training was the most interesting ____________ of my life.
그 훈련은 내 인생에서 제일 재미있는 도전이었다.

6 Regular exercise can decrease the ____________ of heart disease.
규칙적인 운동은 심장병의 위험을 줄여줄 수 있다.

7 Dinosaurs are ____________ creatures. 공룡은 멸종된 생물이다.

8 Be careful not to get ____________ with cholera. 콜레라에 감염되지 않도록 조심하세요.

9 We ____________ John to apologize to Mary.
우리는 John이 Mary에게 사과해야 한다고 요구했다.

10 He drew perfectly ____________ lines on the paper.
그는 종이 위에다 완벽하게 평행하는 선들을 그렸다.

B 빈 칸에 알맞은 단어를 고르세요.

1 There was some ____________ news last night.
① surprising ② surprised ③ urged ④ considered ⑤ infected

2 Stir the soup ____________ for 3 minutes.
① fountain ② constant ③ usually ④ constantly ⑤ idealy

3 He fell in love with her at first ____________.
① saw ② meet ③ sight ④ challenge ⑤ see

Review Test 08

Day 15 + Day 16 | 월 일 |

A 우리말에 맞게 빈 칸에 알맞은 단어를 쓰시오.

1 a big ______________ 큰 말다툼

2 a regional ______________ 지역 방언

3 ______________ viruses 바이러스를 제거하다

4 ______________ with the flu 감기에 감염시키다

5 global ______________ 세계적인 유행병

6 ______________ over a fence 울타리를 뛰어넘다

7 ______________ beauty 이상적인 아름다움

8 a ______________ disease 희귀병

9 take a ______________ 위험을 감수하다

10 ______________ to each other 서로 평행인

B 다음 영어 풀이에 알맞은 어휘를 〈보기〉에서 고르시오.

보기	postpone	mention	rare	concrete	extinct

1 ____________ : not commonly found, seen, or happening

2 ____________ : to move an event to a later time or date

3 ____________ : all members of a species died out and no longer exist

4 ____________ : to talk or write about something briefly

5 ____________ : not imaginary ; related to a specific thing, quality, or idea

C 다음 단어의 관계가 A:B=C:D가 되도록 알맞은 단어를 골라 빈 칸에 적으시오.

1 survive : ______________ = argue : argument

① survivement ② survival ③ survives
④ survivalent ⑤ survived

2 trust : trusty = worth : ______________

① money ② property ③ worthed
④ worthy ⑤ wealth

3 ______________ : schedule = open : window

① many ② delayed ③ postpone
④ His ⑤ wash

4 relative : relatively = constant : ______________

① constantly ② constants ③ pain
④ constanted ⑤ constantily

5 ______________ : meat = chew : gum

① fruit ② red ③ vegetable
④ chop ⑤ beef

D 문맥에 맞게 다음 문장을 완성하시오.

1	Linda fixed •	• a	fountain in the park.
2	Korea built a research base •	• b	in the Antarctic.
3	There is a beautiful •	• c	to apologize to Mary.
4	Regular exercise can decrease •	• d	the risk of heart disease.
5	We urged John •	• e	a shelf to the wall.

E 문장을 읽고 문맥에 적절한 단어를 고르시오.

1 All dinosaurs died out a long time ago. They are (extinct/rare) now.

2 (Mention/Repetition) is an efficient way to learn new languages.

3 The new manager agreed to (get rid of/look forward to) unnecessary regulations.

4 The old palace will be (realistic/restored) and able to accept visitors soon.

5 When you plan the next picnic, take Sue and Joe (into account/for granted).

F 문장의 빈칸에 알맞은 단어를 〈보기〉에서 찾아 쓰시오. (필요하면 형태를 고치시오.)

보기	personality	well-known	dialect	infect	secondary

1 It is difficult for me to understand my grandmother's ____________.
내게는 할머니의 사투리를 이해하는 것이 어렵다.

2 France is ____________ for its wines.
프랑스는 와인으로 잘 알려져 있다.

3 For him, practicing piano is ____________ to playing soccer with his friends.
그에게는 피아노 연습하는 것은 친구들과 축구를 하는 것에 비하면 부수적이다.

4 Some children were ____________ with a bad cold during the trip.
몇몇 어린이들은 여행기간 동안 심한 감기에 전염되었다.

5 We all like her cheerful and positive ____________.
우리 모두는 그녀의 명랑하고 긍정적인 성격을 좋아한다.

G 그림과 낱말이 <u>잘못</u> 짝이어진 것을 고르시오. ······························ (   )

ⓐ

bump

ⓑ

lung

ⓒ

erase

ⓓ

faucet

H 낱말과 어울리는 그림을 연결하시오.

1 vertical •

2 track •

• ⓐ 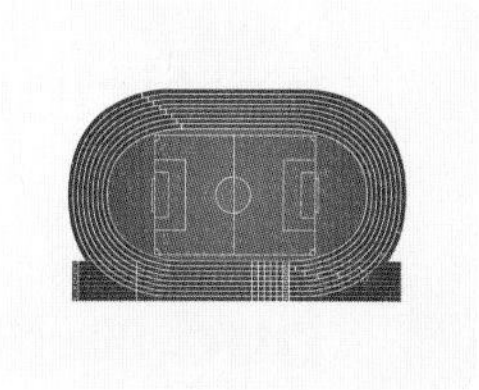

• ⓑ 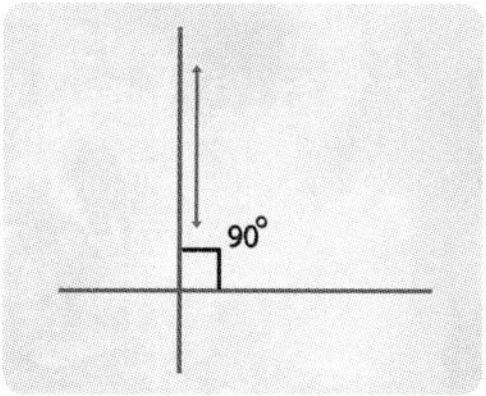

Study More

personality '성격,인격'을 나타내는 어휘들

- [긍정적] : brave 용감한, calm 침착한, decisive 결단력 있는, generous 너그러운
- [부정적] : timid 겁 많은, nervous 불안해하는, indecisive 결단력이 없는, mean 인색한

  The **brave** soldier saved the children. 그 용감한 병사가 아이들을 구했다.

  He is too **timid** to take part in the race. 그는 그 경주에 참가하기에는 너무 소심하다.

Day 17

MP3

481 **reluctant** [rilʌ́ktənt]
형 꺼리는, 주저하는 반 eager 열렬히 바라는
reluctant to agree 동의하기를 주저하는

482 **advantage** [ədvǽntidʒ]
명 이점, 장점
take advantage of ~를 이용하다

483 **inventor** [invéntər]
명 발명가 동 invent 발명하다
the inventor of the light bulb 전구의 발명가

484 **gaze** [geiz]
동 응시하다
gaze into her face 그녀의 얼굴을 응시하다

485 **tortoise** [tɔ́ːrtəs]
명 거북이 유 turtle 바다 거북
a slow tortoise 느린 거북이 rabbit and tortoise 토끼와 거북이

486 **hire** [haiər]
동 고용하다 hire-hired-hired 유 employ 고용하다
hire a driver 운전사를 고용하다 hire a workman 일꾼을 고용하다

487 **participate** [pɑːrtísəpèit]
동 참여하다 participate-participated-participated
participate in the Olympics 올림픽에 참여하다

488 **bud** [bʌd]
명 싹, 눈, 꽃봉오리
a blossom bud 꽃눈

489 **fake** [feik]
형 가짜의 동 위조하다 fake-faked-faked
fake money 위조 지폐 fake items 가짜 상품

490 **banner** [bǽnər]
명 기, 현수막
a national banner 국기 wave a banner 기를 흔들다

491 **greet** [griːt]
동 맞이하다, 환영하다 greet-greeted-greeted 명 greeting 인사
greet with a smile 웃음으로 맞이하다

492 **comment** [kάment]
명 논평 동 논평하다
make a comment 논평하다 comment on the movie 영화를 논평하다

493 **pleasure** [pléʒər]
명 기쁨, 즐거움
the pleasure of everyday life 일상생활의 즐거움

494 **aboard** [əbɔ́ːrd]
부 전 (배, 기차 등에) 탑승한
go aboard 탑승하다 go aboard a ship 배를 타다

495 **ballet** [bæléi]
명 발레
become a ballet dancer 발레 무용수가 되다

Daily Test

| 월 일 |

A 우리말에 맞게 빈 칸에 알맞은 단어를 쓰세요.

1 You should not take ______________ of Jimin's weak point.
너는 지민의 약점을 이용해서는 안 된다.

2 I want to become an ______________. 나는 발명가가 되고 싶어요.

3 She ______________ into in the mirror. 그녀는 거울 속을 응시했다.

4 Why don't they ______________ a new manager? 왜 그들은 새 매니저를 고용하지 않나요?

5 The women ______________ the paintings. 여자는 그 그림을 위조했다.

6 You should remove the ______________ after the party ends.
파티가 끝난 후에 너는 현수막을 제거해야 한다.

7 Grandfather ______________ us warmly. 할아버지는 우리를 따뜻하게 맞아주셨다.

8 We made no ______________ on the novel. 우리는 그 소설에 대해 아무런 논평도 하지 않았다.

9 People went ______________ the plane. 사람들은 비행기에 탑승했다.

10 Jessie will enter the ______________ class next week.
Jessie는 다음주부터 발레 수업에 참여할 것이다.

B 빈 칸에 알맞은 단어를 고르세요.

1 He was ______________ to accept our proposal.
① rely ② reluctant ③ gaze ④ urge ⑤ risk

2 My everyday life is full of ______________.
① inventor ② consider ③ fake ④ ballet ⑤ pleasure

3 I will ______________ in an English speaking contest.
① part ② faucet ③ participate ④ advantage ⑤ comment

Day 17

MP3

496 **relate** [riléit]
동 관련시키다, 관련짓다 relate-related-related 명 relation 관계, 관련
relate the disease to the virus 그 바이러스와 질병을 관련짓다

497 **responsible** [rispánsəbl]
형 ~을 책임지고 있는, 책임감 있는
be responsible for ~에 대해 책임이 있다

498 **economic** [ìːkənámik]
형 경제의
solve the economic problem 경제적 문제를 해결하다

499 **facility** [fəsíləti]
명 편의 시설
sports facilities 운동 시설 shopping facilities 쇼핑 시설

500 **livestock** [láivstɑ̀k]
명 가축
raise livestock 가축을 기르다 livestock farming 목축업

501 **characteristic** [kæ̀riktərístik]
형 특유의 명 특징
her unique characteristics 그녀의 독특한 특징들

502 **escalator** [éskəlèitər]
명 에스컬레이터
get on the escalator 에스컬레이터를 타다

503 **version** [və́ːrʒən]
명 ~판, 버전
the Korean version of the novel 그 소설의 한국어판

504 **explore** [iksplɔ́ːr]
동 탐험하다, 조사하다 explore-explored-explored
explore the Amazon 아마존을 탐험하다

505 **software** [sɔ́(ː)ftwɛ̀ər]
명 소프트웨어
design software 디자인용 소프트웨어

506 **government** [gʌ́vərnmənt]
명 정부
the US government 미국 정부 lead a government 정부를 이끌다

507 **will** [wíl]
명 의지
have a strong will 강한 의지를 가지다

508 **worldwide** [wə́ːrldwáid]
형 세계적인, 세계적으로
a worldwide issue 전 세계적인 화제

509 **actual** [ǽktʃuəl]
형 실제의
the actual height 실제 높이 an actual fact 실제 사실

510 **take off** [teik ɔːf]
동 (옷 등을) 벗다, (비행기 등이) 이륙하다
take off your boots 부츠를 벗다

Daily Test

| 월 일 |

A 우리말에 맞게 빈 칸에 알맞은 단어를 쓰세요.

1 Eating junk food is closely ____________ to obesity.
인스턴트 음식을 먹는 것은 비만과 밀접하게 관련되어 있다.

2 Jieun is ____________ for leading the book club.
지은이는 독서클럽을 이끄는 책임을 맡고 있다.

3 Janet majored in ____________ history. Janet은 경제사를 전공했다.

4 There is a big shopping ____________ in the hotel. 그 호텔에는 큰 쇼핑 시설이 있다.

5 My parents want to raise ____________ in the countryside.
우리 부모님은 시골에서 가축을 기르길 원하신다.

6. The girl fell on the ____________. 그 소녀는 에스컬레이터에서 넘어졌다.

7 Each house in this village has a ____________ appearance.
이 마을에는 각각의 집들이 특유의 모습을 가지고 있다.

8 We will ____________ the secret of the pyramid.
우리는 피라미드의 비밀에 대해 조사해 볼 것이다.

9 I need to install an educational ____________ program.
나는 교육용 소프트웨어 프로그램을 설치해야 해요.

10 My brother works for the ____________. 우리 오빠는 정부에서 일하고 있다.

B 빈 칸에 알맞은 단어를 고르세요.

1 A successful man has some unique ____________.
① fury ② character ③ states ④ characteristics ⑤ migrate

2 The singer achieved ____________ fame at an early age.
① wordly ② banner ③ economic ④ worldwide ⑤ famous

3 The ____________ performance will last two hours.
① facility ② actually ③ explore ④ really ⑤ actual

Day 18

MP3

511 honestly [ɑ́nistli]
부 정직하게
answer honestly 정직하게 답하다 live honestly 정직하게 살다

512 disappear [dìsəpíər]
동 사라지다 disappear-disappeared-disappeared
disappear without a word 말 한 마디 없이 사라지다

513 traditional [trədíʃənəl]
형 전통적인, 전통의
traditional art 전통 예술 wear traditional shoes 전통 신발을 신다

514 chain [tʃein]
명 사슬, 체인 동 묶다
a watch chain 시계줄 chain your bike 자전거를 체인으로 묶다

515 doubt [daut]
동 의심하다 명 의심
doubt his honesty 그의 정직성을 의심하다

516 face [feis]
동 ~을 마주보다, 직면하다 face-faced-faced
face the problem 문제를 직면하다 face the sea 바다를 마주하다

517 species [spíːʃiːz]
명 종
a rare species 희귀종 The Origin of Species 종의 기원

518 except [iksépt]
전 ~을 제외하고
except Monday 월요일을 제외하고 except foreigners 외국인을 제외하고

519 block [blɑk]
동 막다 block-blocked-blocked
block the road 길을 막다 block the door 문을 막다

520 steel [stiːl]
명 강철, 철
the steel industry 철강 산업 be made from steel 강철로 만들어지다

521 least [liːst]
대 가장 작은
at least 최소한의 the least distance 최단 거리

522 rainforest [reinfɔːrist;-faːr-]
명 (열대) 우림
the Amazon rainforest 아마존 열대 우림

523 lie [lai]
동 눕다 lie-lay-lain
lie in bed 침대 위에 눕다 lie on your back 등을 대고 눕다

524 error [érər]
명 오류, 실수
a fatal error 치명적인 실수 trial and error 시행착오

525 current [kə́ːrənt]
형 현재의, 지금의
the current month 이번 달

Daily Test

| 월 일 |

A 우리말에 맞게 빈 칸에 알맞은 단어를 쓰세요.

1 The balloon ____________ from sight. 그 풍선은 시야에서 사라졌다.

2 The Hanbok is a ____________ dress of Korea. 한복은 한국의 전통 의상이다.

3 Linda ____________ a difficult situation. Linda는 어려운 상황에 직면해 있다.

4 I like all sports ____________ basketball. 농구를 제외하고 나는 운동을 좋아한다.

5 Police ____________ the street because of the accident. 경찰은 사고 때문에 도로를 막았다.

6 The ____________ industry is one of Korea's key industries. 철강 산업은 한국의 주요 산업 중의 하나이다.

7 I see that dog at ____________ five times a day. 나는 하루에 적어도 다섯 번은 저 개를 본다.

8 People ____________ on the grass. 사람들은 잔디 위에 누워 있었다.

9 We learned to make delicious cookies by trial and ____________. 우리는 시행착오를 통해 맛있는 쿠키를 만드는 법을 배웠다.

10 What is your ____________ address? 현재 주소는 어디입니까?

B 빈 칸에 알맞은 단어를 고르세요.

1 There is no ____________ that James is kind.

① software ② doubt ③ face ④ responsible ⑤ steel

2 There are many ____________ of cat.

① traditional ② least ③ lie ④ species ⑤ except

3 Answer these questions ____________.

① honest ② speed ③ honestly ④ greet ⑤ facility

Day 18

MP3

526 **acne** [ǽkni]
명 여드름
have acne 여드름이 나다　treat her acne 그녀의 여드름을 치료하다

527 **structure** [strʌ́ktʃər]
명 구조, 구조물
industrial structure 산업 구조　social structure 사회 구조

528 **grain** [grein]
명 곡물, 알갱이
the chief grain of Korea 한국의 주요 곡물　a grain of salt 소금 알갱이

529 **bronze** [brɑnz]
명 청동
a bronze statue 동상　get a bronze medal 동메달을 따다

530 **although** [ɔːlðóu]
접 비록 ~일지라도
although he was young 그가 어렸음에도 불구하고

531 **succeed** [səksíːd]
동 성공하다, 계승하다
succeed in scoring a goal 득점에 성공하다

532 **landscape** [lǽndskèip]
명 풍경
the beautiful landscape of Jeju Island 제주도의 아름다운 풍경

533 **submarine** [sʌ̀bməríːn]
명 잠수함　형 해저의
a nuclear submarine 핵잠수함　a submarine volcano 해저 화산

534 **prevent** [privént]
동 막다, 방지하다　prevent-prevented-prevented
prevent school violence 학교 폭력을 막다

535 **beggar** [bégər]
명 거지
a poor beggar 가엾은 거지　live like a beggar 거지처럼 살다

536 **discount** [diskáunt]
명 할인
get a discount 할인을 받다　discount prices 할인가

537 **pile** [pail]
명 더미　동 쌓다　pile-piled-piled
pile the boxes 상자를 쌓다　a pile of books 책 더미

538 **harbor** [hάːrbər]
명 항구
a large harbor 큰 항구　leave the harbor 항구를 떠나다

539 **resource** [ríːsɔ̀ːrs]
명 자원
natural resources 천연 자원　valuable resources 가치있는 자원

540 **reasonable** [ríːzənəbl]
형 타당한, 합리적인
a reasonable person 합리적인 사람　a reasonable price 합리적인 가격

Daily Test

| 월 일 |

A 우리말에 맞게 빈 칸에 알맞은 단어를 쓰세요.

1 That building has an old wooden ______________.
그 건물은 오래된 목조 구조를 가지고 있다.

2 Hojin got a ______________ medal at the Olympics. 올림픽에서 호진은 동메달을 땄다.

3 ______________ he was tired, he took a walk for two hours.
그는 피곤했음에도 불구하고, 두 시간 동안 산책했다.

4 My father likes to take ______________ photographs.
아버지는 풍경 사진을 찍는 것을 좋아하신다.

5 The ______________ came up to the surface. 표면위로 잠수함이 떠올랐다.

6 It's hard to ______________ every crime. 모든 범죄를 방지하는 것은 힘들다.

7 I gave some food to the ______________. 나는 거지에게 약간의 음식을 주었다.

8 Is there a ______________ for students? 학생 할인이 있나요?

9 The students ______________ clothes on the chair. 학생들은 의자 위에 옷을 쌓았다.

10 There is a large ______________ in our village. 우리 마을에는 큰 항구가 있다.

B 빈 칸에 알맞은 단어를 고르세요.

1 Rice is the chief ______________ of Korea.
① bronze ② grain ③ structure ④ steel ⑤ block

2 Water is the most important natural ______________.
① submarine ② error ③ fountain ④ resource ⑤ landscape

3 The price of the dress was ______________.
① preventing ② beggar ③ reasonable ④ discount ⑤ reason

Review Test 09

Day 17 + Day 18 | 월 일 |

A 우리말에 맞게 빈 칸에 알맞은 단어를 쓰시오.

1 hire a ____________ 운전사를 고용하다

2 a national ____________ 국기

3 a ____________ leader 책임감 있는 지도자

4 the US ____________ 미국 정부

5 reach your ____________ 목적지에 이르다

6 answer ____________ 정직하게 답하다

7 ____________ foreigners 외국인을 제외하고

8 the ____________ distance 최단 거리

9 the beautiful ____________ of Jeju Island 제주도의 아름다운 풍경

10 leave the ____________ 항구를 떠나다

B 다음 영어 풀이에 알맞은 어휘를 〈보기〉에서 고르시오.

보기	reluctant	facility	tortoise	grain	species

1 ____________ : animals or plants that belong to the same family

2 ____________ : to hesitate to do something or to avoid something if possible

3 ____________ : the seed of a plant such as rice or wheat

4 ____________ : a building or service for a particular purpose

5 ____________ : a turtle with a hard shell that lives on land

C 다음 단어의 관계가 A:B=C:D가 되도록 알맞은 단어를 골라 빈칸에 적으시오.

1 invent : ______________ = teach : teacher

① inventer ② inventor ③ machine
④ classroom ⑤ invention

2 happy : unhappy = appear : ______________

① unappear ② appearance ③ disappear
④ appearing ⑤ imappear

3 ______________ : violence = study : physics

① version ② important ③ prevent
④ prevention ⑤ goods

4 take : ______________ = repair : bike

① advantage ② took ③ advent
④ taken ⑤ weather

5 tradition : ______________ = love : lovely

① traditionly ② Hanbok ③ custom
④ traditional ⑤ traditionally

D 문맥에 맞게 다음 문장을 완성하시오.

1 You should not take advantage •	• a	of Jimin's weak point.
2 She gazed •	• b	a characteristic appearance.
3 Each house in this village has •	• c	medal at the Olympics.
4 The balloon disappeared •	• d	into the mirror.
5 Hojin got a bronze •	• e	from sight.

E 문장을 읽고 문맥에 적절한 단어를 고르시오.

1 The little girl was (reluctant/vertical) to go to the dentist.

2 I think no one is (admired/responsible) for the failure of the project.

3 Can you (comment/infect) on my essay?

4 Animals on this island are (facing/performing) extinction.

5 The company (remained/hired) more staff for the customer service department.

F 문장의 빈칸에 알맞은 단어를 〈보기〉에서 찾아 쓰시오. (필요하면 형태를 고치시오.)

보기	participate	structure	explore	worldwide	species

1 Many ____________ of chameleons can change their color when they are in danger.
많은 카멜레온 종들은 위험에 처하면 자신들의 색을 바꿀 수 있다.

2 Everyone in our class was required to ____________ in the quiz.
우리 반 모두가 퀴즈에 참여하도록 요청 받았다.

3 The ____________ of the detective novel was quite complex.
그 탐정소설의 구조는 매우 복잡했다.

4 The unknown singer gained ____________ fame with one song.
그 무명의 가수는 노래 한 곡으로 전 세계적인 명성을 얻었다.

5 The curious students decided to ____________ the cave.
그 호기심 많은 학생들은 동굴을 탐험하기로 결정했다.

G 그림에 해당하는 낱말을 〈보기〉에서 골라 쓰시오.

1 

(   )

2 

(   )

3 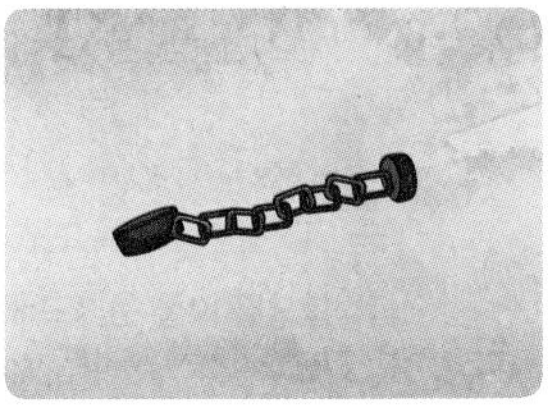

(   )

4 

(   )

5 

(   )

6 

(   )

보기 tortoise block chain pile discount ballet

Study More

혼동하기 쉬운 단어 current vs. currant

- [current] 형 현재/지금의 명 (물이나 전류의) 흐름
  The current of this stream is strong. 이 개울의 물살은 세다.
- [currant] 명 (작고 씨가 없는) 건포도
  redcurrant 건포도 redcurrant jelly 건포도 젤리

Day 19

MP3

541 **discovery** [diskʌ́vəri]
명 발견 동 discover 발견하다
a new discovery 새로운 발견 make a discovery 발견하다

542 **freedom** [frí:dəm]
명 자유, 해방
freedom of expression 표현의 자유

543 **nasal** [néizəl]
형 코의, 콧소리의
a nasal voice 콧소리 nasal accents 콧소리 억양

544 **check** [tʃek]
동 살피다
check your homework 숙제를 점검하다 check the room 방을 살피다

545 **creature** [krí:tʃər]
명 생물
all living creatures 모든 살아있는 것들 strange creatures 이상한 생물들

546 **tragic** [trǽdʒik]
형 비극적인 명 tragedy 비극
a tragic ending 비극적 결말 his tragic death 그의 비극적 죽음

547 **matter** [mǽtər]
동 중요하다 matter-mattered-mattered
Age doesn't matter. 나이는 중요하지 않다.

548 **communicate** [kəmjú:nəkèit]
동 의사소통하다, 연락을 주고받다 명 communication 의사소통, 연락
communicate with each other 서로 의사소통 하다

549 **vowel** [váuəl]
명 모음
a vowel system 모음 체계 begin with a vowel 모음으로 시작하다

550 **justice** [dʒʌ́stis]
명 정의, 공정
justice for workers 노동자를 위한 정의 social justice 사회 정의

551 **respect** [rispékt]
동 존경하다 명 존경심 respect-respected-respected
respect your parents 당신의 부모님을 존경하다

552 **pregnant** [prégnənt]
형 임신한
a heavily pregnant woman 만삭의 여인

553 **recharge** [ri:tʃá:rdʒ]
동 충전하다 명 충전
recharge a battery 전지를 충전하다

554 **instrument** [ínstrəmənt]
명 기구, 악기
medical instruments 의료 기구 a musical instrument 악기

555 **education** [èdʒukéiʃən]
명 교육
English education 영어 교육 elementary education 초등 교육

Daily Test

| 월 일 |

A 우리말에 맞게 빈 칸에 알맞은 단어를 쓰세요.

1 Come on! Let me show you my new ______________.
이리 와봐! 내가 새로 발견한 걸 보여줄게.

2 Before dinner, you should ______________ your homework.
저녁 먹기 전에, 너는 숙제를 점검해야 한다.

3 There are no living ______________ on the island. 그 섬에는 살아있는 생명체가 없다.

4. It doesn't ______________ to me what they say.
그들이 무슨 말을 하는지는 내게 중요하지 않다.

5 We ______________ by telephone. 우리는 전화로 연락을 주고 받았다.

6 Liberty and ______________ are very important things in our lives.
자유와 정의는 우리 삶에 매우 중요한 것이다.

7 We ______________ her as our teacher. 우리는 그녀를 우리의 선생님으로서 존경한다.

8. Suzie is ______________ with her second child. Suzie는 그녀의 두 번째 아이를 임신 중이다.

9. How often do you ______________ your cell phone? 휴대폰은 얼마나 자주 충전하나요?

10 What musical ______________ does Susan play? Susan이 연주하는 악기는 무엇인가요?

B 빈 칸에 알맞은 단어를 고르세요.

1 Romeo and Juliet is famous for its ______________ ending.
① matter ② tragedy ③ happily ④ tragic ⑤ check

2 Hangeul consists of 10 ______________.
① pregnant ② harbor ③ vowels ④ creatures ⑤ respect

3 Everyone has ______________ of religion.
① free ② recharge ③ discovery ④ freedom ⑤ discount

Day 19

MP3

556 **advertise** [ǽdvərtàiz]
동 광고하다 advertise-advertised-advertised
advertise products 상품을 광고하다

557 **countryside** [kʌ́ntrisàid]
명 시골 지역
a peaceful countryside 평화로운 시골

558 **remark** [rimɑ́ːrk]
명 발언, 언급
remark about the play 그 연극에 대한 언급

559 **describe** [diskráib]
동 묘사하다 describe-described-described
describe exactly 정확하게 묘사하다

560 **male** [meil]
형 남자의 반 female 여성의
a male animal 수컷 동물 a male zebra 수컷 얼룩말

561 **shape** [ʃeip]
명 모양 동 ~모양으로 만들다
a circular shape 원형 the shape of a heart 하트 모양

562 **inspire** [inspáiər]
동 격려하다, 분발하게 하다 inspire-inspired-inspired
inspire A with B A에게 B를 불어넣다

563 **continent** [kάntənənt]
명 대륙 형 continental 대륙의, 대륙풍의
the continent of America 미국 대륙 the New Continent 신대륙

564 **diligent** [dílidʒənt]
형 근면한, 성실한 명 diligence 근면
a diligent girl 근면한 소녀 diligent in study 근면하게 공부하다

565 **refill** [ríːfil]
동 다시 채우다, 리필하다 명 다시 채운 것
refill his cup 그의 컵을 다시 채우다 refill the coffee 커피를 리필하다

566 **blond** [blɑnd]
형 금발의
blond hair 금발 머리 a blond girl 금발의 소녀

567 **continue** [kəntínju(ː)]
동 계속하다, 계속되다 continue-continued-continued
continue his study 학업을 계속하다

568 **source** [sɔːrs]
명 원천, 근원
energy source 에너지원

569 **pepper** [pépər]
명 후추
salt and pepper 소금과 후추 pass the pepper 후추를 건네주다

570 **orphan** [ɔ́ːrfən]
명 고아
orphan boys 고아 소년들 a war orphan 전쟁 고아

Daily Test

| 월 일 |

A 우리말에 맞게 빈 칸에 알맞은 단어를 쓰세요.

1 Julie and I spent a lovely time in the ____________.
Julie와 나는 시골에서 아름다운 시간을 보냈다.

2 Frankie made a positive ____________ about the play.
Frankie는 그 연극에 대해 좋은 평을 했다.

3 The police asked me to ____________ the thief.
경찰은 내게 도둑을 묘사해 달라고 요청했다.

4 ____________ students wear green pants and blue ties.
남학생들은 녹색 바지와 파란색 넥타이를 착용하고 있다.

5 Peter ____________ some clay into a ball. Peter는 찰흙으로 공을 빚었다.

6 The teacher ____________ me with confidence.
그 선생님은 내게 자신감을 불어넣어 주셨다.

7 Columbus found the new ____________ in 1492.
콜럼버스는 1492년에 신대륙을 발견했다.

8 She ____________ the glass with orange juice. 그녀는 잔을 오렌지 주스로 다시 채웠다.

9 The short and ____________ boy is my son. 저 키가 작고 금발인 소년이 제 아들입니다.

10 The baseball game ____________ for three hours. 야구 경기는 3시간 동안 계속되었다.

B 빈 칸에 알맞은 단어를 고르세요.

1 Leah is ____________ and works very hard.
① countryside ② diligent ③ shape ④ school ⑤ male

2 He was a war ____________.
① justice ② inspire ③ orphan ④ children ⑤ blond

3 The company ____________ a new computer on TV.
① continent ② remark ③ refilled ④ continues ⑤ advertised

Day 20

MP3

571 **web** [web]
명 거미줄(집), 망
spin a web 거미집을 만들다　a web of relationships 관계망

572 **propose** [prəpóuz]
동 제안하다, 청혼하다　유 offer 제안하다, 권유하다
propose two different options 두 가지 다른 선택권을 제안하다

573 **evidence** [évidəns]
명 증거
concrete evidence 구체적인 증거　scientific evidence 과학적 증거

574 **unfair** [ʌnfέər]
형 부당한, 불공평한
an unfair decision 불공평한 결정　an unfair law 부당한 법

575 **athlete** [ǽθliːt]
명 (운동) 선수　형 athletic 운동 경기의, 체육의
a professional athlete 프로 선수　a great athlete 위대한 운동선수

576 **tribe** [traib]
명 부족, 종족
tribes in Africa 아프리카의 부족들　lead a tribe 부족을 이끌다

577 **convenient** [kənvíːnjənt]
형 편리한, 간편한
convenient to eat 먹기 편한　a convenient location 편리한 장소

578 **artificial** [ɑ̀ːrtəfíʃəl]
형 인공의, 인조의
artificial flowers 조화　an artificial smile 인위적인 웃음

579 **renewable** [rinuːəbl]
형 재생 가능한
renewable forms of energy 재생 가능한 형태의 에너지

580 **quarter** [kwɔ́ːrtər]
명 4분의 1
three quarters 4분의 3　a quarter to seven 7시 15분 전

581 **associate** [əsóuʃiit]
동 관련시키다　명 association 연관성, 협회
associate a cat with misfortune 고양이를 불운과 관련시키다

582 **site** [sait]
명 위치, 장소
a camping site 캠핑장　the site of a new park 새로운 공원의 위치

583 **suppose** [səpóuz]
동 가정하다, 생각(추정)하다　suppose-supposed-supposed
suppose the rumor is true 소문이 사실이라고 가정하다

584 **routine** [ruːtíːn]
명 일과　형 일상적인
the daily routine 하루 일과　routine check 정기 점검

585 **proficiency** [prəfíʃənsi]
명 능숙, 숙달
language proficiency 언어 능숙도

Daily Test

| 월 일 |

A 우리말에 맞게 빈 칸에 알맞은 단어를 쓰세요.

1 I ______________ that the movie be banned. 나는 저 영화를 금지 시킬 것을 제안한다.

2 She found concrete ______________ of the accident. 그녀는 사고에 대해 구체적인 증거를 발견했다.

3 Some ______________ live in the desert. 몇몇 부족들은 사막에서 산다.

4 It's more ______________ to take a taxi. 택시를 타는 것이 더 편리하다.

5 He gave us ______________ flowers. 그는 우리에게 조화를 주었다.

6 People are becoming aware of ______________ energy market. 사람들은 이 재생 가능 에너지 시장에 대해 인식해 가고 있다.

7 Let's divide the watermelon into ______________. 수박을 4등분 합시다.

8 People usually ______________ winter with Christmas. 사람들은 흔히 겨울 하면 크리스마스를 연상한다.

9 I ______________ he's right. 나는 그가 옳다고 생각해.

10 Changing a daily ______________ is hard. 매일의 일상적인 일과를 바꾼다는 것은 힘들다.

B 빈 칸에 알맞은 단어를 고르세요.

1 He is one of the most famous Korean ______________ of all time.

① propose ② athletes ③ supposed ④ artificial ⑤ quarter

2 We will have an English ______________ test next Monday.

① describe ② associate ③ proficiency ④ routine ⑤ tribe

3 I think the rule is very ______________.

① infair ② impair ③ unfair ④ fairly ⑤ unfaired

Day 20

MP3

586 **dull** [dʌl]
형 따분한, 둔한 dull-duller-dullest
a dull lecture 따분한 강의 a dull sound 둔한 소리

587 **architect** [ɑ́:rkitèkt]
명 건축가, 설계자 명 architecture 건축
a principal architect 주요 설계자 a unique architect 독특한 건축가

588 **edge** [edʒ]
명 가장자리, 모서리
the edge of a cliff 벼랑 끝 the edge of a table 탁자 모서리

589 **chief** [tʃi:f]
형 주된 명 우두머리, 장
the chief reason 주된 이유 the chief of the tribe 부족의 족장

590 **pastime** [pǽstàim]
명 기분 전환, 취미, 오락
Korea's national pastime 한국의 국민적인 오락

591 **planet** [plǽnit]
명 행성
the planet Earth 지구라는 행성 other planets 다른 행성들

592 **sled** [sled]
명 썰매
ride a sled 썰매를 타다 travel by dog sled 개 썰매를 타고 여행하다

593 **strength** [streŋkθ]
명 힘, 기운
build up strength 힘을 기르다 economic strength 경제력

594 **handkerchief** [hǽŋkərtʃi(:)f]
명 손수건
Father's handkerchief 아버지의 손수건

595 **feel like ~ing** [fi:l laik iŋ]
~하고 싶다
feel like taking a walk 산책하고 싶다

596 **custom** [kʌ́stəm]
명 관습, 풍습
the old Korean custom 한국의 오랜 풍습

597 **nutrition** [nju:tríʃən]
명 영양
unbalanced nutrition 영양 불균형

598 **flour** [fláuər]
명 밀가루
be made from flour 밀가루로 만들다 buy some flour 밀가루를 사다

599 **familiar** [fəmíljər]
형 익숙한, 친숙한
look familiar 친숙해 보이다 a familiar voice 친숙한 목소리

600 **section** [sékʃən]
명 부분, 구역
a section of road 도로의 한 구역

Daily Test

| 월 일 |

A 우리말에 맞게 빈 칸에 알맞은 단어를 쓰세요.

1 Her speech was ____________ and boring. 그녀의 연설은 따분하고 지루했다.

2 He was a very famous ____________ in Korea. 그는 한국에서 매우 유명한 건축가였다.

3 Don't stand on the ____________ of the cliff. 벼랑 끝에 서 있지 마세요.

4 His ____________ merit is his positive attitude. 그의 주된 장점은 긍정적인 태도이다.

5 The Earth is the third ____________ in the solar system.
지구는 태양계에서 3번째 행성이다.

6 Sarah doesn't have the ____________ to walk. Sarah는 걸을 힘도 없었다.

7 I ____________ taking a nap. 나는 낮잠을 자고 싶어요.

8 Bread is made from ____________ and eggs. 그 빵은 밀가루와 계란으로 만들어진다.

9 The story sounds ____________ to me. 그 얘기는 내게 익숙하게 들린다.

10 You can find the book in the Social Science ____________.
당신은 이 책을 사회 과학 구역에서 찾을 수 있어요.

B 빈 칸에 알맞은 단어를 고르세요.

1 Watching movies is an enjoyable ____________.
① dull ② pastime ③ edge ④ architect ⑤ strength

2 I got some advice on ____________ and diet.
① flour ② nutritious ③ familiar ④ nutrition ⑤ section

3 We have a number of interesting local ____________.
① traditional ② vowels ③ planets ④ remarks ⑤ customs

Review Test 10 Day 19 + Day 20 | 월 일 |

A 우리말에 맞게 빈 칸에 알맞은 단어를 쓰시오.

1 ____________ accents 콧소리 억양

2 _______________ with each other 서로 의사소통 하다

3 a heavily ____________ woman 만삭의 여인

4 ____________ A with B A에게 B를 불어넣다

5 energy ____________ 에너지원

6 spin a ____________ 거미집을 만들다

7 a ____________ location 편리한 장소

8 ____________ forms of energy 재생 가능한 형태의 에너지

9 the ____________ of the tribe 부족의 족장

10 ____________ taking a walk 산책하고 싶다

B 다음 영어 풀이에 알맞은 어휘를 〈보기〉에서 고르시오.

보기	nasal	describe	evidence	dull	routine

1 ____________ : something that makes you believe or accept what you see or hear

2 ____________ : a regular or fixed way of doing something

3 ____________ : of or relating to the nose

4 ____________ : to tell someone how something or someone is or looks like

5 ____________ : not interesting or exciting; boring

C 다음 단어의 관계가 A:B=C:D가 되도록 알맞은 단어를 골라 빈칸에 적으시오.

1 discover : ______________ = create : creature

① discovered ② discovery ③ discovering
④ find ⑤ solution

2 honest : honesty = free : ______________

① freely ② freety ③ independence
④ freedom ⑤ frees

3 fair : ______________ = like : dislike

① disfair ② safe ③ unfair
④ rule ⑤ impair

4 daily : ______________ = delicious : cookies

① routine ② communicate ③ hot
④ unfair ⑤ week

5 empty : bottle = ______________ : flower

① remark ② tree ③ artificial
④ nature ⑤ fail

D 문맥에 맞게 다음 문장을 완성하시오.

1 Come on! Let me show	• •	a evidence of the accident.
2 Liberty and justice are	• •	b into quarters.
3 She found concrete	• •	c you my new discovery.
4 Let's divide the watermelon	• •	d in the Social Science section.
5 You can find the book	• •	e very important things in our lives.

E 문장을 읽고 문맥에 적절한 단어를 고르시오.

1 Where can I (recharge/suppose) my cell phone around here?

2 I (propose/participate) that our meeting be moved to a later date.

3 If you are busy now, I will call you at a time (convenient/responsible) for you.

4 Because she is French, she is not (provided/familiar) with Korean food.

5 It does not (matter/appear) to me whether you go to France or Germany.

F 문장의 빈칸에 알맞은 단어를 〈보기〉에서 찾아 쓰시오. (필요하면 형태를 고치시오.)

보기 respect remark communicate renewable associate

1 Like human beings, whales can also ______________ with each other.
인간과 마찬가지로 고래들도 서로 의사소통을 할 수 있다.

2 He was ___________ by many people as a great teacher.
그는 많은 사람들에게 위대한 선생님으로 존경 받았다.

3 His ___________ on the generation gap caused unnecessary arguments.
세대 차이에 관한 그의 언급은 불필요한 논쟁을 불러 일으켰다.

4 The symptoms you have mentioned are closely ___________ with lack of sleep.
말씀하신 증상들은 수면 부족과 깊이 연관되어 있습니다.

5 Using ___________ resources will greatly decrease our dependence on oil.
재생 가능한 자원을 사용하면 기름에 대한 의존을 크게 줄여줄 것이다.

G 그림과 낱말이 <u>잘못</u> 짝이어진 것을 고르시오. ································ (   )

ⓐ

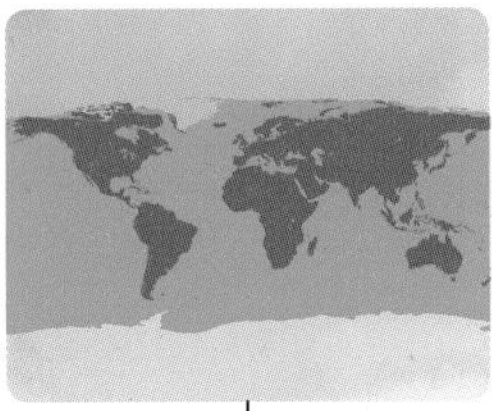

continent

ⓑ

web

ⓒ

instrument

ⓓ

female

H 낱말과 어울리는 그림을 연결하시오.

1 planets •

2 athlete •

• ⓐ

• ⓑ

Study More

quarter '4분의 1'의 다양한 의미

- quarter는 기본적으로 '4분의 1'이라는 의미를 가지고 있으며 개체, 시간, 장소 등 다양한 대상과 쓰인다. 1시간에 대해서 쓰일 때는 15분 단위를 지칭하며 1년에 대해서 쓰일 때는 3개월 단위를 지칭한다.

  cut the apple into **quarters** 사과를 네 조각으로 자르다

  a **quarter** of a mile 4분의 1마일   a quarter to 5 p.m. 5시 15분 전

  the second **quarter** of this year 올해 두 번째 분기(=4월~6월)

Day 21

MP3

601 **wake** [weik]
동 (잠에서) 깨다, 일어나다 wake-woke-woken
Wake up! 일어나! wake from a deep sleep 깊은 잠에서 깨어나다

602 **entrance** [éntrəns]
명 입구 반 exit 출구
the store entrance 상점 입구 the museum entrance 박물관 입구

603 **local** [lóukəl]
형 지역의
local food 그 지역의 음식 a local custom 그 지방의 관습

604 **represent** [rèprizént]
동 대표하다, 나타내다 represent-represented-represented
represent the U.S. 미국을 대표하다 represent freedom 자유를 나타내다

605 **tease** [ti:z]
동 놀리다, 못살게 하다 tease-teased-teased
tease other students 다른 학생들을 놀리다

606 **net** [net]
명 그물
fishing nets 낚시 그물 throw a net 그물을 던지다

607 **misunderstand** [mìsʌndərstǽnd]
동 오해하다 misunderstand-misunderstood-misunderstood
misunderstand his intention 그의 의도를 오해하다

608 **cast** [kæst]
동 던지다, (시선 등을) 보내다 cast-cast-cast
cast a smile 미소를 보내다 cast the rope 밧줄을 던지다

609 **typhoon** [taifú:n]
명 태풍
a large typhoon 거대한 태풍 the path of a typhoon 태풍의 진로

610 **crisis** [kráisəs]
명 위기
a political crisis 정치적 위기

611 **typical** [típikəl]
형 전형적인, 대표적인
a typical answer 전형적인 답 a typical example 전형적인 예시

612 **slim** [slim]
형 날씬한, 마른
a slim body 날씬한 몸 tall and slim 키가 크고 날씬한

613 **observe** [əbzə́:rv]
동 관찰하다, 보다 observe-observed-observed
observe children 아이들을 관찰하다 observe changes 변화를 관찰하다

614 **existence** [igzístəns]
명 존재
be aware of her existence 그녀의 존재를 알다 real existence 실재

615 **particular** [pərtíkjələr]
형 특정한, 특별한
a particular type of book 특정한 종류의 책

Daily Test

| 월 일 |

A 우리말에 맞게 빈 칸에 알맞은 단어를 쓰세요.

1 Sumi always ____________ up early in the morning. 수미는 매일 아침 일찍 일어난다.

2 How can we get to the main ____________? 정문은 어떻게 가나요?

3 The exhibition will be held at a ____________ gallery.
그 전시회는 지역 갤러리에서 열릴 예정이다.

4 She ____________ our country at the Olympics. 그녀는 올림픽에서 우리나라를 대표했다.

5 Don't ____________ your friend. 친구를 놀리지 마세요.

6 Many fish were caught in the ____________. 많은 물고기들이 그물에 걸렸다.

7 We ____________ each other last week. 우리는 지난 주에 서로를 오해했었다.

8 Joe ____________ the dice. Joe가 주사위를 던졌다.

9 The country is facing a serious political ____________.
그 나라는 현재 심각한 정치적 위기를 맞고 있다.

10 People ____________ the movement of the baby elephant.
사람들은 아기 코끼리의 변화를 관찰했다.

B 빈 칸에 알맞은 단어를 고르세요.

1 These questions are too ____________.
① type ② typical ③ local ④ tease ⑤ wake

2 No one noticed the ____________ of such strange rules.
① exist ② create ③ existence ④ misunderstand ⑤ bored

3 We don't have any ____________ plan.
① particular ② observe ③ strength ④ cast ⑤ part

Day 21

MP3

616 quality [kwáləti]
명 질, 품질, 특질 　반 quantity 양
high-quality goods 고품질의 상품　water quality 수질

617 appointment [əpɔ́intmənt]
명 약속
keep an appointment 약속을 지키다

618 overweight [òuvərwéit]
형 과체중의, 비만의
get overweight 살이 찌다　overweight passengers 과체중의 승객들

619 roof [ru(:)f]
명 지붕, 천장
the roof of a house 집의 지붕　the roof of a cave 동굴의 천장

620 plug [plʌg]
명 (전기) 플러그 　동 막다 　plug-plugged-plugged
pull the plug 플러그를 뽑다

621 independence [indipéndəns]
명 독립
independence from Japan 일본으로부터의 독립

622 panic [pǽnik]
명 (갑작스러운) 공포, 공황
go into a panic 공황상태에 빠지다　in panic 공포에 질려

623 crack [krǽk]
동 갈라지다, 금이 가다 　명 갈라진 금 　crack-cracked-cracked
crack a bone in his leg 그의 무릎 뼈에 금이 가다

624 lighting [láitiŋ]
명 조명
natural lighting 자연 조명　street lighting 가로등

625 payment [péimənt]
명 지불
make a payment 지불하다　part payment 부분 지불

626 crowd [kraud]
명 군중 　동 (장소를) 메우다, 붐비다
a crowd of 300 300명의 군중　gather a crowd 관중을 끌다

627 bullet [búlit]
명 총알
bullet-proof glass 방탄 유리　take a bullet 총에 맞다

628 warmth [wɔːrmθ]
명 온기, 따뜻함
the warmth of the sunshine 햇살의 온기

629 exit [égzit]
동 나가다, 퇴장하다 　명 출구 　exit-exited-exited
an emergency exit 비상구　exit the stage 무대를 퇴장하다

630 cart [kaːrt]
명 수레, 카트
push the cart 카트를 밀다　a grocery cart 식료품 카트

Daily Test

| 월 일 |

A 우리말에 맞게 빈 칸에 알맞은 단어를 쓰세요.

1 We need to improve the ______________ of our proucducts.
우리는 우리상품의 질을 향상시킬 필요가 있다.

2 I am ______________. I have to start exercising! 나 너무 살쪘어. 난 운동 해야겠어.

3 We painted the ______________ of the house. 우리는 집의 지붕을 칠했다.

4 The concert hall has ______________ on the floor. 콘서트 홀 바닥에는 금이 가 있었다.

5 John and I will go to the ______________ ceremony next week.
John과 나는 다음주에 점등 행사를 보러 갈 것이다.

6 The ______________ period has ended. 지불 기간이 끝났다.

7 The park is very ______________ today. 공원이 오늘 매우 붐빈다.

8 Mike ran as fast as a ______________. Mike는 총알처럼 빠르게 달렸다.

9 There is an ______________ sign over there. 저기 출구 표시가 있네요.

10 Horses pulled the ______________ along. 말들이 수레를 끌고 갔다.

B 빈 칸에 알맞은 단어를 고르세요.

1 I have an ______________ for an interview tomorrow.
① quality ② appoint ③ appointment ④ crack ⑤ bullet

2 Korea gained ______________ from Japan in 1945.
① roof ② independent ③ independence ④ cart ⑤ cast

3 There was ______________ in her smile.
① warmth ② warmly ③ warming ④ warm ⑤ warn

Day 22

MP3

631 **attention** [ətènʃʌ́n]
명 주의, 주목
pay attention to the teacher 선생님께 주목하다

632 **elevator** [éləvèitər]
명 엘리베이터, 승강기
go up by elevator 엘리베이터를 타고 올라가다

633 **fairy** [fέ(:)əri]
명 요정 형 상상의
a beautiful fairy 아름다운 요정 read a fairy tale 동화를 읽다

634 **invade** [invéid]
동 침략하다, 침공하다 invade-invaded-invaded
invade the neighboring country 이웃나라를 침략하다

635 **cancer** [kǽnsər]
명 암
get cancer 암에 걸리다 die of cancer 암으로 죽다

636 **native** [néitiv]
형 출생지의, 원주민(의)
native language 모국어 native art 원주민 예술

637 **disgust** [disgʌ́st]
명 역겨움, 혐오감
be disgusted with ~에 대한 혐오감을 느끼다

638 **debate** [dibéit]
명 토론 동 토론하다 debate-debated-debated
have a debate 토론을 하다 a public debate 공개 토론

639 **vain** [vein]
형 헛된, 소용없는
a vain hope 헛된 희망 a vain effort 헛된 노력

640 **swear** [swεər]
동 맹세하다 swear-swore-sworn
swear to God 신에게 맹세하다

641 **labor** [léibər]
명 노동(력)
mental labor 정신 노동 import foreign labor 외국 노동력을 수입하다

642 **professional** [prəféʃənəl]
형 전문적인, 직업의 명 전문가, 전문직 종사자
professional skills 전문적인 기술 professional education 직업 교육

643 **figure** [fígjər]
명 수치, 인물
sales figure 판매 수치 an important figure 중요한 인물

644 **option** [ápʃən]
명 선택, 선택권
have color options 색깔 선택권을 갖다

645 **various** [vέ(:)əriəs]
형 여러 가지의, 다양한
various shapes 다양한 모양 in various ways 다양한 방식으로

Daily Test

| 월 일 |

A 우리말에 맞게 빈 칸에 알맞은 단어를 쓰세요.

1 People paid ______________ to his words. 사람들은 그의 말에 주목했다.

2 The ______________ changed the girl into a mouse. 요정은 소녀를 쥐로 변하게 했다.

3 The king decided to ______________ the neighboring country.
왕은 그들의 이웃나라를 침략하기로 결정했다.

4 Lung ______________ is hard to treat. 폐암은 치료하기 어렵다.

5 Her ______________ language is English. 그녀의 모국어는 영어이다.

6 I participated in a school English ______________. 나는 학교 영어 토론에 참가했다.

7 All of Jungmin's efforts ended in ______________. 정민의 모든 노력은 허사로 끝났다.

8 I ______________ that I will never make the same mistake.
같은 실수를 하지 않겠다고 맹세해요.

9 Computer programming requires long hours of mental __________.
컴퓨터 프로그래밍은 장시간의 정신 노동을 필요로 한다.

10 Let us know the latest unemployment ______________.
우리에게 최근 실업률 수치를 알려 주세요.

B 빈 칸에 알맞은 단어를 고르세요.

1 Her dream is to become a ______________ dancer.
① profession ② professional ③ job ④ work ⑤ debate

2 Jane has no ______________ but to do it.
① native ② vain ③ choose ④ swear ⑤ option

3 Skirts come in ______________ sizes and lengths.
① labor ② attention ③ various ④ native ⑤ vary

Day 22

MP3

646 **measure** [méʒər]
동 측정하다 measure-measured-measured
measure the distance 거리를 측정하다　measure a room 방을 재다

647 **tropical** [rinu:əbl]
형 열대의, 열대 지방의
live on a tropical island 열대 섬에서 살다

648 **smoke** [smouk]
명 연기 동 담배를 피우다 smoke-smoked-smoked
toxic smoke 유독성 연기　quit smoking 담배를 끊다

649 **hard-working** [hɑːrd wə́ːrkiŋ]
형 열심히 일하는, 근면한
hard-working people 열심히 일하는 사람들

650 **semester** [siméstər]
명 학기
the fall semester 가을 학기　during the semester 학기 중에

651 **vehicle** [víːikl]
동 탈 것, 차량
a motor vehicle 자동차　drive a vehicle 차를 운전하다

652 **awkward** [ɔ́ːkwərd]
형 (기분이) 어색한, 서투른
awkward behavior 어색한 행동　an awkward situation 어색한 상황

653 **stranger** [stréindʒər]
명 낯선 사람, 처음인 사람　형 strange 낯선, 이상한
a complete stranger 전혀 모르는 사람

654 **blossom** [blάsəm]
명 꽃 동 꽃이 피다 blossom-blossomed-blossomed
cherry blossom 벚꽃　the blossoming season 개화기

655 **selfish** [sélfiʃ]
형 이기적인　유 self-centered 자기 중심적인
a selfish man 이기적인 남자　selfish behavior 이기적인 행동

656 **brief** [briːf]
형 짧은, 간결한
a brief silence 짧은 침묵　a brief meeting 짧은 회의

657 **noisy** [nɔ́izi]
형 시끄러운
Don't be noisy. 시끄럽게 하지 마세요.　noisy students 시끄러운 학생들

658 **set up** [set ʌp]
동 설립하다　유 establish 설립하다,수립하다
set up a new business 새로운 사업을 시작하다

659 **right** [rait]
형 올바른, 옳은
the right answer 정답　do the right thing 올바른 일을 하다

660 **organize** [ɔ́ːrgənàiz]
동 준비하다, 조직하다 organize-organized-organized
organize a meeting 회의를 준비하다

Daily Test

| 월 일 |

Ⓐ 우리말에 맞게 빈 칸에 알맞은 단어를 쓰세요.

1 How can we ______________ the ship's speed? 우리는 어떻게 배의 속도를 측정할 수 있을까?

2 The country has a ______________ climate. 그 나라는 열대성 기후이다.

3 My father has decided to stop ______________. 아버지는 담배를 끊기로 결심하셨다.

4 The spring ______________ will start in March. 봄 학기는 3월에 시작 할 것이다.

5 Parking a ______________ is not allowed here. 여기는 주차를 할 수 없다.

6 His gesture was ______________. 그의 손짓은 어색했다.

7 Peter is ______________, so his friends don't like him.
Peter는 이기적이어서 그의 친구들은 그를 싫어한다.

8 There was a ______________ silence. 짧은 침묵이 있었다.

9 The university ______________ new departments for foreign students.
그 대학은 외국인 학생들을 위해 새로운 학과들을 설립했다.

10 We are ______________ a baseball game. 우리는 야구 경기를 준비하고 있다.

Ⓑ 빈 칸에 알맞은 단어를 고르세요.

1 The trees are in ______________.

① awkward ② smoke ③ blossom ④ flower ⑤ seed

2 He is a ______________ to us.

① semester ② stranger ③ selfish ④ brief ⑤ students

3 It is too ______________ for the baby to sleep.

① vain ② noise ③ tropical ④ native ⑤ noisy

A 우리말에 맞게 빈 칸에 알맞은 단어를 쓰시오.

1 the store ____________ 상점 입구

2 ____________ other students 다른 학생들을 놀리다

3 a ____________ example 전형적인 예시

4 keep an ____________ 약속을 지키다

5 an emergency ____________ 비상구

6 read a ____________ tale 동화를 읽다

7 ____________ education 직업 교육

8 have color ____________ 색깔 선택권을 갖다

9 ____________ the distance 거리를 측정하다

10 ____________ behavior 이기적인 행동

B 다음 영어 풀이에 알맞은 어휘를 〈보기〉에서 고르시오.

보기	option	typical	debate	typhoon	native

1 ____________ : having usual or average features

2 ____________ : one of two or more choices available

3 ____________ : the place where a person was born

4 ____________ : a formal discussion where people of different opinions argue against each other

5 ____________ : a large and strong storm which is also called a hurricane

C 다음 단어의 관계가 A:B=C:D가 되도록 알맞은 단어를 골라 빈칸에 적으시오.

1 exist : ______________ = organize : organization

① existing ② existation ③ existence
④ exit ⑤ enter

2 gather : ______________ = collect : stamps

① crowd ② gathered ③ cloud
④ voice ⑤ time

3 ______________ : artists = difficult : question

① variety ② various ③ dress
④ color ⑤ much

4 excite : excitement = warm : ______________

① warment ② cold ③ warmth
④ spring ⑤ weather

5 ______________ : destroy = rain : flood

① heart ② body ③ cancer
④ flu ⑤ typhoon

D 문맥에 맞게 다음 문장을 완성하시오.

1	The country is facing •	• a	as a bullet.
2	Mike ran as fast •	• b	unemployment figures.
3	Lung cancer is •	• c	hard to treat.
4	Let us know the latest •	• d	a serious political crisis.
5	We are organizing •	• e	a baseball game.

E 문장을 읽고 문맥에 적절한 단어를 고르시오.

1 It is (typical/vain) for children to like toys.

2 Do you have any (particular/popular) color in mind?

3 We hurried to the cafe to make (attention/appointment) on time.

4 We'd better check the sound (reality/quality) of the headphones before buying them.

5 Although Bill is a child, he plays the violin like a (professional/architect).

F 문장의 빈칸에 알맞은 단어를 〈보기〉에서 찾아 쓰시오. (필요하면 형태를 고치시오.)

보기	native	awkward	local	hard-working	represent

1 He asked me a very ____________ question.
그는 내게 아주 곤란한 질문을 했다.

2 Koreans are known as _______________ people.
한국인은 열심히 일하는 사람들로 알려져 있다.

3 I will attend the meeting to ____________ our school.
나는 그 모임에 학교를 대표해서 참석한다.

4 Eric works as reporter at a ____________ newspaper company.
Eric은 지역 신문사에서 기자로 일한다.

5 He is very interested in the ____________ cultures of South America.
그는 남아메리카의 토착문화에 아주 관심이 많다.

G 그림에 해당하는 낱말을 〈보기〉에서 골라 쓰시오.

1 

(   )

2 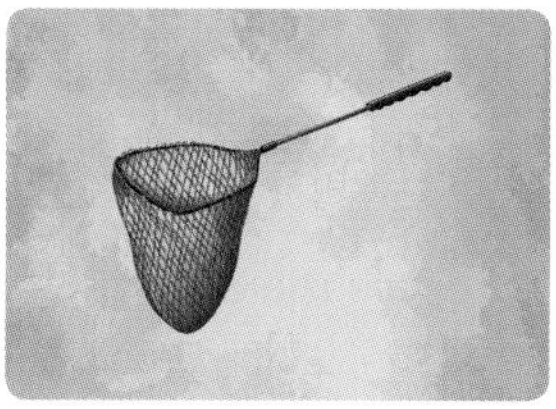

(   )

3 

(   )

4 

(   )

5 

(   )

6 

(   )

보기	wake	roof	cart	vehicle	net	observe

Study More

appointment의 다양한 뜻

- [명사] : '(업무 관련) 약속'
  Jill made an **appointment** with her teacher. Jill은 선생님과 만나기로 약속을 했다.
- [명사] : '임명, 선정'
  The team announced the **appointment** of a new director. 그 팀은 새로운 감독의 임명을 발표했다.

Day 23

MP3

661 **imagination** [imæ̀dʒənéiʃən]
명 상상, 상상력
a rich imagination 풍부한 상상력

662 **transfer** [trǽnsfər]
동 이동하다, 환승하다 transfer-transferred-transferred
transfer to another city 다른 도시로 가다

663 **border** [bɔ́:rdər]
명 국경, 경계지역 +territory 명 지역, 영토
cross the border 국경을 넘다 at a border 국경에서

664 **demand** [dimǽnd]
동 요구하다 명 요구 demand-demanded-demanded
demand an apology 사과를 요구하다 make a demand 요구하다

665 **be tired of** [bi taiərd əv]
~에 싫증이 나다, ~에 질리다
be tired of dancing 춤추는 데 싫증이 나다

666 **row** [rou]
명 열, 줄
a row of students 일렬로 서 있는 학생들 in a row 연이어

667 **arrest** [ərést]
동 체포하다 명 체포 arrest-arrested-arrested
arrest for murder 살인 혐의로 체포하다 under arrest 체포된 상태

668 **attractive** [ətrǽktiv]
형 매력적인
look attractive 매력있어 보이다 an attractive woman 매력적인 여성

669 **manager** [mǽnidʒər]
명 경영자, 관리자 동 manage 경영하다, 관리하다
a hotel manager 호텔 경영인 a stage manager 무대 감독

670 **reality** [ri(:)ǽləti]
명 현실
face reality 현실을 직시하다 accept reality 현실을 받아들이다

671 **niece** [ni:s]
명 조카딸 명 nephew 남자 조카
my beautiful niece 내 예쁜 조카딸

672 **compose** [kəmpóuz]
동 구성하다, 작곡하다
compose piano music 피아노 음악을 작곡하다

673 **prefer** [prifə́:r]
동 선호하다
prefer A to B B보다 A를 선호하다

674 **salary** [sǽləri]
명 급여, 월급 유 wage 임금, 급료
get a high salary 높은 급여를 받다 a monthly salary 월급

675 **decline** [dikláin]
동 감소하다, 쇠퇴하다 명 감소, 쇠퇴
a sharp decline 대폭하락, 폭락 in decline 쇠퇴하여

Daily Test

| 월 일 |

A 우리말에 맞게 빈 칸에 알맞은 단어를 쓰세요.

1 You should use your ______________ to write an interesting novel. 재미있는 소설을 쓰기 위해서 상상력을 발휘해야 한다.

2 Mihyun ______________ to another school last week. 미현은 지난주에 다른 학교로 전학을 갔다.

3 Sue ______________ practicing the piano. Sue는 피아노 연습하는 것에 싫증이 났다.

4 The police ______________ the thief last night. 지난 밤 경찰이 그 도둑을 체포했다.

5 We complained to the hotel ______________. 우리는 호텔 매니저에게 불만을 말했다.

6 Cindy refused to face ______________. Cindy는 현실을 마주하길 거부했다.

7 I want to learn how to ______________ music. 나는 음악을 작곡하는 법을 배우고 싶어요.

8 I ______________ reading books to watching movies. 나는 영화를 보는 것보다 책 읽는 것을 선호한다.

9 Helen saves part of her ______________ every month. Helen은 매달 월급의 일부를 저축하고 있다.

10 The number of race participants ______________ sharply. 경주 참가자 수가 급격하게 줄었다.

B 빈 칸에 알맞은 단어를 고르세요.

1 Her voice is very ______________.

① attractive ② attraction ③ attract ④ attractively ⑤ attracted

2 There is a town near the ______________.

① prefer ② border ③ compose ④ board ⑤ arrest

3 People ______________ an immediate explanation.

① demands ② declining ③ brief ④ demanded ⑤ describe

Day 23

MP3

676 **general** [dʒénərəl]

형 일반적인

general opinions 일반적인 의견　　the general public 일반 대중

677 **organic** [ɔːrgǽnik]

형 유기농의

organic vegetables 유기농 채소　　eat organic food 유기농 식품을 먹다

678 **coast** [koust]

명 해안

along the coast 해안을 따라서　　the western coast 서부 해안

679 **stomach** [stʌ́mək]

명 위, 복부

on an empty stomach 공복 시에　　stomach cancer 위암

680 **indeed** [indíːd]

부 정말, 확실히

Thank you indeed! 정말 고마워!　　very hot indeed 정말 덥다

681 **progress** [prɑ́gres]

명 진전　동 진보하다, 앞으로 나아가다

make progress 진전을 이루다　　progress in knowledge 지식이 향상되다

682 **greenhouse** [gríːnhàus]

명 온실

greenhouse plants 온실 식물　　the greenhouse effect 온실 효과

683 **skyscraper** [skáiskrèipər]

명 고층 건물

a tall skyscraper 고층 건물　　build a skyscraper 고층 건물을 짓다

684 **thrill** [θril]

명 전율, 오싹함　　형 thrilling 황홀한, 아주 신나는

feel a thrill 전율을 느끼다　　a movie full of thrills 오싹한 영화

685 **suitable** [sjúːtəbl]

형 적절한, 알맞은　　유 appropriate 적절한

a suitable topic for discussion 토론을 위한 알맞은 주제

686 **instant** [ínstənt]

형 즉각적인　명 순간

an instant response 즉각적인 반응　　for an instant 순간

687 **fond** [fɑnd]

형 애정을 느끼는, 좋아하는

be fond of ~을 좋아하다　　be fond of going hiking 야영가는 것을 좋아하다

688 **dare** [dɛər]

동 감히 ~하다　dare-dared-dared

dare to ask for money 감히 돈을 요구하다

689 **beat** [biːt]

동 이기다　beat-beat-beaten

beat him at tennis 테니스에서 그를 이기다

690 **slow down** [slou daun]

늦추다

slow down the tempo 박자를 늦추다

Daily Test

| 월 일 |

A 우리말에 맞게 빈 칸에 알맞은 단어를 쓰세요.

1 This topic will be difficult for ______________ readers.
일반 독자들에게 이 주제는 어려울 것이다.

2 There was a heavy storm on the north ______________ last weekend.
지난 주말에 북부 해안에 심한 폭풍이 왔다.

3 It is a wonderful day ______________. 오늘 날씨 정말 좋아요.

4 I hope they've made some ______________. 난 그들이 좀 진전이 있었으면 좋겠어요.

5 They have a plan to build a ______________ in front of the tower.
그들은 탑 앞에 초고층 빌딩을 세울 계획을 갖고 있다.

6 She loves the ______________ of going downhill at high speed.
그녀는 빠른 속도로 내리막을 내려오는 것에 오싹함을 즐긴다.

7 This English book is ______________ for kids under seven.
이 영어책은 7세 이하 아이들이 읽기에 적합하다.

8 The performance was an ______________ success. 공연은 즉각적인 성공을 거두었다.

9 Julie ______________ me in the English debate contest.
Julie는 영어 토론대회에서 나를 이겼다.

10 There is a crosswalk ahead. You should ______________.
횡단보도가 앞에 있어. 속도를 줄여야 해.

B 빈 칸에 알맞은 단어를 고르세요.

1 My sister is ______________ of riding her bike in summer.
① fond ② love ③ like ④ general ⑤ coast

2 Eating ______________ food is good for your health.
① organism ② health ③ organic ④ reality ⑤ prefer

3 He does not ______________ to call to her.
① rare ② dear ③ suitable ④ beat ⑤ dare

Day 24

MP3

691 **emergency** [imə́ːrdʒənsi]
명 비상
the emergency exit 비상구 / an emergency room 응급실

692 **seriously** [sí(ː)əriəsli]
부 심각하게, 진지하게
think seriously 진지하게 생각하다 / talk seriously 진지하게 이야기하다

693 **force** [fɔːrs]
명 힘 동 억지로 ~하게 하다, 강요하다 force-forced-forced
a force of nature 자연의 힘

694 **bloom** [bluːm]
명 꽃 동 꽃이 피다
come into bloom 꽃이 피기 시작하다

695 **amusement** [əmjúːzmənt]
명 오락, 놀이
go to an amusement park 놀이공원에 가다

696 **direct** [dirékt]
형 직접적인 동 감독하다, 안내하다 direct-directed-directed
a direct effect 직접적인 영향 / direct the movie 그 영화를 감독하다

697 **name** [neim]
동 이름을 붙이다 name-named-named
name him after his father 그의 아버지를 따서 이름 짓다

698 **newborn** [njúːbɔ́ːrn]
형 갓 난
a newborn baby 갓 태어난 아기

699 **crowded** [kráudid]
형 붐비는, 복잡한
a crowded bus 붐비는 버스 / crowded streets 붐비는 거리

700 **dirt** [dəːrt]
명 먼지, 때 / 형 dirty 더러운
be covered in dirt 먼지로 뒤덮인 / wash the dirt off 먼지를 씻어내다

701 **position** [pəzíʃən]
명 위치, 지위
change the position 위치를 바꾸다 / a lying position 누워있는 자세

702 **stand for** [stænd fər]
~을 나타내다
stand for peace 평화를 상징하다

703 **eye-catching** [ai kǽtʃiŋ]
형 단번에 눈길을 끄는
an eye-catching design 눈길을 끄는 디자인

704 **swallow** [swálou]
동 삼키다 swallow-swallowed-swallowed
swallow food 음식을 삼키다 / swallow a pill 알약을 삼키다

705 **collection** [kəlékʃən]
명 수집품, 소장품
a coin collection 동전 수집품 / a collection of records 음반 수집품

Daily Test

| 월 일 |

A **우리말에 맞게 빈 칸에 알맞은 단어를 쓰세요.**

1 She was ______________ ill. 그녀는 심하게 아팠다.

2 James ______________ his daughter to clean her room.
James는 그의 딸이 방을 치우도록 강요했다.

3 The party had lots of ______________ for children.
그 파티에는 아이들을 위한 많은 오락거리가 있었다.

4 A man ______________ me to Sam's office. 한 남자가 나를 Sam의 사무실까지 안내해주었다.

5 John was ______________ after his grandfather. John은 할아버지를 따서 이름이 지어졌다.

6 The number of ______________ babies is decreasing these days.
요즘 신생아의 수가 감소하고 있다.

7 Linda changed the ______________ of her bed. Linda는 그녀의 침대 위치를 바꿨다.

8 WHO ______________ World Health Organization. WHO는 세계 보건 기구를 의미한다.

9 The new car advertisement is ______________. 새로운 자동차 광고가 눈길을 사로잡는다.

10 Yuri couldn't ______________ the pill. Yuri는 그 알약을 삼키지 못했다.

B **빈 칸에 알맞은 단어를 고르세요.**

1 Where is the ______________ exit?
① thrill ② emergency ③ instant ④ emerge ⑤ swallow

2 Oh, his coat is covered in ______________!
① direct ② dirty ③ clean ④ force ⑤ dirt

3 Her hobby is making a ______________ of coins.
① position ② collection ③ collect ④ amusement ⑤ name

Day 24

MP3

706 □ **urban** [ə́ːrbən]

형 도시의 반 rural 시골의

urban life 도시생활 urban development 도시 개발

707 □ **purse** [pəːrs]

명 지갑 유 wallet (접이식) 지갑

200 dollars in a purse 지갑 속 200달러

708 □ **resident** [rézidənt]

명 주민, 거주자

a resident of Korea 한국 거주자

709 □ **recreation** [rèkriéiʃən]

명 오락, 휴양, 레크리에이션

leisure and recreation 여가와 오락 recreation facilities 휴양 시설

710 □ **part** [pɑːrt]

동 ~와 헤어지다 part-parted-parted

part from his family 그의 가족과 헤어지다

711 □ **bare** [bɛər]

형 벌거벗은, 노출된

bare hands 맨손 walk in bare feet 맨발로 걷다

712 □ **honor** [ánər]

명 명예 형 명예의

lose honor 명예를 잃다 a great honor 큰 영광

713 □ **get away with** [get əwéi wið]

~를 교묘히 모면하다, ~을 가지고 도망가다

get away with punishment 처벌을 교묘히 모면하다

714 □ **function** [fʌ́ŋkʃən]

명 기능 동 작동하다, 기능을 하다

perform a function 기능을 수행하다

715 □ **stream** [striːm]

명 개울, 시내

a large stream 큰 개울 go across a stream 개울을 건너다

716 □ **thinker** [θíŋkər]

명 사색가, 생각하는 사람

a creative thinker 창의적으로 생각하는 사람

717 □ **treat** [triːt]

동 대하다, 치료하다 treat-treated-treated

treat him with respect 존경심을 갖고 그를 대하다

718 □ **moonlight** [múːnlàit]

명 달빛

walk in the moonlight 달빛 아래서 걷다 a moonlight sonata 월광곡

719 □ **pretend** [priténd]

동 ~인 척 하다 pretend-pretended-pretended

pretend to ~인 체 하다 pretend to know 아는 척 하다

720 □ **sprinkle** [spríŋkl]

동 뿌리다

sprinkle the fish with salt 생선에 소금을 뿌리다

Daily Test

| 월 일 |

A **우리말에 맞게 빈 칸에 알맞은 단어를 쓰세요.**

1 ____________ pollution is a serious problem in many countries. 도시 공해는 여러 나라에서 심각한 문제이다.

2 Julia plays table tennis for ____________. Julia는 오락 삼아 탁구를 친다.

3 Can you catch fish with your ____________ hands? 맨 손으로 물고기를 잡을 수 있나요?

4 It is a great ____________ to meet you. 당신을 만나게 되어 큰 영광이었어요.

5 Sue and her friends ____________ at the station. Sue와 친구들은 역에서 헤어졌다.

6 Don't lie to me! I won't let you ____________ it. 내게 거짓말 하지마. 그냥 넘어가도록 놔두지 않을 거야.

7 Andy is a quick ____________. Andy는 두뇌 회전이 빠르다.

8 ____________ people as you would like to be treated. 대접 받고 싶은 대로 남을 대하라.

9 She and I walked together in the ____________. 달빛 아래에서 그녀와 나는 함께 걸었다.

10 ____________ some salt and pepper on the soup. 수프에 소금과 후추를 약간 뿌리세요.

B **빈 칸에 알맞은 단어를 고르세요.**

1 The ____________ of the village voted for a new governor.

① purse ② dirt ③ honor ④ stream ⑤ residents

2 My old radio still ____________ well.

① treat ② functions ③ known ④ direction ⑤ honor

3 He ____________ to be sad.

① sprinkles ② pretends ③ intend ④ bares ⑤ pretend

Review Test 12

Day 23 + Day 24 | 월 일 |

A 우리말에 맞게 빈 칸에 알맞은 단어를 쓰시오.

1 cross the ______________ 국경을 넘다

2 look ____________ 매력 있어 보이다

3 get a high ______________ 높은 급여를 받다

4 ____________ opinions 일반적인 의견

5 a ____________ topic for discussion 토론을 위한 알맞은 주제

6 think ____________ 진지하게 생각하다

7 ____________ him after his father 그의 아버지를 따서 이름 짓다

8 ______________ a pill 알약을 삼키다

9 ____________ facilities 휴양 시설

10 ____________to laugh 웃는 척 하다

B 다음 영어 풀이에 알맞은 어휘를 〈보기〉에서 고르시오.

보기	border	stream	urban	swallow	demand

1 ____________ : the line that separates one country from another

2 ____________ : a need for something to be sold or supplied

3 ____________ : a small body of flowing water

4 ____________ : of or relating to cities

5 ____________ : to move food or drink from the mouth to the stomach

C 다음 단어의 관계가 A:B=C:D가 되도록 알맞은 단어를 골라 빈칸에 적으시오.

1 imagine : ______________ = collect : collection

① imagination ② imaginary ③ image
④ imagines ⑤ imagenation

2 ill : illness = real : ______________

① realness ② realism ③ fake
④ reality ⑤ true

3 manage : ______________ = write : writer

① manager ② problem ③ management
④ students ⑤ managed

4 nephew : ______________ = brother : sister

① aunt ② niece ③ uncle
④ family ⑤ neice

5 ______________ : dirty = reality : real

① dirt ② clean ③ dust
④ room ⑤ mud

D 문맥에 맞게 다음 문장을 완성하시오.

1 You should use your imagination •	• a is decreasing these days.
2 The police arrested •	• b World Health Organization.
3 The number of newborn babies •	• c for recreation.
4 WHO stands for •	• d to write an interesting novel.
5 Julia plays table tennis •	• e the thief last night.

E 문장을 읽고 문맥에 적절한 단어를 고르시오.

1 The shopping center was already (crowded/crawled) with shoppers.

2 You are driving too fast. Can you (slow down/turn down) a bit?

3 You can (arrest/transfer) to Line 4 at Seoul Station.

4 It is very windy outside. I (prefer/pretend) to stay in than to go out.

5 This book is easy to read and (responsible/suitable) for young children.

F 문장의 빈칸에 알맞은 단어를 〈보기〉에서 찾아 쓰시오. (필요하면 형태를 고치시오.)

보기 attractive demand function seriously indeed

1 ____________ for ice cream is getting higher due to the hot weather.
더운 날씨 때문에 아이스크림에 대한 수요가 높아지고 있다.

2 This beach is ____________ to campers and windsurfers.
이 해변은 야영객들과 윈드서핑을 하는 사람들에게 매력적이다.

3 Liam is thinking ____________ about changing his major.
Liam은 전공을 바꾸는 것을 진지하게 생각하고 있다.

4 ____________, many students have difficulty in expressing their opinions.
실제로 많은 학생들이 자신들의 의견을 표현하는 것을 어려워한다.

5 This cell phone has a lot of ____________, but I only use some of them.
이 휴대폰은 많은 기능을 가지고 있지만 나는 그 중 몇 개만 사용한다.

Ⓖ 그림과 낱말이 잘못 짝이어진 것을 고르시오. .... (   )

ⓐ

crowded

ⓑ

skyscraper

ⓒ

stomach

ⓓ

amusement

Ⓗ 낱말과 어울리는 그림을 연결하시오.

1 stream •   • ⓐ

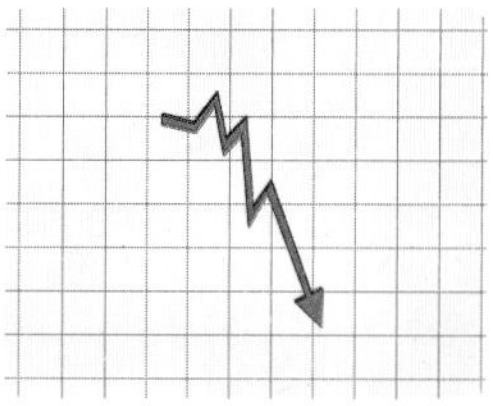

2 decline •   • ⓑ

Study More

part를 포함하는 숙어

- [part] 명 '부분, 구성원' 동 '(~와) 헤어지다, 갈라지다'
- [take part in ~] : '~에 참여하다/~에 참가하다'
  Lewis **took part in** a singing contest. Lewis는 노래 경연대회에 참가했다.
- [part company (with/from ~)] : '~와 헤어지다'
  They **parted company.** 그들은 헤어졌다.

Day 25

MP3

721 **movement** [mú:vmənt]
명 움직임, 활동
the movement of the body 신체의 움직임

722 **stir** [stə:r]
동 젓다 stir-stirred-stirred
stir the tea with a spoon 스푼으로 차를 젓다

723 **assign** [əsáin]
동 배정하다, 할당하다 assign-assigned-assigned
assign roles 역할을 배정하다 assign work 일을 할당하다

724 **bear** [bɛər]
동 참다, 견디다 유 endure 견디다, 참다
bear the pain 고통을 견디다 bear to eat 참고 먹다

725 **crab** [kræb]
명 게
walk like a crab 게처럼 걷다 a crab shell 게딱지

726 **obey** [oubéi]
동 따르다, 순종하다 obey-obeyed-obeyed
obey the rules 법을 따르다 obey her parents 그녀의 부모님께 순종하다

727 **dive** [daiv]
동 (물 속으로) 뛰어들다, 다이빙하다 dive-dived(dove)-dived
dive into the pool 수영장에 뛰어들다 dive deep 물 속 깊이 들어가다

728 **terrific** [tərífik]
형 아주 멋진, 훌륭한
a terrific holiday 아주 멋진 휴일

729 **direction** [dirékʃən]
명 (위치, 이동의) 방향, 지시
the opposite direction 반대 방향 ask for directions 지시를 요청하다

730 **request** [rikwést]
명 요청 동 요청하다 request-requested-requested
refuse a request 요청을 거절하다 request for aid 지원을 요청하다

731 **arise** [əráiz]
동 생기다, 발생하다 arise-arose-arisen
A political crisis has arisen. 정치적 위기가 발생했다.

732 **link** [liŋk]
명 관련성, 연결 동 link 연결하다, 관련짓다
the link between the two discoveries 두 발견의 관련성

733 **scenery** [sí:nəri]
명 경치, 풍경
enjoy the beautiful scenery 아름다운 풍경을 즐기다

734 **threaten** [θrétən]
동 위협(협박)하다 threaten-threatened-threatened
threaten to kill 생명을 협박하다 threaten with ~으로 협박하다

735 **saying** [séiiŋ]
명 말하기, 속담
sayings and doings 언행 a common saying 흔히 하는 말, 속담

Daily Test

| 월 일 |

A 우리말에 맞게 빈 칸에 알맞은 단어를 쓰세요.

1 The dancer's ______________ was fast but soft. 그 댄서의 움직임은 빠르지만 부드러웠다.

2 I ______________ my black tea with a spoon. 나는 스푼으로 내 홍차를 저었다.

3 We need to ______________ some roles in preparation for the seminar. 우리는 세미나 준비를 위해 몇 가지 역할을 지정해야 해요.

4 I wonder how ______________ can walk sideways. 나는 게가 어떻게 옆으로 걸을 수 있는지 궁금하다.

5 He didn't ______________ the traffic rules. 그는 교통 규칙을 따르지 않았다.

6 His performance was ______________! 그의 공연은 아주 멋졌어!

7 We were walking in the opposite ______________. 우리는 반대방향에 서 있었다.

8 Ryan ______________ that we arrive an hour earlier. Ryan은 우리에게 한 시간 일찍 도착하라고 요청했다.

9 Major problems often ______________ from simple mistakes. 심각한 문제는 때때로 사소한 실수에서 발생한다.

10 There is a close ______________ between the two issues. 그 두 문제 사이에는 긴밀한 연관성이 있다.

B 빈 칸에 알맞은 단어를 고르세요.

1 The garden is famous for its grand ______________.

① scene ② scenery ③ movement ④ surprising ⑤ obey

2 I was so afraid of ______________ into the pool.

① dives ② diveing ③ diving ④ dive ⑤ dived

3 There are many substances that ______________ the ecosystem.

① threaten ② assign ③ threat ④ arise ⑤ rise

Day 25

MP3

736 **scale** [skeil]
명 규모, 범위, 등급
on a grand scale 전 세계적 범위에서 / the social scale 사회적 등급

737 **nearby** [níərbài]
형 가까운 곳의, 근처에
a nearby shop 근처 가게 / a nearby river 근처 호수

738 **wound** [wuːnd]
명 상처, 부상 동 부상을 입히다
a head wound 머리 부상 / treat the wound 부상을 치료하다

739 **injury** [índʒəri]
명 부상
a serious injury 심각한 부상 / an injury to the right arm 오른팔 부상

740 **twist** [twist]
동 꼬다, 비틀다, 삐다 twist-twisted-twisted
twist her ankle 그녀의 발목을 삐다 / twist the wire 철사를 구부리다

741 **spot** [spɑt]
명 점, 장소
a quiet spot 조용한 장소 / a black spot on the beak 부리 위에 검은 점

742 **scissors** [sízərz]
명 가위
use scissors 가위를 사용하다 / a pair of scissors 한 쌍의 가위

743 **camping** [kǽmpiŋ]
명 야영, 캠핑
go camping 야영을 가다 / a camping site 야영지

744 **awesome** [ɔ́ːsəm]
형 감탄할만한, 무서운, 놀라운
an awesome sight 놀라운 광경 / an awesome story 무서운 이야기

745 **haircut** [hɛ́ərkʌ̀t]
명 이발, 머리모양
get a haircut 이발하다 / a short haircut 짧은 머리모양

746 **rapid** [rǽpid]
형 급격한, 빠른 부 rapidly 급속히, 빨리
rapid growth 급격한 성장 / make a rapid recovery 빠른 회복을 하다

747 **uneasy** [ʌníːzi]
형 불안한, 걱정되는
an uneasy smile 불안한 미소 / an uneasy peace 불안한 평화

748 **forward** [fɔ́ːrwərd]
부 (위치가) 앞으로
lean forward 앞으로 숙이다 / go forward 전진하다

749 **insert** [insə́ːrt]
동 넣다, 삽입하다 insert-inserted-inserted
insert coins 동전을 끼워 넣다

750 **sweep** [swiːp]
동 ~을 쓸다, 청소하다 sweep-swept-swept
sweep the dirt 먼지를 쓸다 / sweep a room 방을 청소하다

Daily Test

| 월 일 |

A **우리말에 맞게 빈 칸에 알맞은 단어를 쓰세요.**

1 I didn't know the ______________ of the accident. 나는 사고의 규모를 몰랐다.

2 His ______________ healed slowly. 그의 상처는 천천히 나았다.

3 ______________ the wire to form a triangle. 철사를 삼각형 모양으로 구부리세요.

4 I bought a tie with black ______________. 나는 검은 반점이 있는 넥타이를 샀다.

5 We will go ______________ next weekend. 우리는 다음주에 야영을 갈 것이다.

6 Your new album is ______________! 너의 새 앨범은 최고야!

7 I think John needs a ______________. 내 생각엔 John은 머리를 좀 자를 필요가 있는 거 같아.

8 A positive attitude will give you the power to move ______________. 긍정적인 태도는 앞으로 나아갈 힘을 줄 것 입니다.

9 If you want to play the game, ______________ coins. 게임을 하고 싶다면 동전을 넣으세요.

10 Let's ______________ the room. 방을 치우자.

B **빈 칸에 알맞은 단어를 고르세요.**

1 The boy made a ______________ recovery after the operation.
① rapid ② scale ③ forward ④ link ⑤ rapidly

2 He couldn't attend school because of a leg ______________.
① insert ② sweep ③ direction ④ injury ⑤ camping

3 I feel ______________ about Tim's health.
① ineasy ② easily ③ uneasy ④ twist ⑤ difficult

Day 26

MP3

751 ☐ **pattern** [pǽtərn]
명 무늬, 양식
a flower pattern 꽃무늬　the pattern of behavior 행동 양식

752 ☐ **comfort** [kʌ́mfərt]
명 편안, 위로　형 comfortable 편안한
words of comfort 위로의 말　comfort and safety 편안함과 안전

753 ☐ **submit** [səbmít]
동 제출하다　명 submission 제출
submit homework by email 이메일로 숙제를 제출하다

754 ☐ **seasoning** [síːzəniŋ]
명 조미료, 양념
artificial seasoning 인공 조미료　add seasoning 양념을 더하다

755 ☐ **paralyze** [pǽrəlàiz]
동 마비시키다　paralyze-paralyzed-paralyzed
paralyze the left arm 왼팔을 마비시키다

756 ☐ **virtual** [və́ːrtʃuəl]
형 사실상의, (컴퓨터를 이용한) 가상의
virtual reality 가상 현실　a virtual leader 사실상의 지도자

757 ☐ **yummy** [jʌ́mi]
형 아주 맛있는　유 delicious 아주 맛있는
yummy chocolate 아주 맛있는 초콜릿

758 ☐ **tidy** [táidi]
형 깔끔한, 잘 정돈된　유 neat 정돈된, 단정한
a tidy room 잘 정돈된 방　his tidy house 그의 깔끔한 집

759 ☐ **weekly** [wíːkli]
형 매주의, 주 1회의
a weekly magazine 주간 잡지　a weekly test 주간 시험

760 ☐ **impress** [ímpres]
동 감명을 주다　impress-impressed-impressed
impress the audience 군중에게 감명을 주다

761 ☐ **select** [silékt]
동 고르다, 선택하다　select-selected-selected
select an interesting book 재미있는 책을 고르다

762 ☐ **bucket** [bʌ́kit]
명 양동이, 물통
a plastic bucket 플라스틱 양동이　a bucket of water 물 한 동이

763 ☐ **dynasty** [dáinəsti]
명 왕조, 왕가
the Chosun Dynasty 조선 왕조　found a dynasty 왕조를 세우다

764 ☐ **fitness** [fítnis]
명 (신체적인) 건강, 신체단련
a fitness test 체력 테스트　improve your fitness 건강을 증진시키다

765 ☐ **memorize** [méməràiz]
동 암기하다　memorize-memorized-memorized
memorize a poem 시를 암기하다

Daily Test

| 월 일 |

A 우리말에 맞게 빈 칸에 알맞은 단어를 쓰세요.

1 The wallpaper of my room has flower ______________. 내 방 벽지는 꽃무늬로 되어있다.

2 Please ______________ your writing homework to Mr. Perry.
작문 숙제를 Perry 선생님께 제출해 주세요.

3 The drug ______________ his nerves. 그 약은 그의 신경을 마비시켰다.

4 She is the ______________ owner of the company. 그녀는 우리 회사의 사실상의 소유주였다.

5 Mina goes to a ______________ tennis class. 미나는 매주 테니스 수업에 간다.

6 I made delicious cookies to ______________ my mother.
나는 엄마를 감동시키기 위해 맛있는 쿠키를 만들었다.

7 Andy ______________ the cheapest shirts. Andy는 가장 싼 셔츠를 골랐다.

8 The blue ______________ is filled with pebbles. 파란 양동이는 조약돌로 가득 차 있다.

9 Jihyun and I signed up for the ______________ class.
지현과 나는 피트니스 수업에 등록했다.

10 Do you know the best way of ______________ English words?
너는 영단어를 외우는 가장 좋은 방법을 알고 있니?

B 빈 칸에 알맞은 단어를 고르세요.

1 Youngjin's room is always neat and ______________.
① tidy ② tiny ③ pattern ④ bucket ⑤ virtual

2 People want to live in ______________.
① comfortably ② select ③ comfort ④ memorize ⑤ spot

3 The custom dated from the Chosun ______________.
① submit ② impress ③ during ④ for ⑤ Dynasty

Day 26

MP3

766 **attempt** [ətémpt]
명 시도 동 시도하다 attempt-attempted-attempted
make an attempt 시도하다 attempt to escape 도망치려 시도하다

767 **ruin** [rú(:)in]
동 망치다, 파괴하다 명 파멸, 폐허
ruin the city 도시를 폐허로 만들다

768 **globe** [gloub]
명 지구본, 지구, 세계
all over the globe 전 세계에 circle the globe 세계 일주하다

769 **salty** [sɔ́:lti]
형 짭짤한, 소금이 든
drink salty water 소금물을 먹다 a salty taste 짠 맛

770 **elect** [ilékt]
동 선출하다 elect-elected-elected 명 election 선거
elect the class president 반장을 선출하다

771 **oxygen** [ɑ́ksidʒən]
명 산소
an oxygen tank 산소 탱크 receive oxygen 산소호흡을 받다

772 **technology** [teknɑ́lədʒi]
명 기술
medical technology 의학 기술 new technology 신기술

773 **by the way** [bai ðə wei]
그런데
By the way, have we met before? 그런데, 우리가 전에 본 적 있나요?

774 **principal** [prínsəpəl]
형 주요한, 주된
principal reason 주된 이유 principal subjects 주요 과목

775 **store** [stɔ:r]
동 저장하다 store-stored-stored
store information 정보를 저장하다 store food 음식을 저장하다

776 **cheese** [tʃi:z]
명 치즈
make cheese sandwiches 치즈 샌드위치를 만들다

777 **subtract** [səbtrǽkt]
동 빼다 subtract-subtracted-subtracted
subtract 5 from 20 20에서 5를 빼다

778 **gargle** [gɑ́:rgl]
동 (물로) 양치질하다, 입을 헹구다 gargle-gargled-gargled
gargle with salt water 소금물로 입을 헹구다

779 **overestimate** [óuvərestəmit]
동 과대평가하다
overestimate her ability 그녀의 능력을 과대평가하다

780 **toss** [tɔ(:)s]
동 (가볍게) 던지다
toss his hat aside 한 쪽으로 그의 모자를 던지다

Daily Test

| 월 일 |

A 우리말에 맞게 빈 칸에 알맞은 단어를 쓰세요.

1 Helen ____________ to fix her car but failed.
Helen은 그녀의 차를 고치려고 했지만 실패했다.

2 The war completely ____________ the lives of ordinary people.
전쟁은 평범한 사람들의 삶을 완전히 망쳐 버렸다.

3 My dream is to travel all around the ____________.
내 꿈은 전 세계를 여행하는 것이다.

4 Who will be ____________ as the leader of our team? 우리 팀의 리더로 누가 뽑힐까?

5 ____________ is essential to human life. 인간의 삶에 있어 산소는 매우 중요하다.

6 We are talking about the new ____________. 우리는 새로운 기술에 대해 얘기 중이다.

7 ____________, do you still live in Seoul? 그나저나 넌 아직도 서울에 살고 있니?

8 She is looking for a box to ____________ her photographs.
그녀는 자신의 사진을 보관할 박스를 찾고 있다.

9 If you ____________ 30 from 70, you get 40.
당신이 70에서 30을 빼면, 당신은 40을 갖게 된다.

10 The boy ____________ the tennis ball to the dog. 소년은 테니스 공을 개에게 던졌다.

B 빈 칸에 알맞은 단어를 고르세요.

1 The ____________ reason she studies is to please her parents.
① principal ② impress ③ ruin ④ globe ⑤ elect

2 This soup is too ____________.
① oxygen ② salt ③ store ④ spice ⑤ salty

3 The company ____________ the benefits of the new delivery system.
① attempt ② weekly ③ awesome ④ overestimated ⑤ scale

Review Test 13

A 우리말에 맞게 빈 칸에 알맞은 단어를 쓰시오.

1 ____________ the rules 법을 따르다

2 ______________ to kill 생명을 협박하다

3 a black ____________ on the beak 부리 위에 검은 점

4 ____________ growth 급격한 성장

5 ____________ the coin 동전을 끼워 넣다

6 ____________ homework by email 이메일로 숙제를 제출하다

7 a ____________ room 잘 정돈된 방

8 found a ____________ 왕조를 세우다

9 receive ____________ 산소호흡을 받다

10 the ____________ reason 주된 이유

B 다음 영어 풀이에 알맞은 어휘를 〈보기〉에서 고르시오.

보기	dive	gargle	obey	pattern	dynasty

1 ____________ : to do what someone or the law tells you to do

2 ____________ : to jump into water, usually with your arms first

3 ____________ : a repeated form or way in which something happens or appears

4 ____________ : a family of rulers who rule a country or empire for many generations

5 ____________ : to wash inside your mouth or throat by moving your tongue

C 다음 단어의 관계가 A:B=C:D가 되도록 알맞은 단어를 골라 빈칸에 적으시오.

1 obey : obeyed = dive : ____________

① drove ② dove ③ pool
④ swimming ⑤ jump

2 comfort : ____________ = availability : available

① comfortable ② comforts ③ uneasy
④ uncomfort ⑤ comforting

3 revolution : revolutionize = memory : ____________

① brain ② remember ③ memorize
④ past ⑤ fade

4 ____________ : date = listen : music

① select ② calendar ③ selection
④ meet ⑤ time

5 make : ____________ = spill : milk

① attempt ② attemption ③ made
④ receive ⑤ direction

D 문맥에 맞게 다음 문장을 완성하시오.

1 I stirred my black tea • • a with a spoon.

2 A positive attitude will give you • • b owner of the company.

3 She is the virtual • • c to store her photographs.

4 She is looking for a box • • d the power to move forward.

5 The boy tossed • • e the tennis ball to the dog.

E 문장을 읽고 문맥에 적절한 단어를 고르시오.

1 The accident (arose/raised) from a mistake.

2 We will reply to your (request/respect) by next Friday.

3 Because we don't have a car, we walked to a(n) (awkward/nearby) restaurant.

4 Patience was the (vain/principal) element behind his success.

5 The audience was deeply (impressed/tossed) by the performance of the pianist.

F 문장의 빈칸에 알맞은 단어를 〈보기〉에서 찾아 쓰시오. (필요하면 형태를 고치시오.)

보기 rapid awesome terrific movement overestimate

1 The view from the mountain top was ____________.
산 정상에서 내려다보는 광경은 굉장했다.

2 Isabel's ____________ idea made our plan complete.
Isabel의 훌륭한 아이디어는 우리의 계획을 완벽하게 만들었다.

3 Korea has seen ____________ changes in many fields of industry.
한국은 산업의 여러 분야에서 빠른 변화를 목격했다.

4 People tend to ____________ the impact of technology.
사람들은 기술의 영향력을 과대평가하는 경향이 있다.

5 He played a major role in the antiwar ____________.
그는 반전 운동에서 중요한 역할을 했다.

G 그림에 해당하는 낱말을 〈보기〉에서 골라 쓰시오.

1 
(　　　　　　)

2 
(　　　　　　)

3 
(　　　　　　)

4 
(　　　　　　)

5 
(　　　　　　)

6 
(　　　　　　)

보기 wound　direction　globe　sweep　bucket　crab

Study More

'scissors'처럼 항상 복수형으로 쓰이는 명사들

- 영어에서 짝을 이루어서 기능을 하는 개체들은 복수형으로 자주 쓰인다.
  trousers 바지　jeans 청바지　glasses 안경　clothes 옷, 의복　shoes 신발, 구두
- 한 쌍이나 한 벌로 사용되는 개체들의 수량을 나타낼 때는 'a pair of ~'를 주로 사용한다.
  a pair of trousers 바지 한 벌　**a pair of** shoes 구두 한 켤레,

Day 27

MP3

781 **foggy** [fɔ́(:)gi]
형 안개가 낀
a foggy day 안개가 낀 날　　a foggy street 안개가 낀 거리

782 **scientific** [sàiəntífik]
형 과학적인, 과학의
a scientific fact 과학적인 사실　　a scientific discovery 과학적인 발견

783 **celebrate** [séləbrèit]
동 축하하다　celebrate-celebrated-celebrated
celebrate a victory 승리를 축하하다

784 **poverty** [pávərti]
명 가난, 빈곤
live in poverty 가난하게 살다　　extreme poverty 극도의 빈곤

785 **fall in love** [fɔːl in lʌv]
사랑에 빠지다
fall in love at first sight 첫 눈에 사랑에 빠지다

786 **weekday** [wíːkdèi]
명 평일
each weekday 평일마다　　during the weekdays 평일에

787 **grateful** [gréitfəl]
형 고마워하는, 감사하는
a grateful letter 감사의 편지　　grateful to ~에 감사하는

788 **lip** [lip]
명 입술
the lower lip 아랫입술　　thin-lipped 입술이 얇은

789 **supper** [sʌ́pər]
명 저녁
have supper 저녁을 먹다　　make supper 저녁식사를 준비하다

790 **aerobic** [ɛəróubik]
형 유산소의　명 에어로빅
aerobic exercise 유산소 운동

791 **carbon** [káːrbən]
명 탄소
reduce carbon emissions 탄소 배출량을 줄이다

792 **preface** [préfis]
명 서문
write a preface for a book 책에 서문을 쓰다

793 **microwave** [máikrəwèiv]
명 전자레인지
use the microwave 전자레인지를 사용하다

794 **conquer** [káŋkər]
동 정복하다　conquer-conquered-conquered　명 conquest 정복
conquer an enemy 적을 정복하다

795 **emit** [imít]
동 내뿜다, 내다　명 emission 배출, 배출물
emit heat 열을 내뿜다　　emit gas 가스를 내뿜다

Daily Test

| 월 일 |

A 우리말에 맞게 빈 칸에 알맞은 단어를 쓰세요.

1 Today is ______________ and cold. 오늘은 안개가 끼고 춥다.

2 The country has a high rate of ______________. 그 나라는 빈곤율이 높다.

3 We ______________ Jack's graduation. 우리는 Jack의 졸업을 축하했다.

4 Ann seems to have ______________ with James. Ann은 James와 사랑에 빠진 것처럼 보인다.

5 This flower shop is open on every ______________. 그 꽃가게는 매일 문을 열어요.

6 I'm so ______________ to meet you again. 나는 너를 다시 만나게 되서 감사해.

7 We reduced our ______________ emissions to protect our environment. 환경을 보호하기 위해 우리는 탄소 배출량을 줄였다.

8 The author clearly stated the objective of the book in the ______________. 그 저자는 서문에 책의 목적을 명확하게 밝혔다.

9 He ______________ Everest in 1993. 그는 1993년에 에베레스트를 정복했다.

10 Many cars ______________ carbon dioxide. 많은 차들이 이산화탄소를 배출한다.

B 빈 칸에 알맞은 단어를 고르세요.

1 After ______________, we usually watch a movie.
① foggy ② supper ③ grateful ④ preface ⑤ emit

2 Tom's upper ______________ is swollen.
① floor ② poverty ③ carbon ④ toss ⑤ lip

3 Hangeul is one of the ______________ writing systems in the world.
① science ② beauty ③ scientific ④ weekday ⑤ alone

Day 27

MP3

796 □ **property** [prápərti]
명 재산, 소유물
government property 정부 재산　public property 공유 재산

797 □ **wagon** [wǽgən]
명 4륜차, 마차, 수레
a four-wheeled wagon 사륜 마차

798 □ **emerge** [imə́ːrdʒ]
동 나오다, 드러나다, 나타나다　명 emergence 출현, 발생
emerge from the empty room 빈 방에서 나오다

799 □ **script** [skript]
명 대본, 원고
write a script 원고를 쓰다　a film script 영화 대본

800 □ **swing** [swiŋ]
동 흔들리다, 흔들다　명 그네
play on the swing 그네를 타며 놀다　swing her leg 그녀의 다리를 흔들다

801 □ **discipline** [dísəplin]
명 규율, 훈육　동 훈육하다
strict discipline 엄격한 규율　discipline a child 아이를 훈육하다

802 □ **wireless** [wáiərlis]
형 무선의　반 wired 유선의
wireless communication 무선 통신

803 □ **crayon** [kréiɑn]
명 크레용
draw a picture with crayons 크레용으로 그림을 그리다

804 □ **revolution** [rèvəljúːʃən]
명 혁명　형 revolutionary 혁명의, 혁명적인
the French Revolution 프랑스 혁명

805 □ **paragraph** [pǽrəgræ̀f]
명 단락
the theme of the paragraph 문단의 주제

806 □ **package** [pǽkidʒ]
명 포장, 짐꾸리기, 소포
deliver a package 소포를 배달하다

807 □ **waterfall** [wɔ́ːtərfɔ̀ːl]
명 폭포
an artificial waterfall 인공 폭포

808 □ **clearly** [klíərli]
부 뚜렷하게, 명확하게
speak clearly 명확하게 말하다　clearly visible 뚜렷하게 보이는

809 □ **sponge** [spʌndʒ]
동 (해면,스펀지로) 몸, 얼굴을 닦다　sponge-sponged-sponged
sponge down his body 스펀지로 그의 몸을 닦다

810 □ **take over** [teik óuvər]
인수하다, 인계받다
take over the record company 그 음반 회사를 인수하다

Daily Test

| 월 일 |

A **우리말에 맞게 빈 칸에 알맞은 단어를 쓰세요.**

1 Nick decided to give back the whole of his ____________ to society.
Nick은 그의 전 재산을 사회에 환원하기로 결심했다.

2 Tony pulled a ____________ up the hill. Tony는 수레를 언덕 위로 끌고 올라갔다.

3 She is writing a new film ____________ these days.
그녀는 요즘 새 영화대본을 쓰는 중이다.

4 Students in this school are educated under strict ____________.
이 학교의 학생들은 엄격한 규율 하에 교육을 받는다.

5 Our summer camp provides free ____________ Internet access.
우리의 여름 캠프는 무료 인터넷 접속을 제공한다.

6 One day, I received a ____________ from my old friend.
어느 날, 오랜 친구로부터 난 소포 하나를 받았다.

7 Angel Falls in Venezuela is the highest ____________ in the world.
베네수엘라의 앙헬 폭포는 세계에서 가장 높은 폭포이다.

8 This ____________ doesn't connect with the main theme.
이 단락은 중심 주제와 연결되지 않아요.

9 I'd like to ____________ my dirty face. 나는 더러워진 내 얼굴을 닦고 싶어요.

10 There are a lot of people who want to ____________ the job.
그 일을 이어받기를 원하는 사람들이 많이 있었다.

B **빈 칸에 알맞은 단어를 고르세요.**

1 This was the beginning of a technological ____________.
① waterfall ② wagon ③ property ④ revolution ⑤ supper

2 The speaker ____________ presented his points.
① sponge ② clear ③ real ④ clearly ⑤ wireless

3 Suddenly, a strange man ____________ from the fog.
① discipline ② emerged ③ preface ④ celebrate ⑤ store

Day 28

MP3

811 **performance** [pərfɔ́:rməns]
명 공연
enjoy the performance 공연을 즐기다

812 **victim** [víktim]
명 피해자, 희생자
a war victim 전쟁 희생자 fall victim to ~의 희생자가 되다

813 **detective** [ditéktiv]
명 형사, 탐정
a private detective 사립 탐정 a detective novel 추리 소설

814 **charm** [tʃɑ:rm]
명 매력 형 charming 매력적인, 멋진
a girl of great charm 대단히 매력적인 소녀

815 **strengthen** [stréŋkθən]
동 강화되다, 강력해지다
strengthen his position 그의 위치를 강화시키다

816 **bacon** [béikən]
명 베이컨
smoked bacon 훈제 베이컨 eat lots of bacon 베이컨을 많이 먹다

817 **climb** [klaim]
동 오르다, 올라가다 climb-climbed-climbed
climb up the stairs 계단을 오르다 climb a mountain 산을 오르다

818 **slave** [sleiv]
명 노예
work like a slave 노예처럼 일하다 free slaves 노예를 해방하다

819 **norm** [nɔ:rm]
명 규범, 표준 유 standard 규범, 기준
social norm 사회 규범 differ from the norm 표준과 다르다

820 **adopt** [ədɑ́pt]
동 입양하다, 채택하다 adopt-adopted-adopted
adopt a child 아이를 입양하다 adopt his idea 그의 아이디어를 채택하다

821 **apply** [əplái]
동 지원하다 apply-applied-applied 명 application 지원
apply to university 대학에 지원하다

822 **look down on** [luk daun ən]
~을 내려다보다, 얕보다
look down on lazy people 게으른 사람을 얕보다

823 **complex** [kɑ́mpleks]
형 복잡한 유 complicated 복잡한
a complex structure 복잡한 구조

824 **encounter** [inkáuntər]
동 ~와 우연히 마주치다 encounter-encountered-encountered
encounter an old friend on the street 거리에서 오랜 친구를 우연히 만나다

825 **destiny** [déstəni]
명 운명
a tragic destiny 비극적 운명

Daily Test

| 월 일 |

A 우리말에 맞게 빈 칸에 알맞은 단어를 쓰세요.

1 The ______________ starts at 12 p.m. 그 공연은 오후 12시에 시작한다.

2 I'm reading his new ______________ novel. 나는 그의 새 추리 소설을 읽는 중이다.

3 John ______________ up the stairs slowly. John은 천천히 계단을 올라갔다.

4 Sarah is a ______________ to fashion. Sarah는 유행의 노예이다.

5 Minji is planning to ______________ a child. 민지는 아이를 입양하고자 계획하고 있다.

6 Sorry, it's too late to ______________ for the job.
죄송합니다, 그 일자리에 지원하기에는 너무 늦었어요.

7 He ______________ people younger than him. 그는 자기보다 어린 사람을 얕보았다.

8 The human eye has a highly ______________ structure.
인간의 눈은 아주 복잡한 구조를 가지고 있다.

9 She ______________ a bear in the forest. 그녀는 숲에서 곰과 마주쳤다.

10 I believe in ______________. 나는 운명을 믿어요.

B 빈 칸에 알맞은 단어를 고르세요.

1 Most people in the village fell ______________ to the flu.
① victim ② present ③ down ④ slave ⑤ script

2 There are various ways to ______________ your body.
① weak ② strong ③ adopt ④ strengthen ⑤ power

3 People should follow the social ______________.
① destiny ② norms ③ complex ④ apply ⑤ wagon

Day 28

MP3

826 **laboratory** [lǽbrətɔ̀:ri]
명 실험실, 연구소
a chemical laboratory 화학 실험실

827 **intention** [inténʃən]
명 의도, 목적 | 동 intend 의도하다
intention to find a solution 해결책을 찾을 의사

828 **expert** [ikspə́:rt]
명 전문가
a language expert 언어 전문가 | an expert in science 과학 전문가

829 **nutrient** [njú:triənt]
명 영양소, 영양분
the essential nutrient 필수 영양소

830 **satisfied** [sǽtisfaid]
형 만족하는, 만족스러워하는
a satisfied smile 만족해하는 미소 | be satisfied with ~에 만족하다

831 **nuclear** [njú:kliər]
형 핵의, 원자력의
nuclear bombs 핵폭탄 | a nuclear power station 원자력 발전소

832 **put into practice** [put íntə prǽktis]
~을 실행하다
put the plan into practice 계획을 실행에 옮기다

833 **inspect** [inspékt]
동 조사하다, 검사하다
inspect in detail 자세히 조사하다

834 **genetic** [dʒənétik]
형 유전의, 유전학의 | 명 gene 유전자
genetic factors 유전적 요인 | genetic condition 유전적 상태

835 **switch** [switʃ]
동 전환되다, 바꾸다 명 스위치 switch-switched-switched
switch the system 시스템을 바꾸다 | switch the date 날짜를 바꾸다

836 **realize** [rí(:)əlàiz]
동 깨닫다, 실현하다 realize-realized-realized
realize the danger of fire 불의 위험성을 깨닫다

837 **arrow** [ǽrou]
명 화살 | *bow 명 활
like an arrow 화살처럼 | shoot an arrow 화살을 쏘다

838 **mechanic** [məkǽnik]
명 정비사
become a car mechanic 자동차 정비사가 되다

839 **in spite of** [in spait əv]
~에도 불구하고 | 유 despite ~에도 불구하고
in spite of his age 그의 나이에도 불구하고

840 **stool** [stu:l]
명 (등받이가 없는) 의자, 스툴
a piano stool 피아노 의자 | sit on a stool 의자에 앉다

Daily Test

| 월 일 |

A 우리말에 맞게 빈 칸에 알맞은 단어를 쓰세요.

1 We had class in the physics ____________. 우리는 물리 실험실에서 수업이 있었다.

2 That was not my real ____________. 그것은 내 의도가 아니었다.

3 Ann is an ____________ in repairing cars. Ann은 자동차 고치는 데 전문가이다.

4 The ____________ helps to prevent the flu. 그 영양소는 감기를 예방하도록 도와준다.

5 Are you ____________ with your new computer? 새 컴퓨터에 만족 하세요?

6 ____________ energy can be used to produce electricity. 원자력 에너지는 전기를 생산하는데 사용될 수 있다.

7 The new school rules will be ____________ from next month. 다음 달부터 새로운 교칙이 시행됩니다.

8 I got my ____________ license last year. 나는 작년에 정비사 자격증을 땄다.

9 He won the race ____________ his slow start. 그는 느린 출발에도 불구하고 경주에서 우승했다.

10 Dad made a wooden piano ____________ for me. 아빠가 나를 위해 나무로 된 피아노 의자를 만들어 주었다.

B 빈 칸에 알맞은 단어를 고르세요.

1 Time flies like an ____________.

① arrow ② expert ③ laboratory ④ arrows ⑤ bird

2 Engineers are ____________ the new alarm system.

① emitting ② inspecting ③ sponging ④ experting ⑤ satisfying

3 My daughter is continuously ____________ TV channels.

① realizing ② strengthening ③ switching ④ climbing ⑤ adopting

Review Test 14

Day 27 + Day 28 | 월 일 |

A 우리말에 맞게 빈 칸에 알맞은 단어를 쓰시오.

1 make ______________ 저녁식사를 준비하다

2 write a ______________ to a new novel 새 소설에 서문을 쓰다

3 strict ______________ 엄격한 규율

4 speak ______________ 명확하게 말하다

5 ______________ the record company 그 음반 회사를 인수하다

6 a war ______________ 전쟁 희생자

7 social ______________ 사회 규범

8 a ______________ structure 복잡한 구조

9 a ______________ power station 원자력 발전소

10 ______________ factors 유전적 요인

B 다음 영어 풀이에 알맞은 어휘를 〈보기〉에서 고르시오.

보기	expert	property	mechanic	conquer	preface

1 ______________ : a short introduction to a book or writing

2 ______________ : to defeat a country, enemy, or rival and take control of it

3 ______________ : something (such as land or money) that is owned by someone

4 ______________ : someone who has great knowledge in something

5 ______________ : a person who repairs cars and machines

C 다음 단어의 관계가 A:B=C:D가 되도록 알맞은 단어를 골라 빈칸에 적으시오.

1 science : ______________ = drama : dramatic

① scientist ② scientific ③ subject
④ English ⑤ experiment

2 approve : approval = ______________ : celebration

① celebrating ② congratulate ③ celebrate
④ present ⑤ birthday

3 write : ______________ = prove : theory

① script ② broadcast ③ wrote
④ road ⑤ descript

4 narrow : pipe = ______________ : novel

① detail ② detection ③ detective
④ demonstrate ⑤ describe

5 strength : ______________ = length : lengthen

① strong ② power ③ strengthes
④ weak ⑤ strengthen

D 문맥에 맞게 다음 문장을 완성하시오.

1	This flower shop is open	a	carbon dioxide.
2	Many cars emit	b	my real intention.
3	This paragraph doesn't	c	connect with the main theme.
4	That was not	d	put into practice from next month.
5	The new school rules will be	e	on every weekday.

E 문장을 읽고 문맥에 적절한 단어를 고르시오.

1 The engineer carefully (sponged/inspected) the washing machine.

2 I (encountered/conquered) a group of foreign tourists on my way to school.

3 (In favor of/In spite of) the injury, he played until the end of the game.

4 For a five-year-old child, the (stool/globe) was too high to sit on.

5 We (adopted/subtracted) his suggestion to make a better plan.

F 문장의 빈칸에 알맞은 단어를 〈보기〉에서 찾아 쓰시오. (필요하면 형태를 고치시오.)

보기	nutrient	realize	emerge	grateful	scientific

1 We are very ____________ for your kind help.
당신의 친절한 도움에 감사합니다.

2 A big tiger ____________ from the forest and looked at the hunters.
큰 호랑이가 숲에서 나타나서 사냥꾼들을 쳐다 보았다.

3 Max ____________ that he did something wrong to his friends.
Max는 자신이 친구들에게 무언가 잘못을 했다는 것을 깨달았다.

4 What do you think is the most important ____________ discovery this century?
이번 세기에 가장 중요한 과학적 발견은 무엇이라고 생각합니까?

5 Fruit and vegetables contain many ____________ for our body.
과일과 채소는 우리 몸에 필요한 많은 영양소를 담고 있다.

G **그림과 낱말이 잘못 짝이어진 것을 고르시오.** ································· (　　　　　)

ⓐ

laboratory

ⓑ

property

ⓒ

climb

ⓓ

microwave

H **낱말과 어울리는 그림을 연결하시오.**

1 bacon •　　　　• ⓐ

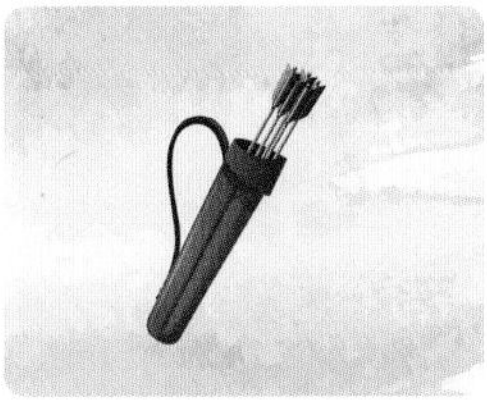

2 arrow •　　　　• ⓑ

Study More

property의 다양한 의미

- [명사] : '재산, 소유물, 부동산, 토지'
  She is a well-known **property** dealer. 그녀는 잘 알려진 부동산 중개인이다.
- [명사] : '사물의 속성'
  Human cultures share similar **properties**. 인간의 문화는 비슷한 속성을 가진다.

Day 29

MP3

841 **cabbage** [kǽbidʒ]
명 양배추
make cabbage soup 양배추 수프를 만들다

842 **utilize** [júːtəlàiz]
동 이용하다, 활용하다 utilize-utilized-utilized
utilize wind energy 풍력 에너지를 이용하다

843 **saw** [sɔː]
동 톱질하다, 톱으로 자르다 saw-sawed-sawn/sawed
saw the timber in half 목재를 톱질해서 반으로 자르다

844 **turn out** [təːrn aut]
~인 것으로 드러나다, ~인 것으로 밝혀지다
turn out to be a lie 거짓말로 밝혀지다

845 **foundation** [faundéiʃən]
명 기초, 근거, 토대
an important foundation 중요한 기초

846 **wag** [wæg]
동 흔들다
wag a tail 꼬리를 흔들다 wag his finger 그의 손가락을 흔들다

847 **commonly** [kámənli]
부 흔히, 보통
commonly used 흔히 사용되는

848 **be worried about** [bi wə́ːrid əbáut]
~에 대해 걱정하다
be worried about her accident 그녀의 사고에 대해 걱정하다

849 **fold** [fould]
동 접다 fold-folded-folded
fold the paper 종이를 접다 fold its wings 날개를 접다

850 **beard** [biərd]
명 턱수염
grow a beard / wear a beard 턱수염을 기르다

851 **infant** [ínfənt]
명 유아, 아기 형 유아의
infant years 유년기 infant food 유아식

852 **latest** [léitist]
형 (가장) 최근의, 최신의
the latest trend 최신 유행 his latest movie 그의 최신 영화

853 **dedication** [dèdəkéiʃən]
명 헌신, 전념
dedication to your country 나라에 대한 헌신

854 **pioneer** [pàiəníər]
명 선구자, 개척자
pioneer of modern architecture 현대 건축의 선구자

855 **once in a while** [wʌns in a hwail]
가끔, 때때로 유 occasionally 가끔
ride a bike once in a while 가끔 자전거를 타다

Daily Test

| 월 일 |

A 우리말에 맞게 빈 칸에 알맞은 단어를 쓰세요.

1 Mina made ______________ soup for dinner. 미나는 저녁으로 양배추 수프를 만들었다.

2 We can ______________ water as an energy source. 우리는 에너지원으로서 물을 활용할 수 있다.

3 Jinsu ______________ and hammered to build a hut. 오두막을 짓기 위해 진수는 톱질과 망치질을 했다.

4 What he said ______________ to be true. 그가 말한 것은 사실로 드러났다.

5 The black dog barked at us while ______________ its tail. 그 검은 개는 우리를 보고 꼬리를 흔들면서 짖었다.

6 He seems to ______________ something. 그는 무언가 걱정하는 것처럼 보인다.

7 Noah ______________ his clothes and put them in the closet. Noah는 옷을 개서 옷장에 넣었다.

8 The ______________ is sleeping in the room. 아기는 방에서 자고 있다.

9 Did you hear the ______________ news? 최신 뉴스 들었니?

10 The company was a ______________ of modern architecture. 그는 현대식 건축의 선구자였다.

B 빈 칸에 알맞은 단어를 고르세요.

1 Health is an important ______________ of all virtues.

① infant ② found ③ cabbage ④ foundation ⑤ utilize

2 This expression is ______________ used in Korea.

① wag ② expert ③ commonly ④ latest ⑤ really

3 James showed great ______________ to his country.

① dedicate ② fold ③ dedication ④ stool ⑤ pioneer

Day 29

MP3

856 **compare** [kəmpɛ́ər]
동 비교하다 compare-compared-compared
compare two movies 두 영화를 비교하다

857 **touch** [tʌtʃ]
동 감동시키다 touch-touched-touched
touch a person 사람을 감동시키다 touch her heart 그녀를 감동시키다

858 **beast** [biːst]
명 짐승, 야수
Beauty and the Beast 미녀와 야수 wild beasts 야생 짐승들

859 **illegal** [ilíːgəl]
형 불법적인
illegal document sharing 불법 문서 공유 an illegal act 불법 행위

860 **hopeless** [hóuplis]
형 희망이 없는
live a hopeless life 희망 없는 삶을 살다

861 **preview** [príːvjùː]
명 시사(회)
give a preview 시사회를 열다 a press preview 언론 시사회

862 **growth** [grouθ]
명 성장
rapid growth 급격한 성장 economic growth 경제 성장

863 **retire** [ritaiə(r)]
동 은퇴하다 명 retirement 은퇴
retire as professor of mathematics 수학 교수에서 은퇴하다

864 **dumb** [dʌm]
형 어리석은, 말문이 막힌 dumb-dumber-dumbest
a dumb idea 어리석은 생각

865 **eyelid** [áilìd]
명 눈꺼풀
the upper eyelid 윗 눈꺼풀

866 **adapt** [ədǽpt]
동 맞추다, 적응하다 유 adjust 조절하다
adapt to ~에 맞추다, ~에 적응하다

867 **kneel** [niːl]
동 무릎을 꿇다 kneel-knelt-knelt
kneel down 꿇어 앉다 kneel in prayer 무릎 꿇고 기도하다

868 **litter** [lítər]
명 쓰레기
a piece of litter 쓰레기 조각 dispose of litter 쓰레기를 버리다

869 **long for** [lɔ(ː)ŋ fər]
동 열망하다, 갈망하다
long for victory 승리를 열망하다 long for peace 평화를 갈망하다

870 **marginal** [máːrdʒənəl]
형 미미한, 중요하지 않은 명 margin 여백, 가장자리
marginal progress 미미한 진전 marginal issues 중요하지 않은 사항

Daily Test

| 월 일 |

A 우리말에 맞게 빈 칸에 알맞은 단어를 쓰세요.

1 We ______________ the two reports. 우리는 두 개의 보고서를 비교했다.

2 The movie ______________ many people deeply.
그 영화는 많은 사람들에게 깊은 감동을 주었다.

3 In some U.S. states, it is ______________ to leave a child alone in a car.
미국의 몇몇 주에서는 어린아이를 혼자 차 안에 두는 것은 불법이다.

4 The boy is smart but sometimes asks ______________ questions.
그 소년은 똑똑하지만 때로는 어리석은 질문을 한다.

5 Many birds have three ______________. 많은 새들은 세 개의 눈꺼풀을 가지고 있다.

6 Jude ______________ to the new school within a short time.
Jude는 새로운 학교에 금방 적응했다.

7 The little girl ______________ down on the ground to see the ants.
개미를 보기 위해 땅에 무릎을 꿇고 앉았다.

8 You should not drop any ______________ in this park.
이 공원에서는 어떤 쓰레기도 버릴 수 없다.

9 People in this country ______________ peace. 이 나라의 국민들은 평화를 원한다.

10 Shall we discuss those ______________ issues next week?
중요하지 않은 문제들은 다음 주에 의논할까요?

B 빈 칸에 알맞은 단어를 고르세요.

1 Her situation is ______________.
① touch ② hopeless ③ long for ④ hopely ⑤ kneel

2 Many famous people attended the ______________ of the movie.
① illegal ② preview ③ over ④ compare ⑤ energy

3 Sunlight is essential for the plant's ______________.
① dumb ② grow ③ rate ④ adapt ⑤ growth

Day 30

MP3

871 **critical** [krítikəl]
형 비판적인, 비난하는
a critical comment 비난하는 논평　a critical opinion 비판적인 의견

872 **evolve** [iválv]
동 전개시키다, 진화하다　evolve-evolved-evolved
evolve from apes 유인원으로부터 진화하다

873 **merchant** [mə́ːrtʃənt]
명 상인
a fish merchant 생선 상인　The Merchant of Venice 베니스의 상인

874 **financial** [finǽnʃəl]
형 재정적인
a financial crisis 재정적인 위기

875 **imitate** [ímitèit]
동 모방하다, 흉내를 내다　imitate-imitated-imitated
imitate a horse 말 흉내를 내다

876 **penalty** [pénəlti]
명 처벌, 형벌, 벌금
determine penalties 형을 결정하다　the death penalty 사형

877 **poster** [póustər]
명 벽보, 포스터
draw an election poster 선거용 포스터를 그리다

878 **prevention** [privénʃən]
명 예방, 방지
crime prevention 범죄 예방　prevention of obesity 비만 방지

879 **constant** [kánstənt]
형 끊임없는, 일정한
constant complaints 끊임없는 불평　constant pain 만성적인 통증

880 **alter** [ɔ́ːltər]
동 변경하다, 바꾸다　alter-altered-altered
alter the limit 한계를 변경하다　alter the course 항로를 바꾸다

881 **cultural** [kʌ́ltʃərəl]
형 문화의, 문화적인
cultural difference 문화적 차이　cultural treasure 문화재

882 **conclusion** [kənklúːʒən]
명 결론
come to a conclusion 결론이 나다

883 **atmosphere** [ǽtməsfìər]
명 대기, 공기
the upper atmosphere 상층부 대기

884 **policy** [pálisi]
명 정책, 방침
change the education policy 교육 정책을 바꾸다

885 **fame** [feim]
명 명성
achieve fame 명성을 얻다　fortune and fame 돈과 명예

Daily Test

| 월 일 |

A 우리말에 맞게 빈 칸에 알맞은 단어를 쓰세요.

1 Some people believe that human beings ____________ from apes.
몇몇 사람들은 인간이 유인원으로부터 진화했다고 믿는다.

2 Mr. Park gave us useful ____________ advice.
Mr. Park은 우리에게 유용한 재정적 조언을 해주었다.

3 Tiffany paid a ____________ for breaking the speed limit.
Tiffany는 속도를 지키지 않아서 벌금을 냈다.

4 Doing regular exercise is useful for the ____________ of obesity.
규칙적인 운동을 하는 것은 비만 방지에 유용하다

5 We had ____________ snow for a week. 일주일 동안 끊임없이 눈이 왔다.

6 Jessica ____________ her travel plan because of the storm.
Jessica는 태풍 때문에 그녀의 여행 계획을 바꿨다.

7 This is the most interesting ____________ event in New York.
이 축제는 뉴욕의 가장 재미있는 문화 행사이다.

8 We didn't agree with that ____________. 우리는 그 결론에 대해 동의하지 않았다.

9 The discussion club has a friendly ____________. 그 토론 동아리는 친절한 분위기였다.

10 We don't care for ____________ or wealth. 우리는 명예나 부를 신경쓰지 않는다.

B 빈 칸에 알맞은 단어를 고르세요.

1 The government changed the education ____________ again.
① politics ② policy ③ evolve ④ penalty ⑤ constant

2 People wrote ____________ comments about the movie.
① prevention ② alter ③ wealth ④ litter ⑤ critical

3 He ____________ the monkey.
① imitated ② fame ③ culture ④ went ⑤ evolve

Day 30

MP3

886 **electronic** [ilektránik]
형 전자의
play the electronic piano 전자 피아노를 연주하다

887 **distinguish** [distíŋgwiʃ]
동 구별하다 distinguish-distinguished-distinguished
distinguish between tortoises and turtles 육지거북과 바다거북을 구별하다

888 **establish** [istǽbliʃ]
동 설립하다 establish-established-established
establish a company 회사를 설립하다

889 **specific** [spisífik]
형 특수한, 명백한
a specific purpose 특수한 목적　a specific reason 명백한 이유

890 **informal** [infɔ́:rməl]
형 비공식의
an informal meeting 비공식 모임　an informal visit 비공식 방문

891 **consume** [kənsjú:m]
동 쓰다, 소비하다 consume-consumed-consumed
consume time and energy 시간과 에너지를 소비하다

892 **potential** [pəténʃəl]
형 잠재적인 명 가능성, 잠재력
potential ability 잠재력　potential customers 잠재적 고객들

893 **standard** [stǽndərd]
명 기준, 수준
high standards 높은 수준　meet standards 기준을 충족하다

894 **greedy** [grí:di]
형 탐욕스러운
greedy for ~에 탐욕스러운　greedy for money 돈에 욕심이 많은

895 **trial** [tráiəl]
명 시도
make a trial 시도하다　trial and error 시행착오

896 **receipt** [risí:t]
명 영수증
write a receipt 영수증을 쓰다　get a receipt 영수증을 받다

897 **obvious** [ábviəs]
형 분명한, 명백한
obvious truth 명백한 진실　obvious facts 명백한 사실

898 **primary** [práimeri]
형 주된, 주요한
the primary aim 주요 목표　primary interest 주된 관심사

899 **keep ~ing** [ki:p iŋ]
계속해서 ~하다
keep crying 계속해서 울다　keep running 계속 뛰다

900 **certainly** [sə́:rtənli]
부 틀림없이, 분명히, (대답으로서) 그럼요, 물론이지요
almost certainly 거의 확실하게　Yes, certainly. 네, 물론이지요.

Daily Test

| 월 일 |

A 우리말에 맞게 빈 칸에 알맞은 단어를 쓰세요.

1 Can I borrow your ______________ dictionary? 너의 전자사전을 좀 빌릴 수 있을까?

2 I can't ______________ Jason from his brother. 나는 Jason과 그의 형을 구별 못하겠어.

3 The school was ______________ in 1980. 그 학교는 1980년에 설립 되었다.

4 Can you be more ______________? 더 자세한 걸 원하세요?

5 My new car ______________ less gas than my old car.
내 새 자동차는 내 예전 차보다 연료를 덜 소비한다.

6 You should believe in your own ______________. 넌 너 자신의 잠재력을 믿어야 한다.

7 We want to improve our ______________ of living.
우리는 우리의 생활수준이 더 향상되길 원합니다.

8 I ______________ for three hours. 나는 3시간 동안 계속 걸었다.

9 Here is your ______________ for the book. 여기 책 영수증 있습니다.

10 Eating junk food is a ______________ cause of obesity.
인스턴트 음식을 먹는 것은 비만의 주요 원인이다.

B 빈 칸에 알맞은 단어를 고르세요.

1 It's a process of ______________ and error.
① try ② trial ③ potential ④ distinguish ⑤ receipt

2 It's ______________ to everyone that the performance was great.
① alter ② religious ③ marginal ④ obvious ⑤ electronic

3 The king was ______________ for money and power.
① greedy ② specific ③ greed ④ cultural ⑤ time

Review Test 15 Day 29 + Day 30

| 월 일 |

A 우리말에 맞게 빈 칸에 알맞은 단어를 쓰시오.

1 ____________ a tail 꼬리를 흔들다

2 ____________ years 유년기

3 ____________ as professor of mathematics 수학 교수에서 은퇴하다

4 ____________ in prayer 무릎 꿇고 기도하다

5 ____________ victory 승리를 열망하다

6 ____________ of obesity 비만 방지

7 ____________ the limit 한계를 변경하다

8 the upper ____________ 상층부 대기

9 a ____________ reason 명백한 이유

10 ____________ customers 잠재적 고객들

B 다음 영어 풀이에 알맞은 어휘를 〈보기〉에서 고르시오.

보기	utilize	kneel	receipt	pioneer	primary

1 ____________ : someone who does something important first

2 ____________ : to use something for a particular purpose

3 ____________ : most important; basic or main

4 ____________ : to lower your body so that your knees are touching the floor

5 ____________ : a piece of paper showing that you paid for something

C 다음 단어의 관계가 A:B=C:D가 되도록 알맞은 단어를 골라 빈칸에 적으시오.

1 ______________ : movie = sufficient : food

① watch ② latest ③ make
④ director ⑤ rainy

2 cancel : cancellation = dedicate : ______________

① dictation ② memorial ③ dedicated
④ parents ⑤ dedication

3 legal : ______________ = formal : informal

① unligal ② illegal ③ speed
④ dislegal ⑤ imlegal

4 hope : ______________ = use : useless

① hopeless ② hopeful ③ hopiless
④ hopely ⑤ hopes

5 ordinary : people = opposite : ______________

① complex ② feed ③ responsible
④ otherwise ⑤ conclusion

D 문맥에 맞게 다음 문장을 완성하시오.

1 We can utilize water • • a many people deeply.

2 Did you hear • • b as an energy source.

3 The movie touched • • c those marginal issues next week?

4 Shall we discuss • • d our standard of living.

5 We want to improve • • e the latest news?

E 문장을 읽고 문맥에 적절한 단어를 고르시오.

1 Tyler (imitated/obeyed) the singer's voice perfectly.

2 (Keep/Put off) running! The finish line is just ahead of you.

3 The school's new language program (turned out/turned on) to be successful.

4 Unfortunately, the original plan has been (altered/consumed) several times.

5 If you buy the printer, don't forget to get a (receipt/trial).

F 문장의 빈칸에 알맞은 단어를 〈보기〉에서 찾아 쓰시오. (필요하면 형태를 고치시오.)

보기	primary	distinguish	constant	compare	consume

1 The use of language ______________ human beings from animals.
언어를 사용하는 것은 인간과 동물을 구별하게 해준다.

2 My father wants to buy a car that ____________ less fuel.
아버지는 연료를 더 적게 소비하는 차를 사고 싶어 하신다.

3 The ____________ goal of today's meeting is to talk about the school trip.
오늘 모임의 주요한 목적은 수학 여행에 대해서 이야기하는 것이다.

4 We were annoyed by the neighbor's ____________ noise.
우리는 이웃집의 거듭된 소음에 짜증이 났다.

5 He ____________ two bags and bought the one with more pockets.
그는 두 가방을 비교하고 나서 주머니가 더 많은 것을 샀다.

G 그림에 해당하는 낱말을 〈보기〉에서 골라 쓰시오.

1 

(   )

2 

(   )

3 

(   )

4 

(   )

5 

(   )

6 

(   )

보기 fold growth cabbage merchant beard litter

Study More

atmosphere의 다양한 의미

- [명사] : '(지구나 행성의) 대기, 공기'
  Some planets have no **atmosphere**. 어떤 행성들에는 대기가 없다.
- [명사] : '분위기, 기운'
  The **atmosphere** of the meeting was very pleasant. 모임의 분위기는 아주 즐거웠다.

Index

A

aboard 104
absolute 62
absorb 58
accent 12
accept 20
accidentally 86
achieve 82
acne 110
actual 106
actually 68
adapt 178
admiral 20
adopt 168
advantage 104
adventurous 24
advertise 118
adviser 82
aerobic 164
aim 50
allowance 84
alter 180
although 110
amaze 34
amusement 144
anger 46
animation 36
announcement 94
annoy 14
Antarctic 96
appearance 84
appetite 56
apply 168
appointment 129
approach 8
appropriate 62
architect 122
argument 92
arid 12
arise 152
arrest 140
arrow 170
artificial 120
as long as 74
assign 152
associate 120
athlete 120
atmosphere 180
attempt 158
attention 132
attractive 140
audience 32
author 58
available 92
awesome 154
awful 58
awkward 134

B

backpack 14
backward 44
bacon 168
ballet 104
bank 96
banner 104
bare 146
be tired of 140
be up to 24
be worried about 176
bear 152
beard 176
beast 178
beat 142
beggar 110
below 72
bet 68
billion 74
bind 62
blackboard 68
block 108
blond 118
bloody 44
bloom 144
blossom 134
book 60
boost 22
border 140
boss 12
bother 8
bottom 22
bowl 46
break 20
breathtaking 26
brick 72
brief 134
bronze 110
bucket 156
bud 104
buddy 8
budget 72
bullet 130
bump 92
by the way 158

C

cabbage 176
calm 26
camp 48
campaign 80
camping 154
cancer 132
carbon 164
carpenter 58
carrot 36
cart 130
case 22
cash 12
cast 128
catch up with 96
celebrate 164
ceramic 24
certain 84
certainly 182
chain 108
challenge 98
champion 56
channel 24
characteristic 106
charge 36
charm 168
cheat 8
check 116
cheese 158
chemical 86
chest 60
chief 122
chilly 68
chop 94
chore 68
classmate 68
clearly 166
climb 168
closely 14
clue 32
coast 142
code 82
collapse 14
collection 144
combine 22
comfort 156
command 50
comment 104
commodity 34
commonly 176
communicate 116
comparable 48
compare 178
compass 74
compete 20
complex 168
compose 140
concentrate 68

conclusion	180
concrete	96
condiment	44
conduct	80
confidence	34
confuse	58
congratulation	84
connection	82
conquer	164
consider	98
constant	180
constantly	98
construct	8
consume	182
contact	48
continent	118
continue	118
convenient	120
cotton	34
countryside	118
coupon	14
crab	152
crack	130
crawl	38
crayon	166
creative	22
creature	116
crisis	128
critical	180
crosswalk	50
crowd	130
crowded	144
cultural	180
current	108
custom	122

D

dare	142
deal	60
debate	132
deceive	60
decision	26
declare	68
decline	140
decorate	20
dedication	176
deeply	10
delay	70
delete	26
delivery	26
demand	140
department	70
describe	118
despite	38
destiny	168
detail	48
detective	168
dialect	92
diligent	118
direct	144
direction	152
director	92
dirt	144
disabled	56
disadvantage	36
disappear	108
discipline	166
discount	110
discovery	116
discuss	12
disgust	132
display	74
distance	56
distinguish	182
dive	152
diverse	62
dizzy	70
documentary	12
dot	8
doubt	108
draw	80
drugstore	92
drum	50
dull	122
dumb	178
durable	82
dust	38
dynasty	156

E

earthquake	58
easily	12
economic	106
edge	122
education	116
effective	46
elbow	10
elect	158
electricity	72
electronic	182
elevator	132
embarrass	32
emerge	166
emergency	144
emit	164
emphasize	62
empire	84
enable	58
encounter	168
encourage	56
enemy	34
engine	98
enlarge	62
entrance	128
envy	46
erase	94
error	108
erupt	80
escalator	106
establish	182
even though	70
evidence	120
evolve	180
examine	84
except	108
exclude	36
exhibit	80
existence	128
exit	130
expect	38
expedite	8
expense	82
experiment	82
expert	170
explore	106
extinct	98
extreme	96
eye-catching	144
eyelid	178

F

face	108
facility	106
fairy	132
fake	104
fall in love	164
fame	180
familiar	122
fancy	38
fantasy	32
faucet	98
fault	12
fear	56
fearful	10
feel like ~ing	122
figurative	60
figure	132
filter	32
finally	12
financial	180
fingerprint	72
fitness	156
fix	94
flavor	86
flour	122

flow 92
foggy 164
fold 176
folk 62
fond 142
force 144
form 84
former 20
forward 154
foundation 176
fountain 98
frame 70
freedom 116
fully 70
function 146

G

galaxy 56
gap 46
gargle 158
gate 10
gaze 104
general 142
generous 70
genetic 170
genius 84
get away with 146
get rid of 94
gifted 10
ginseng 38
giraffe 60
gladly 32
globe 158
government 106
gradually 48
grain 110
grand 58
graphic 14
grassland 82
grateful 164
greedy 182
greenhouse 142
greet 104
growth 178

H

haircut 154
handkerchief 122
handle 36
harbor 110
hard-working 134
harm 82
hatch 82
head 36
heritage 24
hierarchy 12
highlight 68
high-tech 46
highway 56
hire 104
historic 36
honestly 108
honor 146
hopeless 178
humanism 60
hurricane 72

I

ideal 96
ignore 50
illegal 178
illusion 84
image 10
imagination 140
imitate 180
immigrant 36
impossible 74
impress 156
impression 80
impressive 62
improve 48
in charge of 32
in spite of 170
include 32
income 38
incredible 34
indeed 142
independence 130
individual 22
indoor 34
industry 70
infant 176
infect 98
influential 24
informal 182
inherent 26
injury 153
insert 154
inspect 170
inspire 118
instant 142
instrument 116
insult 72
intellectual 80
intelligent 46
intention 170
international 8
invade 132
inventor 104
investigate 44
involve 62
issue 48

J

jar 86
jewel 46
journey 72
jury 86
justice 116

K

keep ~ing 182
keep track of 22
keep up with 24
kin 44
kindness 20
kneel 178
knowledge 14

L

labor 132
laboratory 170
landmark 34
landscape 110
last 86
latest 176
layer 22
leader 10
leap 96
least 108
lecture 48
legendary 32
leisure 20
liberal 12
lid 74
lie 108
lifetime 58
lift 8
lighting 130
link 152
lip 164
liquid 80
literal 8
litter 178
livestock 106
local 128
log 82
long for 178
look down on 168
loss 86

lunar 84
lung 96
lyrics 70

M

magical 50
maintain 60
make up for 84
maker 38
make-up 80
male 118
manage 56
manager 140
maple 44
marginal 178
mascot 44
mass media 20
match 22
matter 116
maximum 68
meadow 10
measure 134
mechanic 170
meet 98
memorize 156
mention 94
merchant 180
metal 82
method 32
microwave 164
migrant 94
migrate 86
mince 94
minimum 68
misunderstand 128
mixture 44
monthly 44
moonlight 146
mop 84
movement 152

N

name 144
nasal 116
national 74
native 132
natural 20
nearby 153
negative 10
net 128
newborn 144
niece 140
noisy 134
norm 168
notice 80
novel 14
nuclear 170
nutrient 170
nutrition 122

O

obey 152
observe 128
obtain 62
obvious 182
occur 82
odd 38
offer 84
officer 26
official 38
once in a while 176
online 48
opposite 70
optical 74
option 132
orchestra 50
organic 142
organism 56
organization 38
organize 134
original 24
orphan 118
overestimate 158
overseas 48
overweight 129
oxygen 158

P

package 166
pandemic 94
panic 130
paragraph 166
parallel 98
paralyze 156
part 146
participate 104
particular 128
pass away 60
passion 74
pastime 122
pattern 156
payment 130
peasant 94
pedal 86
penalty 180
pepper 118
perform 48
performance 168
period 32
personality 92
perspective 74
physical 22
pile 110
pioneer 176
pipe 24
place 14
planet 122
plant 20
pleasure 104
plenty 48
plug 130
pole 74
policy 180
pollution 50
population 70
portable 94
position 144
post 80
poster 180
postpone 96
potential 182
poverty 164
precious 34
preface 164
prefer 140
pregnant 116
present 26
presentation 50
preserve 60
press 80
pretend 146
prevent 110
prevention 180
preview 178
prey 26
primary 182
principal 158
private 36
probably 14
product 8
professional 132
proficiency 120
progress 142
project 92
proper 38
property 166
proportion 60
propose 120
protect 84
prove 56
proverb 86
provide 38
publish 32
purse 146
put into practice 170

Q

quality 129
quantity 62
quarter 120
question 14

R

rainfall 20
rainforest 108
rapid 154
rare 96
rate 92
raw 86
realistic 96
reality 140
realize 170
reasonable 110
receipt 182
recharge 116
recover 46
recreation 146
refill 118
reflect 50
refund 46
refuse 68
regular 34
relate 106
relative 94
reluctant 104
rely on 74
remain 80
remark 118
renewable 120
rent 82
repetition 92
replay 34
reply 44
reporter 10
represent 128
request 152
rescue 62
research 44
resident 146
resource 110
respect 116
responsible 106
restore 92
result 50
reveal 72
revolution 166
rhythm 10
rich 56
right 134
risk 98
role 60
roof 129
root 46
rough 36
route 10
routine 120
row 140
rubber 24
ruin 158
ruler 72
rush 74
rush 68

S

salary 140
salty 158
satellite 70
satisfied 170
saw 176
saying 152
scale 153
scenery 152
scientific 164
scientist 46
scissors 154
scold 26
score 26
scrape 72
scratch 12
scream 8
script 166
sculpture 58
seasoning 156
secondary 94
section 122
select 156
selfish 134
semester 134
sensor 56
sentence 50
separate 36
seriously 144
set up 134
shame 12
shape 118
sheet 50
shelter 72
shock 8
shower 14
shut 46
shuttle 70
sight 98
signal 68
silly 26
silver 22
since 48
sincere 68
site 120
sketch 26
skyscraper 142
slave 168
sled 122
slice 22
slim 128
slip 72
slippery 94
slow down 142
smoke 134
soda 32
software 106
solution 70
source 118
space 74
spare 58
species 108
specific 182
speed 10
spin 92
sponge 166
spot 154
spray 8
sprinkle 146
stand for 144
standard 182
starfish 44
starve 80
state 86
status 62
stay up 80
steel 108
stick 96
still 22
stir 152
stomach 142
stool 170
store 158
stranger 134
stream 146
strength 122
strengthen 168
stress 86
stressful 20
string 58
structure 110
studio 22
submarine 110
submit 156
subtract 158
succeed 110
successful 34
suck 86

suffer 44
suitable 142
summarize 72
sunlight 10
sunshine 12
supper 164
supply 14
suppose 120
surprising 98
surround 60
survey 36
survive 94
swallow 144
swear 132
sweep 154
swing 166
switch 170
symptom 60
system 50

T

take ~ into account 96
take off 106
take over 166
talented 82
tap 68
target 20
tax 72
tease 128
technology 158
terrific 152
territory 32
thanks to 58
theme 10
theory 48
think over 58
thinker 146
threaten 152
thrill 142
thumb 14
thunder 50
tidy 156
token 8
tomb 44
tortoise 104
toss 158
totally 36
touch 178
track 98
traditional 108
tragic 116
trait 74
transfer 140
treasure 24
treat 146
tremble 38
trial 182
tribe 120
tropical 134
turn out 176
twist 153
typhoon 128
typical 128

U

uncomfortable 24
underground 26
understanding 70
uneasy 154
unfair 120
unhappy 20
universe 24
unlike 60
urban 146
urge 98
used to 44
utilize 176

V

vain 132
valid 62
various 132
vehicle 134
version 106
vertical 96
victim 168
virtual 156
vision 56
vital 34
vivid 14
vowel 116

W

wag 176
wagon 166
wake 128
wallpaper 24
warmth 130
waterfall 166
waterproof 92
weaken 22
wealthy 56
weapon 62
wear 34
web 120
wedding 38
weekday 164
weekly 156
weird 26
well-known 92
wetland 32
wheel 46
wheelchair 48
will 106
windmill 58
wing 12
wire 34
wireless 166
wisely 24
wooden 46
work 84
worldwide 106
worse 86
worth 96
wound 153

Y

youth 36
yummy 156

Answer Key

정답 및 해설

Answer Key

Day 01

Daily Test 1 P. 09

A
1 scream
2 expedite
3 constructed
4 cheated
5 bother
6 lifted
7 approached
8 literal
9 international
10 product

B
1 ① buddies
2 ② shock
3 ② sprayed

Daily Test 2 P. 11

A
1 gifted
2 sunlight
3 theme
4 speed
5 leader
6 elbows
7 fearful
8 meadow
9 negative
10 gate

B
1 ③ deeply
2 ① route
3 ③ rhythm

Day 02

Daily Test 1 P. 13

A
1 sunshine
2 scratch
3 documentary
4 shame
5 accent
6 boss
7 arid
8 discuss
9 liberal
10 hierarchy

B
1 ① fault
2 ④ easily
3 ② cash

Daily Test 2 P. 15

A
1 novel
2 knowledge
3 placed
4 probably
5 supply
6 graphic
7 backpack
8 vivid
9 questioned
10 annoyed

B
1 ① thumbs
2 ③ closely
3 ④ collapsed

Review Test 01

Day 01 + Day 02 P. 16

A
1 dot
2 lift
3 expedite
4 image
5 meadow
6 sunshine
7 fault
8 scratch
9 liberal
10 supply

B
1 token
2 arid
3 backpack
4 thumb
5 international

C
1 ① construct
2 ③ buddy
3 ⑤ leader
4 ② deeply
5 ② fearful

D
1 c
2 a
3 e
4 b
5 d

E
1 negative
2 screamed

3 placed
4 gifted
5 collapsed

해석
1. 친구들의 부정적인 지적에 대해 걱정하지 마세요.
2. 그녀는 커다란 코끼리가 그녀의 근처에 왔을 때 소리를 질렀다.
3. 나는 내 휴대전화를 어디다 두었는지 모르겠어요.
4. 내 어린 남동생은 재능이 있는 학생이다. 그는 이미 5개 국어를 할 줄 안다.
5. 그 낡은 집은 폭설 때문에 무너졌다.

F
1 expedite
2 international
3 arid
4 vivid
5 annoyed

G
1 wing
2 lift
3 speed
4 backpack
5 question
6 thumb

Day 03

Daily Test 1 P. 21

A
1 accepted
2 rainfall
3 target
4 leisure
5 plant
6 Admiral
7 decorated
8 natural
9 compete
10 broke out

B
1 ③ kindness
2 ② caused
3 ② stressful

Daily Test 2 P. 23

A
1 keep track of
2 creative
3 Combine
4 individuals
5 physical
6 layer
7 match
8 weakened
9 still
10 case

B
1 ① slice
2 ① bottom
3 ② boosted

Day 04

Daily Test 1 P. 25

A
1 treasure
2 ceramic
3 influential
4 adventurous
5 Channel
6 keeps up with
7 is up to
8 uncomfortable
9 universe
10 rubber

B
1 ④ wisely
2 ② heritages
3 ⑤ original

Daily Test 2 P. 27

A
1 breathtaking
2 inherent
3 delete
4 presented
5 underground
6 sketch
7 delivery
8 scolded
9 weird
10 officer

B
1 ③ score
2 ⑤ decision
3 ⑤ calm

Review Test 02

Day 03+ Day 04 P. 28

A
1 target
2 disaster
3 broke out
4 keep track of

5 still
6 adventurous
7 heritage
8 score
9 scold
10 weird

B
1 former
2 leisure
3 break out
4 original
5 weird

C
1 ① accept
2 ④ bottom
3 ① uncomfortable
4 ④ physical
5 ③ leisure

D
1 b
2 d
3 a
4 e
5 c

E
1 up to you
2 natural
3 caused
4 keep up with
5 presented

해석

1. 네가 우리 책 동아리에 가입할 지 안 할 지는 너에게 달려있다.
2. 네가 관중들 앞에서 말하는 것에 대해 걱정하는 건 자연스러운 거야.
3. 그 사고는 그가 야생동물을 무서워하게 만들었다.
4. Jamie는 새로운 기술을 잘 파악하기 위해 규칙적으로 신문을 읽는다.
5. Mr. Johnson은 부모님들에게 새로운 방과 후 프로그램을 선보였다.

F
1 weakened
2 decorated
3 influential
4 weird
5 plant

G
ⓒ scold

H
1 ⓑ
2 ⓐ

Day 05

Daily Test 1 P. 33

A
1 clue
2 territory
3 published
4 methods
5 audience
6 includes
7 period
8 soda
9 embarrassed
10 filter

B
1 ③ gladly
2 ① legendary
3 ③ wetland

Daily Test 2 P. 35

A
1 Regular
2 amazed
3 indoor
4 replayed
5 cotton
6 confidence
7 incredible
8 vital
9 precious
10 worn

B
1 ① enemy
2 ③ commodity
3 ② successful

Day 06

Daily Test 1 P. 37

A
1 separated
2 totally
3 private
4 survey
5 youth
6 handle
7 disadvantage
8 headed
9 charged
10 historic

B
1 ① excluded
2 ② Immigrants
3 ④ rough

Daily Test 2 P. 39

A
1 odd
2 Ginseng
3 income
4 official
5 organization
6 dust
7 crawl
8 Despite
9 provide
10 tremble

B
1 ① maker
2 ② proper
3 ② expected

Review Test 03

Day 05+ Day 06 P. 40

A
1 gladly
2 audience
3 embarrass
4 incredible
5 vital
6 immigrant
7 youth
8 disadvantage
9 official
10 despite

B
1 commodity
2 territory
3 method
4 income
5 tremble

C
1 ① legendary
2 ⑤ exclude
3 ① regular
4 ② provide
5 ④ successful

D
1 b
2 e
3 a
4 d
5 c

E
1 in charge of
2 amazed
3 includes
4 vital
5 fancy

해석

1. Tom은 판매부서를 담당하고 있다.
2. 아이들은 무지개를 보고서 놀랐다.
3. 입장료에는 4인 무료 점심 식사가 포함된다.
4. 당신의 도움이 뮤지컬의 성공에 필수적이었어요.
5. 그녀는 부드러운 깃털이 달린 화려한 모자를 쓰고 있어요.

F
1 published
2 Despite
3 survey
4 clue
5 commodities

G
1 wedding
2 cotton
3 carrot
4 crawl
5 dust
6 soda

Day 07

Daily Test 1 P. 45

A
1 bloody
2 maple
3 backward
4 tomb
5 investigating
6 reply
7 research
8 monthly
9 condiments
10 kin

B
1 ⑤ mixture
2 ① suffered
3 ② used to

Daily Test 2 P. 47

A
1 high-tech
2 recovering
3 roots
4 intelligent
5 refund
6 shut
7 wheel
8 envy
9 anger
10 effective

B
1 ① bowls
2 ② gap
3 ② wooden

Day 08

Daily Test 1 P. 49

A
1 improve
2 contact
3 since
4 issue
5 lecture
6 online
7 performed
8 plenty
9 comparable
10 theory

B
1 ② overseas
2 ③ dctails
3 ② gradually

Daily Test 2 P. 51

A
1 orchestra
2 result
3 system
4 magical
5 aim
6 commanded
7 presentation
8 crosswalk
9 pollution
10 ignored

B
1 ② thunder
2 ⑤ sheets
3 ② reflected

Review Test 04

Day 07+ Day 08 P. 52

A
1 backward
2 reply
3 kin
4 recover
5 wheel
6 contact
7 since
8 perform
9 sheet
10 reflect

B
1 condiment
2 refund
3 gap
4 orchestra
5 ignore

C
1 ② mixture
2 ① wooden
3 ① monthly
4 ⑤ comparable
5 ③ lecture

D
1 a
2 e
3 c
4 d
5 b

E
1 reflects
2 backward
3 refund
4 gap
5 investigated

해석

1. 난 이 에세이가 사회적 이슈에 대한 Tom의 관점을 반영한다고 생각한다.
2. 내 어린 여동생은 이제 10에서 1까지 거꾸로 셀 수 있어요.
3. 그가 산 장난감이 결함이 있었기 때문에, Sam은 환불을 요청했다.
4. 그들은 그들의 의견간에 큰 차이를 느꼈다.
5. 과학자들은 그 지역에 홍수의 원인에 대해 조사했다.

F
1 overseas
2 theory
3 pollution
4 research
5 envies

G
ⓐ maple

H
1 ⓐ
2 ⓑ

Day 09

Daily Test 1 P. 57

A
1 organism
2 encouraged
3 galaxy
4 distance

5 rich
6 sensor
7 vision
8 managed
9 wealthy
10 prove

B
1 ① highway
2 ③ appetite
3 ② disabled

Daily Test 2 P. 59

A
1 confused
2 grand
3 carpenter
4 windmill
5 earthquake
6 string
7 author
8 sculptures
9 absorbs
10 enabled

B
1 ① spare
2 ② Thanks to
3 ② think over

Day 10

Daily Test 1 P. 61

A
1 proportion
2 role
3 surrounded
4 deceive
5 symptoms
6 passed away
7 Unlike
8 figurative
9 preserve
10 book

B
1 ① Maintaining
2 ⑤ deals
3 ② chest

Daily Test 2 P. 63

A
1 bind
2 enlarge
3 diverse
4 folk
5 emphasized
6 quantity
7 obtained
8 involve
9 appropriate
10 impressive

B
1 ① valid
2 ③ status
3 ② rescued

Review Test 05

Day 09+ Day 10 P. 64

A
1 organism
2 encourage
3 sensor
4 confuse
5 awful
6 surround
7 deceive
8 figurative
9 diverse
10 appropriate

B
1 giraffe
2 encourage
3 proportion
4 organism
5 highway

C
1 ① distance
2 ② author
3 ⑤ giraffe
4 ③ preserve
5 ④ book

D
1 c
2 a
3 e
4 d
5 b

E
1 proved
2 emphasized
3 Thanks to
4 enabled
5 valid

해석

1. 그 과학자는 성공적으로 그의 이론을 입증했다.
2. 새로운 교장선생님은 서로를 돕는 것에 중요성을 강조했다.
3. 컴퓨터 그래픽의 개발 덕분에 우리는 어느 것에 대해서든 영화를 만들 수 있다.
4. 장학금은 그가 대학을 갈 수 있게 하였다.
5. 당신이 해외로 여행을 갈 때, 당신은 유효한 여권이 필요합니다.

F

1 managed
2 diverse
3 appropriate
4 proportion
5 absolute

G

1 champion
2 string
3 windmill
4 bind
5 appetite
6 weapon

Day 11

Daily Test 1 P. 69

A

1 declared
2 refused
3 tap
4 maximum
5 minimum
6 actually
7 classmates
8 signal
9 highlights
10 sincere

B

1 ② chilly
2 ③ concentrate
3 ⑤ tapped

Daily Test 2 P. 71

A

1 satellites
2 delay
3 solution
4 fully
5 department
6 generous
7 lyrics
8 industry
9 opposite
10 understanding

B

1 ② shuttle
2 ④ population
3 ④ Even though

Day 12

Daily Test 1 P. 73

A

1 journey
2 shelters
3 ruler
4 taxes
5 fingerprints
6 slip
7 electricity
8 insult
9 summarized
10 scrape

B

1 ① budget
2 ② below
3 ④ reveal

Daily Test 2 P. 75

A

1 passion
2 National
3 display
4 Billions
5 perspective
6 optical
7 rush
8 trait
9 rely on
10 lid

B

1 ③ as long as
2 ① Pole
3 ④ impossible

Review Test 06

Day 11 + Day 12 P. 76

A

1 refuse
2 signal
3 chore
4 department
5 understanding
6 shelter
7 slip
8 reveal
9 as long as
10 trait

B

1 perspective
2 lid
3 pole
4 budget
5 bet

C

1 ① passionate
2 ② solution
3 ④ actually

4 ⑤ maximum
5 ③ national

D
1 a
2 e
3 d
4 b
5 c

E
1 perspective
2 declared
3 refused
4 concentrate
5 opposite

해석

1. 우리는 다른 관점에서 그 문제를 볼 필요가 있어요.
2. 그녀는 그녀가 말한 것이 진짜라고 단언했다.
3. 그 남자는 나와 얘기하는 것을 거절했다.
4. 두통 때문에 그녀는 숙제에 집중하지 못했다.
5. 시작의 반대는 끝이다.

F
1 delayed
2 scraped
3 highlighted
4 reveals
5 traits

G
ⓑ lyrics

H
1 ⓐ
2 ⓑ

Day 13

Daily Test 1 P. 81

A
1 liquid
2 make-up
3 conducted
4 impression
5 exhibited
6 starving
7 notice
8 erupt
9 remains
10 press

B
1 ④ stayed up
2 ② drawing
3 ③ intellectual

Daily Test 2 P. 83

A
1 occurred
2 experiment
3 hatch
4 durable
5 rent
6 connection
7 achieved
8 metal
9 adviser
10 harm

B
1 ① expense
2 ③ talented
3 ② log

Day 14

Daily Test 1 P. 85

A
1 lunar
2 allowance
3 make up for
4 formed
5 appearance
6 illusion
7 Empire
8 examined
9 offered
10 work

B
1 ① protect
2 ② genius
3 ④ mopping

Daily Test 2 P. 87

A
1 jury
2 states
3 worse
4 accidentally
5 raw
6 chemical
7 migrate
8 stressed
9 lasted
10 loss

B
1 ① proverb
2 ② flavor
3 ③ sucks

Review Test 07

Day 13+ Day 14 P. 88

A
1 impression
2 stay up
3 talented
4 code
5 expense
6 allowance
7 examine
8 mop
9 jury
10 accidentally

B
1 appearance
2 empire
3 illusion
4 expense
5 jar

C
1 ① connection
2 ④ conduct
3 ① protect
4 ③ offered
5 ② empire

D
1 b
2 c
3 a
4 e
5 d

E
1 talented
2 occur
3 examined
4 make up for
5 certain

해석

1. 그녀는 천재에요. 나는 그렇게 재능 있는 화가를 본 적이 없어요.
2. 이 산에서, 봄에 종종 눈사태가 일어납니다.
3. 그 의사는 조심스럽게 환자의 손을 살폈다.
4. Susan은 지나간 시간을 만회하기 위해 열심히 일했다.
5. 우리는 그가 경기에서 이길 거라고 확신해요.

F
1 achieved
2 impression
3 exhibited
4 raw
5 chemical

G
1 draw
2 eruption
3 hatch
4 liquid
5 lunar
6 bike pedal

Day 15

Daily Test 1 P. 93

A
1 argument
2 repetition
3 spinning
4 director
5 dialects
6 project
7 available
8 bumped
9 well-known
10 flows

B
1 ① rate
2 ④ personality
3 ③ restoring

Daily Test 2 P. 95

A
1 slippery
2 fixed
3 get rid of
4 mentioned
5 announcement
6 Chop
7 peasant
8 survived
9 erased
10 minced

B
1 ① portable
2 ③ migrant
3 ② pandemic

Day 16

Daily Test 1 P. 97

A
1 catch up with
2 Antarctic
3 postponed
4 leap
5 take / into account
6 ideal
7 bank
8 stick

9 vertical
10 concrete

B
1 ⑤ realistic
2 ② worth
3 ② extreme

Daily Test 2 P. 99

A
1 meet
2 faucet
3 consider
4 fountain
5 challenge
6 risk
7 extinct
8 infected
9 urged
10 parallel

B
1 ① surprising
2 ④ constantly
3 ③ sight

Review Test 08

Day 15+ Day 16 P. 100

A
1 argument
2 dialect
3 get rid of
4 infect
5 pandemic
6 leap
7 ideal
8 rare
9 risk
10 parallel

B
1 rare
2 postpone
3 extinct
4 mention
5 concrete

C
1 ② survival
2 ④ worthy
3 ③ postpone
4 ① constantly
5 ④ chop

D
1 e
2 b
3 a
4 d
5 c

E
1 extinct
2 Repetition
3 get rid of
4 restored
5 into account

해석
1. 모든 공룡들은 오래 전에 죽었다. 그들은 현재 멸종했다.
2. 반복은 새로운 언어를 배우는 효과적인 방법이다.
3. 새로운 관리자는 불필요한 규제를 없애는 데 동의했다.
4. 오래된 궁은 보수 될 것이고 곧 방문객을 받을 거에요.
5. 네가 다음 소풍을 계획 할 때, Sue와 Joe를 고려해 줘.

F
1 dialect
2 well-known
3 secondary
4 infected
5 personality

G
ⓒ erase

H
1 ⓑ
2 ⓐ

Day 17

Daily Test 1 P. 105

A
1 advantage
2 inventor
3 gazed
4 hire
5 faked
6 banner
7 greeted
8 comments
9 aboard
10 ballet

B
1 ② reluctant
2 ⑤ pleasure
3 ③ participate

Daily Test 2 P. 107

A
1 related
2 responsible

3 economic
4 facility
5 livestock
6 escalator
7 characteristic
8 explore
9 software
10 government

B
1 ④ characteristics
2 ④ worldwide
3 ⑤ actual

Day 18

Daily Test 1 P. 109

A
1 disappeared
2 traditional
3 faced
4 except
5 blocked
6 steel
7 least
8 lay
9 error
10 current

B
1 ② doubt
2 ④ species
3 ③ honestly

Daily Test 2 P. 111

A
1 structure
2 bronze
3 Although
4 landscape
5 submarine
6 prevent
7 beggar
8 discount
9 piled
10 harbor

B
1 ② grain
2 ④ resource
3 ③ reasonable

Review Test 09

Day 17+ Day 18 P. 112

A
1 driver
2 banner
3 responsible
4 government
5 destination
6 honestly
7 except
8 least
9 landscape
10 harbor

B
1 species
2 reluctant
3 grain
4 facility
5 tortoise

C
1 ② inventor
2 ③ disappear
3 ③ prevent
4 ① advantage
5 ④ traditional

D
1 a
2 d
3 b
4 e
5 c

E
1 reluctant
2 responsible
3 comment
4 facing
5 hired

해석

1. 어린 소녀는 치과에 가기를 꺼려했다.
2. 나는 아무도 그 프로젝트의 실패에 대한 책임이 없다고 생각한다.
3. 내 에세이에 대해 의견을 말 해 주겠니?
4. 이 섬에 동물들은 멸종을 직면하고 있다.
5. 그 회사는 고객 서비스 부서를 위해 더 많은 직원을 고용했다.

F
1 species
2 participate
3 structure
4 worldwide
5 explore

G
1 ballet
2 tortoise
3 chain
4 discount
5 block
6 pile

Day 19

Daily Test 1 P. 117

A
1 discovery
2 check
3 creatures
4 matter
5 communicated
6 justice
7 respect
8 pregnant
9 recharge
10 instrument

B
1 ④ tragic
2 ③ vowels
3 ④ freedom

Daily Test 2 P. 119

A
1 countryside
2 remark
3 describe
4 Male
5 shaped
6 inspired
7 continent
8 refilled
9 blond
10 continued

B
1 ② diligent
2 ③ orphan
3 ⑤ advertised

Day 20

Daily Test 1 P. 121

A
1 propose
2 evidence
3 tribes
4 convenient
5 artificial
6 renewable
7 quarters
8 associate
9 suppose
10 routine

B
1 ② athletes
2 ③ proficiency
3 ③ unfair

Daily Test 2 P. 123

A
1 dull
2 architect
3 edge
4 chief
5 planet
6 strength
7 feel like
8 flour
9 familiar
10 section

B
1 ② pastime
2 ② nutrition
3 ⑤ customs

Review Test 10

Day 19+ Day 20 P. 124

A
1 nasal
2 communicate
3 pregnant
4 inspire
5 source
6 web
7 convenient
8 renewable
9 chief
10 feel like

B
1 evidence
2 routine
3 nasal
4 describe
5 dull

C
1 ② discovery
2 ④ freedom
3 ③ unfair
4 ① routine
5 ③ artificial

D
1 c
2 e
3 a
4 b
5 d

E
1 recharge
2 propose
3 convenient

4 familiar
5 matter

해석

1. 이 근처 어디서 제 휴대전화를 충전할 수 있을까요?
2. 나는 우리 회의를 좀 더 늦은 날짜로 옮기는 걸 제안해요.
3. 당신이 만약 지금 바쁘다면, 나는 당신이 편할 때 전화 할게요.
4. 그녀가 프랑스인이기 때문에, 그녀는 한국 음식에 익숙하지 않다.
5. 나는 네가 프랑스를 가던지 독일을 가던지 중요하지 않아.

F

1 communicate
2 respected
3 remark
4 associated
5 renewable

G

ⓑ web

H

1 ⓑ
2 ⓐ

Day 21

Daily Test 1 P. 129

A

1 wakes
2 entrance
3 local
4 represented
5 tease
6 net
7 misunderstood
8 cast
9 crisis
10 observed

B

1 ② typical
2 ③ existence
3 ① particular

Daily Test 2 P. 131

A

1 quality
2 overweight
3 roof
4 cracks
5 lighting
6 payment
7 crowded
8 bullet
9 exit
10 cart

B

1 ③ appointment
2 ③ independence
3 ① warmth

Day 22

Daily Test 1 P. 133

A

1 attention
2 fairy
3 invade
4 cancer
5 native
6 debate
7 vain
8 swear
9 labor
10 figures

B

1 ② professional
2 ⑤ option
3 ③ various

Daily Test 2 P. 135

A

1 measure
2 tropical
3 smoking
4 semester
5 vehicle
6 awkward
7 selfish
8 brief
9 set up
10 organizing

B

1 ③ blossom
2 ② stranger
3 ⑤ noisy

Review Test 11

Day 21 + Day 22 P. 136

A

1 entrance
2 tease
3 typical
4 appointment
5 exit
6 fairy
7 professional
8 options
9 measure
10 selfish

B
1 typical
2 option
3 native
4 debate
5 typhoon

C
1 ③ existence
2 ① crowd
3 ② various
4 ③ warmth
5 ⑤ typhoon

D
1 d
2 a
3 c
4 b
5 e

E
1 typical
2 particular
3 appointment
4 quality
5 professional

해석
1. 아이들이 장난감을 좋아하는 건 일반적이다.
2. 당신은 마음속으로 특정 색깔을 떠올렸나요?
3. 우리는 제시간에 약속에 가기 위해서 카페로 서둘렀다.
4. 우리는 헤드폰을 사기 전에 그것의 음질을 확인하는 게 좋겠어.
5. Bill이 어린이임에도 불구하고, 그는 전문가처럼 바이올린을 연주한다.

F
1 awkward
2 hard-working
3 represent
4 local
5 native

G
1 cart
2 net
3 observe
4 roof
5 wake
6 vehicle

Day 23

Daily Test 1 P. 141

A
1 imagination
2 transferred
3 was tired of
4 arrested
5 manager
6 reality
7 compose
8 prefer
9 salary
10 declined

B
1 ① attractive
2 ② border
3 ④ demanded

Daily Test 2 P. 143

A
1 general
2 coast
3 indeed
4 progress
5 skyscraper
6 thrill
7 suitable
8 instant
9 beat
10 slow down

B
1 ① fond
2 ③ organic
3 ⑤ dare

Day 24

Daily Test 1 P. 145

A
1 seriously
2 forced
3 amusements
4 directed
5 named
6 newborn
7 position
8 stands for
9 eye-catching
10 swallow

B
1 ② emergency
2 ⑤ dirt
3 ② collection

Daily Test 2 P. 147

A
1 Urban
2 recreation
3 bare
4 honor
5 parted
6 get away with

7 thinker
8 Treat
9 moonlight
10 Sprinkle

B
1 ⑤ residents
2 ② functions
3 ② pretends

Review Test 12

Day 23+ Day 24 P. 148

A
1 border
2 attractive
3 salary
4 general
5 suitable
6 seriously
7 name
8 swallow
9 recreation
10 pretend

B
1 border
2 demand
3 stream
4 urban
5 swallow

C
1 ① imagination
2 ④ reality
3 ① manager
4 ② niece
5 ① dirt

D
1 d
2 e
3 a
4 b
5 c

E
1 crowded
2 slow down
3 transfer
4 prefer
5 suitable

해석
1. 쇼핑 센터는 이미 쇼핑객들로 붐볐다.
2. 넌 너무 빠르게 운전해. 좀 속도를 낮춰주겠니?
3. 당신은 서울역에서 4호선으로 환승할 수 있습니다.
4. 밖에 바람이 정말 많이 불어요. 전 외출보다 안에 있을래요.
5. 이 책은 읽기도 쉽고 어린 아이들에게 적합해요.

F
1 Demand
2 attractive
3 seriously
4 Indeed
5 functions

G
ⓐ crowded

H
1 ⓑ
2 ⓐ

Day 25

Daily Test 1 P. 153

A
1 movement
2 stirred
3 assign
4 crabs
5 obey
6 terrific
7 direction
8 requested
9 arise
10 link

B
1 ② scenery
2 ③ diving
3 ① threaten

Daily Test 2 P. 155

A
1 scale
2 wound
3 Twist
4 spots
5 camping
6 awesome
7 haircut
8 forward
9 insert
10 sweep

B
1 ① rapid
2 ④ injury
3 ③ uneasy

Day 26

Daily Test 1 P. 157

A
1 patterns
2 submit
3 paralyzed
4 virtual
5 weekly
6 impress
7 selected
8 bucket
9 fitness
10 memorizing

B
1 ① tidy
2 ③ comfort
3 ⑤ Dynasty

Daily Test 2 P. 159

A
1 attempted
2 ruined
3 globe
4 elected
5 Oxygen
6 technology
7 By the way
8 store
9 subtract
10 tossed

B
1 ① principal
2 ⑤ salty
3 ④ overestimated

Review Test 13

Day 25+ Day 26 P. 160

A
1 obey
2 threaten
3 spot
4 rapid
5 insert
6 submit
7 tidy
8 dynasty
9 oxygen
10 principal

B
1 obey
2 dive
3 pattern
4 dynasty
5 gargle

C
1 ② dove
2 ① comfortable
3 ③ memorize
4 ① select
5 ① attempt

D
1 a
2 d
3 b
4 c
5 e

E
1 arose
2 request
3 nearby
4 principal
5 impressed

해석
1. 그 사고는 실수로 인해 일어났다.
2. 우리는 다음 주 금요일까지 당신의 요청에 답할게요.
3. 우리가 차가 없기 때문에, 우리는 근처 레스토랑까지 걸어갔다.
4. 인내는 그의 성공에 있어 주된 요인이었다.
5. 관중은 그 피아니스트의 공연에 깊게 감명 받았다.

F
1 awesome
2 terrific
3 rapid
4 overestimate
5 movement

G
1 crab
2 direction
3 bucket
4 sweep
5 wound
6 globe

Day 27

Daily Test 1 P. 165

A
1 foggy
2 poverty
3 celebrated
4 fallen in love
5 weekday
6 grateful
7 carbon
8 preface

9 conquered
10 emit

B
1 ② supper
2 ⑤ lip
3 ③ scientific

Daily Test 2 P. 167

A
1 property
2 wagon
3 script
4 discipline
5 wireless
6 package
7 waterfall
8 paragraph
9 sponge
10 take over

B
1 ④ revolution
2 ④ clearly
3 ② emerged

Day 28

Daily Test 1 P. 169

A
1 performance
2 detective
3 climbed
4 slave
5 adopt
6 apply
7 looked down on
8 complex
9 encountered
10 destiny

B
1 ① victim
2 ④ strengthen
3 ② norms

Daily Test 2 P. 171

A
1 laboratory
2 intention
3 expert
4 nutrient
5 satisfied
6 Nuclear
7 put into practice
8 mechanic
9 in spite of
10 stool

B
1 ① arrow
2 ② inspecting
3 ③ switching

Review Test 14

Day 27+ Day 28 P. 172

A
1 supper
2 preface
3 discipline
4 clearly
5 take over
6 victim
7 norm
8 complex
9 nuclear
10 genetic

B
1 preface
2 conquer
3 property
4 expert
5 mechanic

C
1 ② scientific
2 ③ celebrate
3 ① script
4 ③ detective
5 ⑤ strengthen

D
1 e
2 a
3 c
4 b
5 d

E
1 inspected
2 encountered
3 In spite of
4 stool
5 adopted

해석

1. 엔지니어는 조심스럽게 세탁기를 점검했다.
2. 나는 학교 가는 길에 한 무리의 외국인 관광객을 마주쳤다.
3. 부상에도 불구하고, 그는 경기가 끝날 때까지 뛰었다.
4. 5살 아이에게, 그 의자는 너무 높아서 위에 앉을 수 없어요.
5. 우리는 더 나은 계획을 짜기 위해서 그의 제안을 받아들였다.

F
1 grateful
2 emerged

3 realized
4 scientific
5 nutrients

G
ⓑ property

H
1 ⓑ
2 ⓐ

Day 29

Daily Test 1 P. 177

A
1 cabbage
2 utilize
3 sawed
4 turned out
5 wagging
6 be worried about
7 folded
8 infant
9 latest
10 pioneer

B
1 ④ foundation
2 ③ commonly
3 ③ dedication

Daily Test 2 P. 179

A
1 compared
2 touched
3 illegal
4 dumb
5 eyelids
6 adapted
7 knelt
8 litter
9 long for
10 marginal

B
1 ② hopeless
2 ② preview
3 ⑤ growth

Day 30

Daily Test 1 P. 181

A
1 evolved
2 financial
3 penalty
4 prevention
5 constant
6 altered
7 cultural
8 conclusion
9 atmosphere
10 fame

B
1 ② policy
2 ⑤ critical
3 ① imitated

Daily Test 2 P. 183

A
1 electronic
2 distinguish
3 established
4 specific
5 consumes
6 potential
7 standard
8 kept walking
9 receipt
10 primary

B
1 ② trial
2 ④ obvious
3 ① greedy

Review Test 15

Day 29+ Day 30 P. 184

A
1 wag
2 infant
3 retire
4 kneel
5 long for
6 prevention
7 alter
8 atmosphere
9 specific
10 potential

B
1 pioneer
2 utilize
3 primary
4 kneel
5 receipt

C
1 ② latest
2 ⑤ dedication

3 ② illegal
4 ① hopeless
5 ⑤ conclusion
5 litter
6 merchant

D
1 b
2 e
3 a
4 c
5 d

E
1 imitated
2 Keep
3 turned out
4 altered
5 receipt

해석

1. Tyler는 그 가수의 목소리를 완벽하게 따라 했다.
2. 계속 달려! 결승선이 바로 네 앞에 있어.
3. 학교의 새로운 언어 프로그램은 성공적이라고 판명됐다.
4. 불행하게도, 원래의 계획은 몇 번 바뀌었다.
5. 당신이 인쇄기를 산다면, 영수증을 받는 걸 잊지 마세요.

F
1 distinguishes
2 consumes
3 primary
4 constant
5 compared

G
1 cabbage
2 fold
3 growth
4 beard

WORD MAX 3 5300

Workbook

WorldCom Edu

Workbook

WORD MAX 3 5300

WorldCom Edu

Workbook

Day 01

| 월 일 |

영어 단어에 해당하는 한국어 뜻을 함께 적으세요.

scream	비명을 지르다; 비명	scream	비명을 지르다; 비명
dot	점		
expedite	신속하게 처리하다, 촉진하다		
construct	건설하다, 구성하다		
cheat	속이다, 부정행위를 하다		
bother	괴롭히다, 귀찮게 하다		
lift	(들어) 올리다; 올리기		
approach	접근하다; 접근, 접촉, 진입로		
token	표시, 상징		
buddy	친구, 동료		
literal	문자 그대로의		
international	국제적인		
product	생산품, 상품		
shock	충격; 충격을 주다		
spray	뿌리다; 분무기, 스프레이		
gifted	재능이 있는		
sunlight	햇빛, 햇살		
theme	주제, 테마		
image	이미지, 인상		
speed	속도		
leader	지도자, 대표		
deeply	깊게		
elbow	팔꿈치		
fearful	무서운, 걱정하는		
route	길, 경로, 노선		
meadow	목초지, 초원		
negative	부정적인		
reporter	기자		
gate	문, 입구, 탑승구		
rhythm	리듬, 율동		

다음 단어에 해당하는 영어 단어 또는 우리말을 쓰세요.

O____개 X____개

영어	한국어
approach	
bother	
buddy	
cheat	
construct	
deeply	
dot	
elbow	
expedite	
fearful	
gate	
gifted	
image	
international	
leader	
lift	
literal	
meadow	
negative	
product	
reporter	
rhythm	
route	
scream	
shock	
speed (nn)	
spray	
sunlight	
theme	
token	

한국어	영어
동 비명을 지르다 명 비명	
동 뿌리다 명 분무기, 스프레이	
형 국제적인	
명 리듬, 율동	
명 점	
동 (들어) 올리다 명 올리기	
명 팔꿈치	
형 재능이 있는	
동 신속하게 처리하다, 촉진하다	
동 건설하다, 구성하다	
형 무서운, 걱정하는	
명 햇빛, 햇살	
형 문자 그대로의	
명 목초지, 초원	
동 속이다, 부정행위를 하다	
명 속도	
동 괴롭히다, 귀찮게 하다	
명 주제, 테마	
명 친구, 동료	
형 부정적인	
명 충격 동 충격을 주다	
명 문, 입구, 탑승구	
명 이미지, 인상	
동 접근하다 명 접근, 접촉, 진입로	
명 지도자, 대표	
부 깊게	
명 생산품, 상품	
명 기자	
명 길, 경로, 노선	
명 표시, 상징	

Workbook

Day 02

| 월 일 |

영어 단어에 해당하는 한국어 뜻을 함께 적으세요.

sunshine	햇빛, 햇살	sunshine	햇빛, 햇살
scratch	긁다, 할퀴다; 긁힌 자국, 상처		
documentary	다큐멘터리, 기록물		
fault	잘못, 결함, 결점		
shame	수치심, 부끄러움		
accent	억양, 말투		
wing	날개		
easily	쉽게		
boss	상사, 사장		
arid	매우 건조한, 무미 건조한		
discuss	의논하다, 상의하다		
liberal	자유로운, 진보적인		
hierachy	계급(제), 계층		
cash	현금		
finally	마침내		
novel	소설		
knowledge	지식		
shower	소나기, 샤워; 샤워하다		
place	두다, 놓다		
coupon	쿠폰, 할인권		
probably	아마(도)		
supply	공급하다; 공급		
graphic	생생한, 사실적인		
backpack	배낭; 배낭을 지고 걷다		
vivid	생생한, 선명한		
thumb	엄지		
closely	가까이, 밀접하게		
question	질문하다		
annoy	짜증나게 하다		
collapse	(건물 등이)무너지다, 쓰러지다 붕괴, 쓰러짐		

다음 단어에 해당하는 영어 단어 또는 우리말을 쓰세요.

O____개 X____개

영어	한국어
sunshine	
accent	
annoy	
arid	
backpack	
boss	
closely	
collapse	
coupon	
discuss	
documentary	
easily	
fault	
finally	
graphic	
hierachy	
knowledge	
liberal	
novel	
place	
probably	
question	
scratch	
shame	
shower	
cash	
supply	
thumb	
vivid	
wing	

한국어	영어
명 소설	
명 다큐멘터리, 기록물	
명 엄지	
동 의논하다, 상의하다	
동 공급하다 명 공급	
명 날개	
형 생생한, 선명한	
명 햇빛, 햇살	
명 수치심, 부끄러움	
부 마침내	
동 짜증나게 하다	
동 긁다, 할퀴다 명 긁힌 자국, 상처	
명 억양, 말투	
명 쿠폰, 할인권	
부 쉽게	
형 생생한, 사실적인	
명 계급(제), 계층	
명 붕괴, 쓰러짐 동 (건물 등이)무너지다, 쓰러지다	
명 지식	
형 매우 건조한, 무미 건조한	
부 가까이, 밀접하게	
부 아마(도)	
형 자유로운, 진보적인	
동 두다, 놓다	
명 상사, 사장	
동 질문하다	
명 소나기, 샤워 동 샤워하다	
명 현금	
명 배낭 동 배낭을 지고 걷다	
명 잘못, 결함, 결점	

Workbook

Day 03

| 월 일 |

영어 단어에 해당하는 한국어 뜻을 함께 적으세요.

accept	받아들이다	accept	받아들이다
former	이전의, 전임의		
rainfall	강우(량)		
mass media	대중 매체		
target	목표, 과녁		
leisure	여가; 한가한		
kindness	친절, 다정함		
plant	공장		
admiral	해군 장성, 제독		
decorate	장식하다		
natural	자연의, 자연스러운		
unhappy	불행한		
compete	경쟁하다		
break out	(부정적인 사건이) 발생하다		
stressful	스트레스가 많은		
keep track of	~을 파악하다, 기억하다		
studio	스튜디오, 촬영소		
creative	창조적인, 창의력이 있는		
combine	결합하다, 혼합하다		
individual	각각의, 개인의		
physical	신체적인		
slice	(얇은) 조각		
layer	층, 겹		
silver	은		
match	어울리다		
weaken	약화시키다		
still	조용한, 가만히 있는		
case	경우, 사건		
boost	신장시키다, 북돋우다		
bottom	밑, 바닥		

다음 단어에 해당하는 영어 단어 또는 우리말을 쓰세요.

O___개 X___개

영어	한국어
accept	
admiral	
boost	
bottom	
break out	
case	
former	
combine	
compete	
creative	
decorate	
individual	
keep track of	
kindness	
layer	
leisure	
mass media	
match	
natural	
physical	
plant	
rainfall	
silver	
slice	
still	
stressful	
studio	
target	
unhappy	
weaken	

한국어	영어
동 경쟁하다	
~을 파악하다, 기억하다	
명 여가 형 한가한	
형 조용한, 가만히 있는	
형 불행한	
명 스튜디오, 촬영소	
형 이전의, 전임의	
명 (얇은) 조각	
형 자연의, 자연스러운	
동 신장시키다, 북돋우다	
명 목표, 과녁	
동 약화시키다	
동 받아들이다	
명 층, 겹	
형 스트레스가 많은	
명 친절, 다정함	
명 경우, 사건	
명 공장	
형 창조적인, 창의력이 있는	
명 강우(량)	
형 신체적인	
명 해군 장성, 제독	
동 결합하다, 혼합하다	
명 대중 매체	
명 은	
형 각각의, 개인의	
동 장식하다	
동 어울리다	
(부정적인 사건이) 발생하다	
명 밑, 바닥	

Workbook

Day 04 | 월 일 |

영어 단어에 해당하는 한국어 뜻을 함께 적으세요.

wisely	현명하게	wisely	현명하게
treasure	보물		
ceramic	도자기, 질그릇; 도자기의, 요업의		
influential	영향력 있는		
adventurous	모험심이 강한		
wallpaper	벽지		
channel	(TV) 채널		
keep up with	~와 연락하고 지내다		
heritage	유산		
pipe	관, 배관		
be up to	~에 달려 있다.		
uncomfortable	불편한		
universe	우주		
rubber	고무; 고무의		
original	원래의		
breathtaking	놀랄만한, 아슬아슬한		
inherent	고유의, 내재된		
score	점수; 득점하다		
delete	삭제하다		
present	주다, 수여하다		
silly	어리석은, 바보 같은		
underground	지하의		
sketch	밑그림; 스케치를 하다		
delivery	배달		
scold	꾸짖다		
prey	먹이, 사냥감		
weird	기이한, 기묘한		
officer	장교, 경찰관		
calm	차분한, 침착한		
decision	결정		

다음 단어에 해당하는 영어 단어 또는 우리말을 쓰세요.

O____개 X____개

영어	한국어
adventurous	
be up to	
breathtaking	
calm	
ceramic	
channel	
decision	
delete	
delivery	
heritage	
influential	
inherent	
keep up with	
officer	
original	
pipe	
present	
prey	
rubber	
scold	
score	
silly	
sketch	
treasure	
uncomfortable	
underground	
universe	
wallpaper	
weird	
wisely	

한국어	영어
명 밑그림 동 스케치를 하다	
명 점수 동 득점하다	
형 영향력 있는	
명 결정	
명 보물	
동 주다, 수여하다	
형 원래의	
동 삭제하다	
형 어리석은, 바보 같은	
명 도자기, 질그릇 형 도자기의, 요업의	
형 지하의	
명 벽지	
형 고유의, 내재된	
~에 달려 있다	
형 차분한, 침착한	
형 모험심이 강한	
형 놀랄만한, 아슬아슬한	
부 현명하게	
형 불편한	
명 배달	
명 유산	
명 고무 형 고무의	
명 먹이, 사냥감	
~와 연락하고 지내다	
명 우주	
명 장교, 경찰관	
명 (TV) 채널	
형 기이한, 기묘한	
명 관, 배관	
동 꾸짖다	

Workbook

Day 05

| 월 일 |

영어 단어에 해당하는 한국어 뜻을 함께 적으세요.

clue	단서	clue	단서
gladly	기쁘게, 고맙게		
territory	지역, 영토		
legendary	전설적인		
publish	출판하다		
method	방법		
audience	관중, 청중		
include	포함하다, 포함시키다		
period	기간, 시대		
soda	소다, 탄산음료		
in charge of	책임이 있는, 담당하는		
embarrass	당황스럽게 만들다		
fantasy	공상, 상상		
filter	여과하다, 거르다; 필터, 여과장치		
wetland	습지		
regular	규칙적인		
amaze	놀라게 하다		
wire	철사, 선		
indoor	실내의		
replay	재경기, 재연; 다시 하다, ~을 재연하다		
cotton	면, 면직물		
confidence	신뢰, 자신감		
enemy	적		
incredible	믿을 수 없는, 믿기 힘든		
vital	필수적인		
landmark	랜드마크, 주요 지형지물		
precious	귀중한, 값비싼		
wear	닳다, 낡다		
successful	성공적인		
commodity	상품, 물품, 원자재		

다음 단어에 해당하는 영어 단어 또는 우리말을 쓰세요. O____개 X____개

영어	한국어
amaze	
audience	
clue	
commodity	
confidence	
cotton	
embarrass	
enemy	
fantasy	
filter	
gladly	
in charge of	
include	
incredible	
indoor	
landmark	
legendary	
method	
period	
precious	
publish	
regular	
replay	
soda	
successful	
territory	
vital	
wear	
wetland	
wire	

한국어	영어
동 놀라게 하다	
명 단서	
명 철사, 선	
명 공상, 상상	
명 면, 면직물	
부 기쁘게, 고맙게	
형 규칙적인	
명 상품, 물품, 원자재	
동 포함하다, 포함시키다	
형 실내의	
명 지역, 영토	
명 재경기, 재연 동 다시 하다, ~을 재연하다	
형 전설적인	
동 닳다, 낡다	
동 당황스럽게 만들다	
형 귀중한, 값비싼	
명 방법	
명 신뢰, 자신감	
동 출판하다	
명 습지	
형 믿을 수 없는, 믿기 힘든	
명 관중, 청중	
형 성공적인	
책임이 있는, 담당하는	
명 기간, 시대	
명 랜드마크, 주요 지형지물	
명 소다, 탄산음료	
명 적	
동 여과하다, 거르다 명 필터, 여과장치	
형 필수적인	

Workbook

Day 06

| 월 일 |

영어 단어에 해당하는 한국어 뜻을 함께 적으세요.

separate	분리된, 따로 떨어진; 분리하다	separate	분리된, 따로 떨어진; 분리하다
totally	완전히, 전적으로		
immigrant	이민자, 이주민		
private	사적인		
survey	살피다; (설문) 조사		
animation	만화 영화, 애니메이션		
youth	젊음, 젊은이		
exclude	제외하다, 배제하다		
handle	다루다; 손잡이		
carrot	당근		
disadvantage	약점, 불리한 점		
head	~로 향하다		
charge	요금; 청구하다		
rough	거친, 고르지 못한		
historic	역사적인		
wedding	결혼식, 혼례		
odd	이상한		
ginseng	인삼		
income	수입, 소득		
official	공식적인		
organization	조직, 단체, 기구		
fancy	장식이 많은, 화려한; 공상, 환상		
dust	먼지		
crawl	(엎드려) 기다		
maker	~을 만드는 사람, 제조사		
despite	~에도 불구하고		
provide	제공하다		
proper	적절한		
tremble	떨다, 흔들리다		
expect	기대하다		

다음 단어에 해당하는 영어 단어 또는 우리말을 쓰세요. O____개 X____개

영어	한국어
animation	
carrot	
charge	
crawl	
despite	
disadvantage	
dust	
exclude	
expect	
fancy	
ginseng	
handle	
head	
historic	
immigrant	
income	
maker	
odd	
official	
organization	
private	
proper	
provide	
rough	
separate	
survey	
totally	
tremble	
wedding	
youth	

한국어	영어
동 ~로 향하다	
명 결혼식, 혼례	
명 상품, 물품, 원자재	
명 인삼	
부 완전히, 전적으로	
명 약점, 불리한 점	
명 ~을 만드는 사람, 제조사	
명 당근	
형 이상한	
동 살피다 명 (설문) 조사	
명 공상, 환상 형 장식이 많은, 화려한	
동 다루다 명 손잡이	
전 ~에도 불구하고	
동 제외하다, 배제하다	
동 제공하다	
명 이민자, 이주민	
형 적절한	
형 사적인	
명 요금 동 청구하다	
명 수입, 소득	
명 젊음, 젊은이	
형 거친, 고르지 못한	
명 먼지	
명 만화 영화, 애니메이션	
동 떨다, 흔들리다	
형 역사적인	
형 공식적인	
동 기대하다	
명 조직, 단체, 기구	
동 (엎드려) 기다	

Workbook

Day 07

| 월 일 |

영어 단어에 해당하는 한국어 뜻을 함께 적으세요.

mixture	혼합물	mixture	혼합물
bloody	유혈의, 피의		
maple	단풍나무		
starfish	불가사리		
backward	뒤의; 뒤로		
tomb	무덤		
investigate	조사하다, 수사하다		
mascot	마스코트		
reply	답하다; 대답		
research	조사하다, 연구하다; 조사,연구		
monthly	매월의, 한 달에 한 번의		
suffer	고통받다, 시달리다		
condiment	양념, 조미료		
kin	친족, 친척		
used to	~하곤 했다 , (한때는) ~이었다		
high-tech	첨단 기술의		
recover	회복하다		
root	뿌리, 근원		
intelligent	영리한, 똑똑한		
refund	환불; 환불하다		
scientist	과학자		
shut	(문을) 닫다, (눈을) 감다		
wheel	바퀴		
envy	부러워하다		
anger	화, 분노		
jewel	보석		
gap	갈라진 틈, 격차		
effective	효과적인		
wooden	나무로 된, 목재의		
bowl	그릇, 한 그릇(의 양)		

다음 단어에 해당하는 영어 단어 또는 우리말을 쓰세요. O____개 X____개

영어	한국어
anger	
backward	
bloody	
bowl	
condiment	
effective	
envy	
gap	
high-tech	
intelligent	
investigate	
jewel	
kin	
maple	
mascot	
mixture	
monthly	
shut	
recover	
refund	
reply	
research	
root	
scientist	
starfish	
suffer	
tomb	
used to	
wheel	
wooden	

한국어	영어
명 혼합물	
동 회복하다	
~하곤 했다, (한때는) ~이었다	
명 바퀴	
동 조사하다, 수사하다	
형 첨단 기술의	
명 양념, 조미료	
동 (문을) 닫다, (눈을) 감다	
명 무덤	
명 그릇, 한 그릇(의 양)	
명 뿌리, 근원	
동 답하다 명 대답	
명 과학자	
형 유혈의, 피의	
형 나무로 된, 목재의	
명 마스코트	
형 영리한, 똑똑한	
형 매월의, 한 달에 한 번의	
동 부러워하다	
명 단풍나무	
명 환불 동 환불하다	
명 화, 분노	
명 불가사리	
동 고통받다, 시달리다	
명 보석	
형 뒤의 전 뒤로	
명 친족, 친척	
명 갈라진 틈, 격차	
명 조사, 연구 동 조사하다, 연구하다	
형 효과적인	

Workbook

Day 08

| 월 일 |

영어 단어에 해당하는 한국어 뜻을 함께 적으세요.

wheelchair	휠체어	wheelchair	휠체어
improve	향상시키다		
camp	야영지, 텐트		
contact	연락, 접촉; 접촉하다		
overseas	해외의; 해외로		
since	~이래 줄곧		
issue	주제, 쟁점, 사안		
lecture	강의; 강의하다		
online	온라인의		
detail	세부사항		
perform	수행하다, 공연하다		
plenty	많음, 충분		
comparable	비교할 만한, 비슷한		
theory	이론		
gradually	서서히, 점차적으로		
orchestra	오케스트라, 관현악단		
result	결과		
system	제도, 체계, 조직		
sentence	문장		
magical	마법의, 마법적인		
thunder	천둥(소리), 우레		
aim	목표		
command	명령하다; 명령		
presentation	수여, 발표		
drum	북, 드럼; 두드리다		
sheet	(종이) 한 장, (침대) 시트		
crosswalk	횡단보도		
pollution	오염, 공해		
ignore	무시하다		
reflect	반영하다, 반사하다		

다음 단어에 해당하는 영어 단어 또는 우리말을 쓰세요.

O____개 X____개

영어	한국어
aim	
camp	
command	
comparable	
contact	
crosswalk	
detail	
drum	
gradually	
ignore	
improve	
issue	
lecture	
magical	
online	
orchestra	
overseas	
perform	
plenty	
pollution	
presentation	
reflect	
result	
sentence	
sheet	
since	
system	
theory	
thunder	
wheelchair	

한국어	영어
부 서서히, 점차적으로	
명 (종이) 한 장, (침대) 시트	
명 야영지, 텐트	
명 오케스트라, 관현악단	
명 이론	
동 향상시키다	
명 오염, 공해	
명 세부사항	
명 문장	
명 휠체어	
명 북, 드럼 동 두드리다	
형 온라인의	
명 제도, 체계, 조직	
형 해외의 부 해외로	
명 수여, 발표	
형 비교할 만한, 비슷한	
명 결과	
명 연락, 접촉 동 접촉하다	
형 마법의, 마법적인	
명 강의 동 강의하다	
동 명령하다 명 명령	
명 많음, 충분	
명 주제, 쟁점, 사안	
동 무시하다	
명 천둥(소리), 우레	
명 횡단보도	
전 ~이래 줄곧	
명 목표	
동 수행하다, 공연하다	
동 반영하다, 반사하다	

Workbook

Day 09

| 월 일 |

영어 단어에 해당하는 한국어 뜻을 함께 적으세요.

organism	생물, 유기체	organism	생물, 유기체
encourage	격려하다, 북돋아주다		
fear	공포, 두려움; ~을 두려워하다		
champion	우승자, 챔피언		
highway	고속도로		
galaxy	은하계		
distance	거리		
rich	다채로운, 풍부한		
sensor	센서, 감지기		
vision	시력, 시야		
manage	간신히 ~하다, ~을 잘 해내다		
appetite	식욕		
wealthy	부유한		
prove	증명하다, 입증하다		
disabled	장애가 있는		
confuse	(사람을) 혼란시키다, 혼동시키다		
spare	예비의, 따로 떼어놓는		
grand	웅장한, 화려한		
carpenter	목수		
lifetime	일생, 생애		
windmill	풍차		
awful	끔찍한		
earthquake	지진		
thanks to	~덕분에		
string	끈, 줄		
author	작가		
sculpture	조각품		
absorb	흡수하다, 빨아들이다		
enable	가능하게 하다		
think over	~을 심사숙고하다		

다음 단어에 해당하는 영어 단어 또는 우리말을 쓰세요.

O____개 X____개

영어	한국어
organism	
absorb	
appetite	
author	
awful	
carpenter	
champion	
confuse	
disabled	
distance	
earthquake	
enable	
encourage	
fear	
galaxy	
grand	
highway	
lifetime	
manage	
prove	
rich	
sculpture	
sensor	
spare	
string	
thanks to	
think over	
vision	
wealthy	
windmill	

한국어	영어
동 (사람을) 혼란시키다, 혼동시키다	
형 장애가 있는	
동 가능하게 하다	
형 예비의, 따로 떼어놓는	
명 생물, 유기체	
명 목수	
~을 심사숙고하다	
동 간신히 ~하다, ~을 잘 해내다	
형 웅장한, 화려한	
명 고속도로	
~덕분에	
동 격려하다, 북돋아주다	
명 일생, 생애	
명 센서, 감지기	
명 풍차	
명 시력, 시야	
동 흡수하다, 빨아들이다	
명 공포, 두려움 동 ~을 두려워하다	
형 끔찍한	
명 우승자, 챔피언	
명 지진	
형 다채로운, 풍부한	
명 끈, 줄	
명 식욕	
명 조각품	
동 증명하다, 입증하다	
명 거리	
명 작가	
형 부유한	
명 은하계	

Workbook

Day 10

| 월 일 |

영어 단어에 해당하는 한국어 뜻을 함께 적으세요.

proportion	비율,부분	proportion	비율,부분
giraffe	기린		
deal	다루다		
role	역할		
humanism	인본주의, 휴머니즘		
surround	둘러싸다, 에워싸다		
deceive	속이다, 기만하다		
symptom	증상		
pass away	사망하다, 돌아가시다		
unlike	~와 다른		
figurative	비유적인		
maintain	유지하다		
preserve	보호하다, 보존하다		
book	예약하다		
chest	가슴, 흉부		
bind	묶다		
weapon	무기		
enlarge	확대하다, 확장하다		
diverse	다양한		
folk	(복수취급) 사람들; 민속의		
valid	유효한, 타당한		
emphasize	강조하다		
quantity	양, 수량, 분량		
obtain	얻다		
involve	수반하다, 포함하다		
appropriate	적절한		
absolute	절대의, 절대적인		
status	신분, 지위, 자격		
impressive	인상적인, 감명 깊은		
rescue	구조; 구하다, 구조하다		

다음 단어에 해당하는 영어 단어 또는 우리말을 쓰세요. O____개 X____개

영어	한국어
proportion	
absolute	
appropriate	
bind	
book	
chest	
deal	
deceive	
diverse	
emphasize	
enlarge	
figurative	
folk	
giraffe	
humanism	
impressive	
involve	
maintain	
obtain	
pass away	
preserve	
quantity	
rescue	
role	
status	
surround	
symptom	
unlike	
valid	
weapon	

한국어	영어
동 묶다	
명 비율,부분	
동 예약하다	
형 다양한	
명 기린	
명 가슴, 흉부	
동 다루다	
명 신분, 지위, 자격	
명 무기	
명 역할	
형 절대의, 절대적인	
명 인본주의, 휴머니즘	
동 확대하다, 확장하다	
동 유지하다	
동 둘러싸다, 에워싸다	
형 인상적인, 감명 깊은	
동 속이다, 기만하다	
명 사람들 형 민속의	
동 보호하다, 보존하다	
형 유효한, 타당한	
전 ~와 다른	
형 적절한	
형 비유적인	
명 양, 수량, 분량	
동 강조하다	
동 수반하다, 포함하다	
명 구조 동 구하다, 구조하다	
동 사망하다, 돌아가시다	
동 얻다	
명 증상	

Workbook

Day 11

| 월 일 |

영어 단어에 해당하는 한국어 뜻을 함께 적으세요.

declare	선언하다, 표명하다	declare	선언하다, 표명하다
blackboard	칠판		
refuse	거절하다		
tap	(가볍게) 톡톡 두드리다		
maximum	최고의, 최대의		
minimum	최저의, 최소한의		
actually	실제로, 실은		
classmate	반 친구		
signal	신호; 신호를 보내다		
highlight	강조하다; 가장 흥미로운 부분		
sincere	진실된, 온후한		
bet	내기하다; 내기		
chore	허드렛일, 하기 싫은 일		
seed	쌀쌀한, 추운		
concentrate	집중하다		
satellite	인공위성		
shuttle	정기 왕복 항공기(버스, 열차)		
delay	지연, 지체; 미루다, 연기하다		
solution	해결책, 해법		
fully	완전히, 충분히		
department	부서, 학과		
generous	인심좋은, 관대한		
population	인구		
frame	뼈대, 틀, 액자		
lyrics	(노래의) 가사, 서정시		
industry	산업, 업계		
opposite	건너편에; 반대의		
understanding	이해, 이해력		
dizzy	어지러운, 아찔한		
even though	비록 ~일지라도		

다음 단어에 해당하는 영어 단어 또는 우리말을 쓰세요.

O____개 X____개

영어	한국어
declare	
actually	
bet	
blackboard	
chore	
classmate	
concentrate	
lyrics	
delay	
department	
dizzy	
even though	
frame	
fully	
generous	
highlight	
industry	
maximum	
minimum	
opposite	
population	
refuse	
satellite	
seed	
shuttle	
signal	
sincere	
solution	
tap	
understanding	

한국어	영어
명 인공위성	
동 집중하다	
명 부서, 학과	
동 거절하다	
형 쌀쌀한, 추운	
명 인구	
동 (가볍게) 툭툭 두드리다	
명 허드렛일, 하기 싫은 일	
부 완전히, 충분히	
명 칠판	
명 해결책, 해법	
동 내기하다 명 내기	
형 인심좋은, 관대한	
형 진실된, 온후한	
명 (노래의) 가사, 서정시	
동 강조하다 명 가장 흥미로운 부분	
전 건너편에 형 반대의	
동 선언하다, 표명하다	
명 정기 왕복 항공기(버스, 열차)	
명 뼈대, 틀, 액자	
형 최저의, 최소한의	
비록 ~일지라도	
형 최고의, 최대의	
명 산업, 업계	
명 신호 동 신호를 보내다	
명 지연, 지체 동 미루다, 연기하다	
명 반 친구	
명 이해, 이해력	
부 실제로, 실은	
형 어지러운, 아찔한	

Workbook

Day 12

| 월 일 |

영어 단어에 해당하는 한국어 뜻을 함께 적으세요.

journey	여행	journey	여행
shelter	피난처		
hurricane	허리케인		
ruler	통치자, 지배자		
tax	세금		
fingerprint	지문		
slip	미끄러지다		
budget	예산; 예산을 세우다		
electricity	전기		
insult	모욕; 모욕하다		
summarize	요약하다		
scrape	긁어내다, 벗겨내다		
reveal	드러내다, 밝히다		
below	아래에; ~아래에		
brick	벽돌		
space	우주		
passion	열정		
as long as	~하는 한		
national	국가의, 전국적인		
display	전시하다; 전시		
billion	10억		
perspective	관점, 시각		
optical	시각적인		
rush	서두르다		
trait	특성		
compass	나침반		
pole	막대기, (지구의) 극		
rely on	~에 의존하다, ~에 의지하다		
lid	뚜껑		
impossible	불가능한, 믿기 어려운		

다음 단어에 해당하는 영어 단어 또는 우리말을 쓰세요.

O____개 X____개

영어	한국어
as long as	
below	
billion	
brick	
budget	
compass	
display	
electricity	
fingerprint	
hurricane	
impossible	
insult	
journey	
lid	
national	
optical	
passion	
perspective	
pole	
rely on	
reveal	
ruler	
rush	
scrape	
shelter	
slip	
space	
summarize	
tax	
trait	

한국어	영어
명 열정	
명 전기	
형 불가능한, 믿기 어려운	
동 요약하다	
명 여행	
명 관점, 시각	
명 10억	
동 미끄러지다	
명 뚜껑	
명 우주	
명 피난처	
동 전시하다 명 전시	
명 허리케인	
형 국가의, 전국적인	
명 모욕 동 모욕하다	
~하는 한	
동 드러내다, 밝히다	
~에 의존하다, ~에 의지하다	
명 지문	
형 시각적인	
명 세금	
명 벽돌	
명 통치자, 지배자	
동 서두르다	
명 특성	
동 긁어내다, 벗겨내다	
명 나침반	
명 예산 동 예산을 세우다	
명 막대기, (지구의) 극	
부 아래에 전 ~아래에	

Workbook

Day 13

| 월 일 |

영어 단어에 해당하는 한국어 뜻을 함께 적으세요.

liquid	액체; 액체의	liquid	액체; 액체의
campaign	(사회적) 운동, 캠페인		
make-up	화장품, 화장		
draw	끌어당기다, 잡아 당기다; 무승부		
conduct	(특정 행동을) 하다, 실시하다		
impression	인상, 느낌		
exhibit	전시하다		
starve	굶주리다, 굶어 죽다		
post	우편; 우편을 발송하다		
notice	주의, 공고; 알아차리다, 인지하다		
erupt	폭발하다, 터지다		
stay up	안 자다, 깨어 있다		
remain	여전히 ~이다, 남다		
press	누르다, 바짝 대다		
intellectual	지능의, 지적인		
talented	재능 있는		
occur	발생하다, 일어나다		
experiment	실험; 실험하다		
hatch	부화하다		
code	암호, 부호		
durable	견고한, 오래가는		
rent	집세, 방세; 세를 내다, 빌리다		
grassland	풀밭, 초원		
expense	비용, 돈		
connection	연결, 관련성		
achieve	성취하다, 달성하다		
metal	금속		
adviser	조언자, 상담가		
harm	해를 끼치다; 손해, 피해		
log	통나무		

다음 단어에 해당하는 영어 단어 또는 우리말을 쓰세요. O____개 X____개

영어	한국어
achieve	
adviser	
code	
conduct	
connection	
draw	
durable	
erupt	
exhibit	
expense	
experiment	
starve	
grassland	
harm	
hatch	
impossible	
impression	
intellectual	
liquid	
log	
make-up	
metal	
notice	
occur	
post	
press	
remain	
rent	
stay up	
talented	

한국어	영어
형 재능 있는	
동 발생하다, 일어나다	
동 누르다, 바짝 대다	
명 우편 동 우편을 발송하다	
동 해를 끼치다 명 손해, 피해	
명 액체 형 액체의	
명 실험 동 실험하다	
동 여전히 ~이다, 남다	
명 비용, 돈	
명 화장품, 화장	
명 풀밭, 초원	
명 (사회적) 운동, 캠페인	
명 금속	
안 자다, 깨어 있다	
명 집세, 방세 동 세를 내다, 빌리다	
동 전시하다	
형 견고한, 오래가는	
명 인상, 느낌	
명 통나무	
명 암호, 부호	
동 끌어당기다, 잡아 당기다 명 무승부	
동 폭발하다, 터지다	
명 연결, 관련성	
동 굶주리다, 굶어 죽다	
동 (특정 행동을) 하다, 실시하다	
형 지능의, 지적인	
명 조언자, 상담가	
동 부화하다	
동 성취하다, 달성하다	
명 주의, 공고 동 알아차리다, 인지하다	

Workbook

Day 14

| 월 일 |

영어 단어에 해당하는 한국어 뜻을 함께 적으세요.

congratulation	축하	congratulation	축하
genius	천재, 천재성		
lunar	달의		
allowance	용돈, 수당		
make up for	만회하다, 보상하다		
form	형태, 서식; 형성하다		
appearance	겉모습, 외모		
illusion	환상		
empire	제국		
examine	조사하다, 검토하다		
offer	제공하다, 권하다		
certain	확실한		
protect	보호하다		
work	효과가 있다		
mop	대걸레; 대걸레로 닦다		
jar	병, 항아리		
jury	배심원		
proverb	속담		
state	상태 , (미국의) 주		
flavor	풍미, 맛		
worse	더 나쁜		
accidentally	우연히, 뜻하지않게		
raw	날것의, 익히지 않은		
chemical	화학의		
pedal	(자전거, 자동차의) 페달		
migrate	이주하다		
stress	강조하다		
last	지속되다		
suck	빨다		
loss	손실		

다음 단어에 해당하는 영어 단어 또는 우리말을 쓰세요.

O____개 X____개

영어	한국어	한국어	영어
accidentally		형 확실한	
allowance		명 상태, (미국의) 주	
appearance		명 병, 항아리	
certain		동 강조하다	
chemical		명 축하	
congratulation		명 배심원	
empire		명 대걸레 동 대걸레로 닦다	
examine		명 속담	
flavor		동 조사하다, 검토하다	
form		동 이주하다	
genius		명 제국	
illusion		명 (자전거, 자동차의) 페달	
jar		명 형태, 서식 동 형성하다	
jury		명 풍미, 맛	
last		만회하다, 보상하다	
loss		형 화학의	
lunar		형 달의	
make up for		명 손실	
migrate		명 겉모습, 외모	
mop		명 천재, 천재성	
offer		형 더 나쁜	
pedal		동 지속되다	
protect		부 우연히, 뜻하지않게	
proverb		동 제공하다, 권하다	
raw		명 용돈, 수당	
state		동 빨다	
stress		명 환상	
suck		형 날것의, 익히지 않은	
work		동 효과가 있다	
worse		동 보호하다	

Workbook

Day 15

| 월 일 |

영어 단어에 해당하는 한국어 뜻을 함께 적으세요.

argument	논쟁, 말다툼	argument	논쟁, 말다툼
drugstore	약국		
repetition	반복		
spin	돌다, 회전시키다		
director	지도자, 책임자		
dialect	사투리, 방언		
rate	비율		
project	계획, 연구과제, 사업계획		
personality	성격, 인격		
available	구할 수 있는, 여유가 있는		
bump	~에 부딪치다		
well-known	유명한, 잘 알려진		
flow	흐름; 흐르다		
waterproof	방수의		
restore	복구하다		
secondary	제 2의, 중등 교육의		
relative	친척		
slippery	미끄러운, 미끈거리는		
fix	고정하다		
get rid of	~을 제거하다, 없애다		
mention	언급하다		
announcement	발표, 소식		
chop	(음식을) 다지다, 썰다		
peasant	농부, 소작농		
portable	휴대하기 쉬운, 휴대용의		
survive	살아남다		
erase	지우다		
migrant	이주자		
mince	(고기 등을) 갈다, 잘게 썰다		
pandemic	(전국적인) 유행병; 유행성의		

다음 단어에 해당하는 영어 단어 또는 우리말을 쓰세요. O___개 X___개

영어	한국어
announcement	
argument	
available	
bump	
chop	
slippery	
dialect	
director	
drugstore	
erase	
fix	
flow	
get rid of	
mention	
migrant	
mince	
pandemic	
peasant	
personality	
portable	
project	
rate	
relative	
repetition	
restore	
secondary	
spin	
survive	
waterproof	
well-known	

한국어	영어
형 미끄러운, 미끈거리는	
명 약국	
동 (고기 등을) 갈다, 잘게 썰다	
명 흐름 동 흐르다	
명 친척	
형 유명한, 잘 알려진	
명 이주자	
명 논쟁, 말다툼	
명 (전국적인) 유행병 형 유행성의	
동 ~에 부딪치다	
동 지우다	
명 지도자, 책임자	
동 고정하다	
~을 제거하다, 없애다	
명 사투리, 방언	
동 돌다, 회전시키다	
동 언급하다	
동 복구하다	
명 반복	
명 농부, 소작농	
명 발표, 소식	
명 성격, 인격	
명 계획, 연구과제, 사업계획	
형 제 2의, 중등 교육의	
형 방수의	
동 (음식을) 다지다, 썰다	
명 비율	
동 살아남다	
형 휴대하기 쉬운, 휴대용의	
형 구할 수 있는, 여유가 있는	

Day 16 | 월 일 |

영어 단어에 해당하는 한국어 뜻을 함께 적으세요.

catch up with	따라잡다	catch up with	따라잡다
lung	폐		
realistic	현실적인		
Antarctic	남극의		
postpone	연기하다		
leap	뛰다, 뛰어오르다		
take ~ into account	~을 고려하다		
ideal	이상적인, 가장 알맞은		
bank	둑		
stick	붙이다		
vertical	수직의		
worth	가치가 있는; 가치, 값어치		
extreme	극도의, 극심한		
rare	드문, 희귀한		
concrete	구체적인		
meet	충족시키다		
faucet	수도꼭지		
consider	잘 생각하다, ~로 여기다		
surprising	놀라운, 놀랄		
fountain	분수, 원천		
challenge	도전; 도전하다		
track	길, 트랙; 추적하다		
sight	시력, 보기, 시야		
risk	위험		
extinct	멸종된		
infect	감염시키다		
engine	엔진, 기관차		
constantly	끊임없이, 계속		
urge	촉구하다, 요구하다		
parallel	평행한		

다음 단어에 해당하는 영어 단어 또는 우리말을 쓰세요.

O____개 X____개

영어	한국어	한국어	영어
Antarctic		형 평행한	
bank		형 가치가 있는 명 가치, 값어치	
catch up with		부 끊임없이, 계속	
challenge		동 충족시키다	
concrete		명 폐	
consider		명 엔진, 기관차	
constantly		형 수직의	
engine		형 놀라운, 놀랄	
extinct		형 현실적인	
extreme		명 도전 동 도전하다	
faucet		형 극도의, 극심한	
fountain		형 남극의	
ideal		동 촉구하다, 요구하다	
infect		~을 고려하다	
leap		명 수도꼭지	
lung		동 연기하다	
meet		동 감염시키다	
parallel		형 이상적인, 가장 알맞은	
postpone		명 분수, 원천	
rare		동 뛰다, 뛰어오르다	
realistic		형 멸종된	
risk		형 드문, 희귀한	
sight		명 길, 트랙 동 추적하다	
stick		따라잡다	
surprising		명 위험	
take ~ into account		명 둑	
track		동 잘 생각하다, ~로 여기다	
urge		동 붙이다	
vertical		형 구체적인	
worth		명 시력, 보기, 시야	

Workbook

Day 17

| 월 일 |

영어 단어에 해당하는 한국어 뜻을 함께 적으세요.

reluctant	꺼리는, 주저하는	reluctant	꺼리는, 주저하는
advantage	이점, 장점		
inventor	발명가		
gaze	응시하다		
tortoise	거북이		
hire	고용하다		
participate	참여하다		
bud	싹, 눈, 꽃봉오리		
fake	가짜의; 위조하다		
banner	기, 현수막		
greet	맞이하다, 환영하다		
comment	논평; 논평하다		
pleasure	기쁨, 즐거움		
aboard	(배, 기차 등에) 탑승한		
ballet	발레		
relate	관련시키다, 관련짓다		
responsible	~을 책임지고 있는, 책임감 있는		
economic	경제의		
facility	편의 시설		
livestock	가축		
characteristic	특유의; 특징		
escalator	에스컬레이터		
version	~판, 버전		
explore	탐험하다, 조사하다		
software	소프트웨어		
government	정부		
will	의지		
worldwide	세계적인, 세계적으로		
actual	실제의		
take off	(옷 등을) 벗다, (비행기 등이) 이륙하다		

다음 단어에 해당하는 영어 단어 또는 우리말을 쓰세요.

O____개 X____개

영어	한국어
reluctant	
aboard	
actual	
advantage	
ballet	
banner	
bud	
characteristic	
comment	
take off	
economic	
escalator	
explore	
facility	
fake	
gaze	
government	
greet	
hire	
inventor	
livestock	
participate	
pleasure	
relate	
responsible	
software	
tortoise	
version	
will	
worldwide	

한국어	영어
형 경제의	
명 의지	
명 거북이	
동 관련시키다, 관련짓다	
형 세계적인, 세계적으로	
명 편의 시설	
동 고용하다	
동 응시하다	
명 정부	
명 발레	
동 탐험하다, 조사하다	
명 싹, 눈, 꽃봉오리	
형 ~을 책임지고 있는, 책임감 있는	
명 이점, 장점	
명 가축	
형 가짜의 동 위조하다	
형 실제의	
동 참여하다	
부 전 (배, 기차 등에) 탑승한	
명 기, 현수막	
동 (옷 등을) 벗다, (비행기 등이) 이륙하다	
형 특유의 명 특징	
형 꺼리는, 주저하는	
명 ~판, 버전	
동 맞이하다, 환영하다	
명 에스컬레이터	
명 발명가	
명 소프트웨어	
명 논평 동 논평하다	
명 기쁨, 즐거움	

Workbook

Day 18 | 월 일 |

영어 단어에 해당하는 한국어 뜻을 함께 적으세요.

honestly	정직하게	honestly	정직하게
disappear	사라지다		
traditional	전통적인, 전통의		
chain	사슬, 체인; 묶다		
doubt	의심하다; 의심		
face	~을 마주보다, 직면하다		
species	종		
except	~을 제외하고		
block	막다		
steel	강철, 철		
least	가장 작은		
rainforest	(열대) 우림		
lie	눕다		
error	오류, 실수		
current	현재의, 지금의		
acne	여드름		
structure	구조, 구조물		
grain	곡물, 알갱이		
bronze	청동		
although	비록 ~일지라도		
succeed	성공하다, 계승하다		
landscape	풍경		
submarine	잠수함; 해저의		
prevent	막다, 방지하다		
beggar	거지		
discount	할인		
pile	더미; 쌓다		
harbor	항구		
resource	자원		
reasonable	타당한, 합리적인		

다음 단어에 해당하는 영어 단어 또는 우리말을 쓰세요.

O____개 X____개

영어	한국어
acne	
although	
beggar	
block	
bronze	
chain	
current	
disappear	
discount	
doubt	
error	
except	
face	
grain	
harbor	
honestly	
landscape	
least	
lie	
pile	
prevent	
rainforest	
reasonable	
resource	
species	
steel	
structure	
submarine	
succeed	
traditional	

한국어	영어
명 청동	
명 여드름	
형 전통적인, 전통의	
명 곡물, 알갱이	
동 막다	
형 현재의, 지금의	
동 사라지다	
명 종	
명 구조, 구조물	
명 오류, 실수	
부 정직하게	
접 비록 ~일지라도	
명 강철, 철	
동 성공하다, 계승하다	
전 ~을 제외하고	
명 풍경	
명 사슬, 체인 동 묶다	
명 잠수함 형 해저의	
명 거지	
동 ~을 마주보다, 직면하다	
동 막다, 방지하다	
동 의심하다 명 의심	
명 항구	
동 눕다	
명 할인	
명 (열대) 우림	
형 타당한, 합리적인	
명 더미 동 쌓다	
명 자원	
대 가장 작은	

Workbook

Day 19

| 월 일 |

영어 단어에 해당하는 한국어 뜻을 함께 적으세요.

discovery	발견	discovery	발견
freedom	자유, 해방		
nasal	코의, 콧소리의		
check	살피다		
creature	생물		
tragic	비극적인		
matter	중요하다		
communicate	의사소통하다, 연락을 주고받다		
vowel	모음		
justice	정의, 공정		
respect	존경하다; 존경심		
pregnant	임신한		
recharge	충전하다; 충전		
instrument	기구, 악기		
education	교육		
advertise	광고하다		
countryside	시골 지역		
remark	발언, 언급		
describe	묘사하다		
male	남자의		
shape	모양; ~모양으로 만들다		
inspire	격려하다, 분발하게 하다		
continent	대륙		
diligent	근면한, 성실한		
refill	다시 채운것; 다시 채우다, 리필하다		
blond	금발의		
continue	계속되다		
source	원천, 근원		
pepper	후추		
orphan	고아		

다음 단어에 해당하는 영어 단어 또는 우리말을 쓰세요.

O____개 X____개

영어	한국어
discovery	
advertise	
blond	
check	
communicate	
continent	
continue	
countryside	
creature	
describe	
diligent	
education	
freedom	
inspire	
instrument	
justice	
male	
matter	
nasal	
orphan	
pepper	
pregnant	
recharge	
refill	
remark	
respect	
shape	
source	
tragic	
vowel	

한국어	영어
명 시골 지역	
동 충전하다 명 충전	
형 근면한, 성실한	
동 광고하다	
명 대륙	
형 코의, 콧소리의	
동 계속되다	
명 모음	
동 격려하다, 분발하게 하다	
명 자유, 해방	
형 임신한	
명 발언, 언급	
형 금발의	
동 살피다	
동 묘사하다	
명 기구, 악기	
형 비극적인	
명 생물	
동 다시 채우다, 리필하다 명 다시 채운것	
명 정의, 공정	
명 모양 동 ~모양으로 만들다	
명 발견	
명 원천, 근원	
동 의사소통하다, 연락을 주고받다	
명 후추	
동 중요하다	
형 남자의	
동 존경하다 명 존경심	
명 고아	
명 교육	

Workbook

Day 20 | 월 일 |

영어 단어에 해당하는 한국어 뜻을 함께 적으세요.

web	거미줄(집), 망	web	거미줄(집), 망
propose	제안하다, 청혼하다		
evidence	증거		
unfair	부당한, 불공평한		
athlete	(운동) 선수		
tribe	부족, 종족		
convenient	편리한, 간편한		
artificial	인공의, 인조의		
renewable	재생 가능한		
quarter	4분의 1		
associate	관련시키다		
site	위치, 장소		
suppose	가정하다, 생각(추정)하다		
routine	일과; 일상적인		
proficiency	능숙, 숙달		
dull	따분한, 둔한		
architect	건축가, 설계자		
edge	가장자리, 모서리		
chief	주된; 우두머리, 장		
pastime	기분 전환, 취미, 오락		
planet	행성		
sled	썰매		
strength	힘, 기운		
handkerchief	손수건		
feel like ~ing	~하고 싶다		
custom	관습, 풍습		
nutrition	영양		
flour	밀가루		
familiar	익숙한, 친숙한		
section	부분, 구역		

다음 단어에 해당하는 영어 단어 또는 우리말을 쓰세요.

O____개 X____개

영어	한국어
architect	
artificial	
associate	
athlete	
chief	
convenient	
custom	
dull	
edge	
evidence	
familiar	
feel like ~ing	
flour	
handkerchief	
nutrition	
pastime	
planet	
proficiency	
propose	
quarter	
renewable	
routine	
section	
site	
sled	
strength	
suppose	
tribe	
unfair	
web	

한국어	영어
명 부분, 구역	
명 (운동) 선수	
명 건축가, 설계자	
형 부당한, 불공평한	
형 따분한, 둔한	
명 증거	
형 익숙한, 친숙한	
동 가정하다, 생각(추정)하다	
명 영양	
동 관련시키다	
명 가장자리, 모서리	
동 제안하다, 청혼하다	
명 밀가루	
명 4분의 1	
형 주된 명 우두머리, 장	
명 부족, 종족	
명 능숙, 숙달	
명 썰매	
형 편리한, 간편한	
명 행성	
명 기분 전환, 취미, 오락	
명 거미줄(집), 망	
명 힘, 기운	
명 위치, 장소	
~하고 싶다	
형 인공의, 인조의	
명 손수건	
형 재생 가능한	
명 관습, 풍습	
명 일과 형 일상적인	

Workbook

Day 21

| 월 일 |

영어 단어에 해당하는 한국어 뜻을 함께 적으세요.

wake	(잠에서) 깨다, 일어나다	wake	(잠에서) 깨다, 일어나다
entrance	입구		
local	지역의		
represent	대표하다, 나타내다		
tease	놀리다, 못살게 하다		
net	그물		
misunderstand	오해하다		
cast	던지다, (시선 등을) 보내다		
typhoon	태풍		
crisis	위기		
typical	전형적인, 대표적인		
slim	날씬한, 마른		
observe	관찰하다, 보다		
existence	존재		
particular	특정한, 특별한		
quality	질, 품질, 특질		
appointment	약속		
overweight	과체중의, 비만의		
roof	지붕, 천장		
plug	(전기) 플러그; 막다		
independence	독립		
panic	(갑작스러운) 공포, 공황		
crack	갈라지다, 금이 가다; 갈라진 금		
lighting	조명		
payment	지불		
crowd	군중; (장소를) 메우다, 붐비다		
bullet	총알		
warmth	온기, 따뜻함		
exit	나가다, 퇴장하다; 출구		
cart	수레, 카트		

다음 단어에 해당하는 영어 단어 또는 우리말을 쓰세요. O____개 X____개

영어	한국어
appointment	
bullet	
cart	
cast	
crack	
crisis	
crowd	
entrance	
existence	
exit	
independence	
lighting	
local	
misunderstand	
net	
observe	
overweight	
panic	
particular	
payment	
plug	
quality	
represent	
roof	
slim	
tease	
typhoon	
typical	
wake	
warmth	

한국어	영어
형 지역의	
동 (잠에서) 깨다, 일어나다	
형 과체중의, 비만의	
명 질, 품질, 특질	
명 조명	
형 특정한, 특별한	
명 총알	
동 던지다, (시선 등을) 보내다	
명 약속	
명 입구	
명 군중 동 (장소를) 메우다, 붐비다	
동 오해하다	
명 갈라진 금 동 갈라지다, 금이 가다	
명 존재	
명 온기, 따뜻함	
동 관찰하다, 보다	
명 태풍	
명 (갑작스러운) 공포, 공황	
동 놀리다, 못살게 하다	
명 지붕, 천장	
명 위기	
명 지불	
동 대표하다, 나타내다	
명 독립	
형 전형적인, 대표적인	
명 수레, 카트	
형 날씬한, 마른	
동 나가다, 퇴장하다 명 출구	
명 (전기) 플러그 동 막다	
명 그물	

Workbook

Day 22

| 월 일 |

영어 단어에 해당하는 한국어 뜻을 함께 적으세요.

attention	주의, 주목	attention	주의, 주목
elevator	엘리베이터, 승강기		
fairy	요정; 상상의		
invade	침략하다, 침공하다		
cancer	암		
native	출생지의, 원주민(의)		
disgust	역겨움, 혐오감		
debate	토론; 토론하다		
vain	헛된, 소용없는		
swear	맹세하다		
labor	노동(력)		
professional	전문적인, 직업의; 전문가, 전문직 종사자		
figure	수치, 인물		
option	선택, 선택권		
various	여러 가지의, 다양한		
measure	측정하다		
tropical	열대의, 열대 지방의		
smoke	연기; 담배를 피우다		
hard-working	열심히 일하는, 근면한		
semester	학기		
vehicle	탈 것, 차량		
awkward	(기분이) 어색한, 서투른		
stranger	낯선 사람, 처음인 사람		
blossom	꽃; 꽃이 피다		
selfish	이기적인		
brief	짧은, 간결한		
noisy	시끄러운		
set up	설립하다		
right	올바른, 옳은		
organize	준비하다, 조직하다		

다음 단어에 해당하는 영어 단어 또는 우리말을 쓰세요. O____개 X____개

영어	한국어
attention	
awkward	
blossom	
brief	
cancer	
debate	
disgust	
elevator	
fairy	
figure	
hard-working	
invade	
labor	
measure	
native	
noisy	
option	
organize	
professional	
right	
selfish	
semester	
set up	
smoke	
stranger	
swear	
tropical	
vain	
various	
vehicle	

한국어	영어
형 헛된, 소용없는	
형 (기분이) 어색한, 서투른	
형 이기적인	
동 맹세하다	
형 열심히 일하는, 근면한	
형 여러 가지의, 다양한	
명 꽃 동 꽃이 피다	
동 침략하다, 침공하다	
명 토론 동 토론하다	
명 연기 동 담배를 피우다	
명 요정 형 상상의	
명 선택, 선택권	
명 엘리베이터, 승강기	
형 짧은, 간결한	
명 낯선 사람, 처음인 사람	
명 수치, 인물	
동 측정하다	
명 암	
명 역겨움, 혐오감	
형 시끄러운	
형 출생지의, 원주민(의)	
동 탈 것, 차량	
명 주의, 주목	
형 열대의, 열대 지방의	
동 설립하다	
형 전문적인, 직업의 명 전문가, 전문직 종사자	
명 노동(력)	
명 학기	
동 준비하다, 조직하다	
형 올바른, 옳은	

Workbook

Day 23

| 월 일 |

영어 단어에 해당하는 한국어 뜻을 함께 적으세요.

imagination	상상, 상상력	imagination	상상, 상상력
transfer	이동하다, 환승하다		
border	국경, 경계지역		
demand	요구; 요구하다		
be tired of	~에 싫증이 나다, ~에 질리다		
row	열, 줄		
arrest	체포; 체포하다		
attractive	매력적인		
manager	경영자, 관리자		
reality	현실		
niece	조카딸		
compose	구성하다, 작곡하다		
prefer	선호하다		
salary	급여, 월급		
decline	감소하다, 쇠퇴하다; 감소, 쇠퇴		
general	일반적인		
organic	유기농의		
coast	해안		
stomach	위, 복부		
indeed	정말, 확실히		
progress	진전; 진보하다, 앞으로 나아가다		
greenhouse	온실		
skyscraper	고층 건물		
thrill	전율, 오싹함		
suitable	적절한, 알맞은		
instant	즉각적인; 순간		
fond	애정을 느끼는, 좋아하는		
dare	감히 ~하다		
beat	이기다		
slow down	늦추다		

다음 단어에 해당하는 영어 단어 또는 우리말을 쓰세요.　　O___개　X___개

영어	한국어
arrest	
attractive	
be tired of	
beat	
border	
coast	
compose	
dare	
decline	
demand	
fond	
general	
greenhouse	
imagination	
indeed	
instant	
manager	
niece	
organic	
prefer	
progress	
reality	
row	
salary	
skyscraper	
slow down	
stomach	
suitable	
thrill	
transfer	

한국어	영어
명 온실	
형 매력적인	
늦추다	
동 체포하다 명 체포	
명 감소, 쇠퇴 동 감소하다, 쇠퇴하다	
형 유기농의	
명 진전 동 진보하다, 앞으로 나아가다	
명 급여, 월급	
명 열, 줄	
동 이기다	
형 일반적인	
명 경영자, 관리자	
명 고층 건물	
동 요구하다 명 요구	
명 해안	
동 선호하다	
동 이동하다, 환승하다	
형 적절한, 알맞은	
~에 싫증이 나다, ~에 질리다	
명 위, 복부	
명 전율, 오싹함	
명 현실	
명 국경, 경계지역	
형 애정을 느끼는, 좋아하는	
형 즉각적인 명 순간	
명 조카딸	
부 정말, 확실히	
동 구성하다, 작곡하다	
동 감히 ~하다	
명 상상, 상상력	

Workbook

Day 24 | 월 일 |

영어 단어에 해당하는 한국어 뜻을 함께 적으세요.

emergency	비상	emergency	비상
seriously	심각하게, 진지하게		
force	힘; 억지로 ~하게 하다, 강요하다		
bloom	꽃; 꽃이 피다		
amusement	오락, 놀이		
direct	직접적인; 감독하다, 안내하다		
name	이름을 붙이다		
newborn	갓 난		
crowded	붐비는, 복잡한		
dirt	먼지, 때		
position	위치, 지위		
stand for	~을 나타내다		
eye-catching	단번에 눈길을 끄는		
swallow	삼키다		
collection	수집품, 소장품		
urban	도시의		
purse	지갑		
resident	주민, 거주자		
recreation	오락, 휴양, 레크리에이션		
part	~와 헤어지다		
bare	벌거벗은, 노출된		
honor	명예; 명예의		
get away with	~를 교묘히 모면하다, ~을 가지고 도망가다		
function	기능; 작동하다, 기능을 하다		
stream	개울, 시내		
thinker	사색가, 생각하는 사람		
treat	대하다, 치료하다		
moonlight	달빛		
pretend	~인 척 하다		
sprinkle	뿌리다		

다음 단어에 해당하는 영어 단어 또는 우리말을 쓰세요. O____개 X____개

영어	한국어
amusement	
bare	
bloom	
collection	
crowded	
direct	
dirt	
emergency	
eye-catching	
force	
function	
get away with	
honor	
moonlight	
name	
newborn	
part	
position	
pretend	
purse	
recreation	
resident	
seriously	
sprinkle	
stand for	
stream	
swallow	
thinker	
treat	
urban	

한국어	영어
명 오락, 놀이	
명 개울, 시내	
~을 나타내다	
부 심각하게, 진지하게	
형 벌거벗은, 노출된	
명 주민, 거주자	
명 힘 동 억지로 ~하게 하다, 강요하다	
명 오락, 휴양, 레크리에이션	
명 먼지, 때	
동 ~인 척 하다	
명 비상	
동 ~와 헤어지다	
명 기능 동 작동하다, 기능을 하다	
명 꽃 동 꽃이 피다	
명 지갑	
명 위치, 지위	
형 붐비는, 복잡한	
명 달빛	
형 단번에 눈길을 끄는	
명 사색가, 생각하는 사람	
형 갓 난	
동 삼키다	
동 이름을 붙이다	
명 명예 형 명예의	
~를 교묘히 모면하다, ~을 가지고 도망가다	
명 수집품, 소장품	
동 뿌리다	
동 대하다, 치료하다	
형 도시의	
형 직접적인 동 감독하다, 안내하다	

Workbook

Day 25

| 월 일 |

영어 단어에 해당하는 한국어 뜻을 함께 적으세요.

movement	움직임, 활동	movement	움직임, 활동
stir	젓다		
assign	배정하다, 할당하다		
bear	참다, 견디다		
crab	게		
obey	따르다, 순종하다		
dive	(물 속으로) 뛰어들다, 다이빙하다		
terrific	아주 멋진, 훌륭한		
direction	(위치, 이동의) 방향, 지시		
request	요청; 요청하다		
arise	생기다, 발생하다		
link	관련성, 연결		
scenery	경치, 풍경		
threaten	위협(협박)하다		
saying	말하기, 속담		
scale	규모, 범위, 등급		
nearby	가까운 곳의, 근처에		
wound	상처, 부상; 부상을 입히다		
injury	부상		
twist	꼬다, 비틀다, 삐다		
spot	점, 장소		
scissors	가위		
camping	야영, 캠핑		
awesome	감탄할만한, 무서운, 놀라운		
haircut	이발, 머리모양		
rapid	급격한, 빠른		
uneasy	불안한, 걱정되는		
forward	(위치가) 앞으로		
insert	넣다, 삽입하다		
sweep	~을 쓸다, 청소하다		

다음 단어에 해당하는 영어 단어 또는 우리말을 쓰세요.

O____개 X____개

영어	한국어
arise	
assign	
awesome	
bear	
camping	
crab	
direction	
dive	
forward	
haircut	
injury	
insert	
link	
movement	
nearby	
obey	
rapid	
request	
saying	
scale	
scenery	
scissors	
spot	
stir	
sweep	
terrific	
threaten	
twist	
uneasy	
wound	

한국어	영어
명 요청 동 요청하다	
명 부상	
동 젓다	
형 감탄할만한, 무서운, 놀라운	
명 말하기, 속담	
명 (위치, 이동의) 방향, 지시	
형 가까운 곳의, 근처에	
동 위협(협박)하다	
동 ~을 쓸다, 청소하다	
동 배정하다, 할당하다	
형 불안한, 걱정되는	
명 움직임, 활동	
명 가위	
동 생기다, 발생하다	
명 규모, 범위, 등급	
명 야영, 캠핑	
동 (물 속으로) 뛰어들다, 나이빙하나	
명 게	
명 점, 장소	
명 상처, 부상 동 부상을 입히다	
형 아주 멋진, 훌륭한	
부 (위치가) 앞으로	
동 참다, 견디다	
명 관련성, 연결	
형 급격한, 빠른	
동 따르다, 순종하다	
동 꼬다, 비틀다, 삐다	
동 넣다, 삽입하다	
명 경치, 풍경	
명 이발, 머리모양	

Workbook

Day 26

| 월 일 |

영어 단어에 해당하는 한국어 뜻을 함께 적으세요.

pattern	무늬, 양식	pattern	무늬, 양식
comfort	편안, 위로		
submit	제출하다		
seasoning	조미료, 양념		
paralyze	마비시키다		
virtual	사실상의, (컴퓨터를 이용한) 가상의		
yummy	아주 맛있는		
tidy	깔끔한, 잘 정돈된		
weekly	매주의, 주 1회의		
impress	감명을 주다		
select	고르다, 선택하다		
bucket	양동이, 물통		
dynasty	왕조, 왕가		
fitness	(신체적인) 건강, 신체단련		
memorize	암기하다		
attempt	시도; 시도하다		
ruin	망치다, 파괴하다; 파멸, 폐허		
globe	지구본, 지구, 세계		
salty	짭짤한, 소금이 든		
elect	선출하다		
oxygen	산소		
technology	기술		
by the way	그런데		
principal	주요한, 주된		
store	저장하다		
cheese	치즈		
subtract	빼다		
gargle	(물로) 양치질하다, 입을 헹구다		
overestimate	과대평가하다		
toss	(가볍게) 던지다		

다음 단어에 해당하는 영어 단어 또는 우리말을 쓰세요. O____개 X____개

영어	한국어
attempt	
bucket	
by the way	
cheese	
comfort	
dynasty	
elect	
fitness	
gargle	
globe	
impress	
memorize	
overestimate	
oxygen	
paralyze	
pattern	
principal	
ruin	
salty	
seasoning	
select	
store	
submit	
subtract	
technology	
tidy	
toss	
virtual	
weekly	
yummy	

한국어	영어
동 마비시키다	
명 조미료, 양념	
명 치즈	
명 시도 동 시도하다	
동 암기하다	
명 산소	
형 아주 맛있는	
명 파멸, 폐허 동 망치다, 파괴하다	
명 편안, 위로	
동 빼다	
명 (신체적인) 건강, 신체단련	
동 저장하다	
명 지구본, 지구, 세계	
동 제출하다	
동 (가볍게) 던지다	
형 깔끔한, 잘 정돈된	
형 짭짤한, 소금이 든	
명 왕조, 왕가	
형 사실상의, (컴퓨터를 이용한) 가상의	
그런데	
동 선출하다	
형 매주의, 주 1회의	
동 (물로) 양치질하다, 입을 헹구다	
동 감명을 주다	
명 무늬, 양식	
명 기술	
동 과대평가하다	
동 고르다, 선택하다	
형 주요한, 주된	
명 양동이, 물통	

Workbook

Day 27

| 월 일 |

영어 단어에 해당하는 한국어 뜻을 함께 적으세요.

foggy	안개가 낀	foggy	안개가 낀
scientific	과학적인, 과학의		
celebrate	축하하다		
poverty	가난, 빈곤		
fall in love	사랑에 빠지다		
weekday	평일		
grateful	고마워하는, 감사하는		
lip	입술		
supper	저녁		
aerobic	유산소의; 에어로빅		
carbon	탄소		
preface	서문		
microwave	전자레인지		
conquer	정복하다		
emit	내뿜다, 내다		
property	재산, 소유물		
wagon	4륜차, 마차, 수레		
emerge	나오다, 드러나다, 나타나다		
script	대본, 원고		
swing	흔들리다, 흔들다; 그네		
discipline	규율, 훈육; 훈육하다		
wireless	무선의		
crayon	크레용		
revolution	혁명		
paragraph	단락		
package	포장, 짐꾸리기, 소포		
waterfall	폭포		
clearly	뚜렷하게, 명확하게		
sponge	(해면,스펀지로) 몸, 얼굴을 닦다		
take over	인수하다, 인계받다		

다음 단어에 해당하는 영어 단어 또는 우리말을 쓰세요.

O____개 X____개

영어	한국어
aerobic	
carbon	
celebrate	
clearly	
conquer	
crayon	
discipline	
emerge	
emit	
fall in love	
foggy	
grateful	
lip	
microwave	
package	
paragraph	
poverty	
preface	
property	
revolution	
scientific	
script	
sponge	
supper	
swing	
take over	
wagon	
waterfall	
weekday	
wireless	

한국어	영어
명 4륜차, 마차, 수레	
명 전자레인지	
명 혁명	
명 서문	
명 재산, 소유물	
명 탄소	
사랑에 빠지다	
명 대본, 원고	
동 나오다, 드러나다, 나타나다	
명 평일	
동 축하하다	
명 크레용	
형 과학적인, 과학의	
명 규율, 훈육 동 훈육하다	
형 고마워하는, 감사하는	
명 폭포	
형 유산소의 명 에어로빅	
명 가난, 빈곤	
동 흔들리다, 흔들다 명 그네	
명 포장, 짐꾸리기, 소포	
명 입술	
부 뚜렷하게, 명확하게	
명 단락	
형 안개가 낀	
인수하다, 인계받다	
명 저녁	
동 (해면,스펀지로) 몸, 얼굴을 닦다	
동 내뿜다, 내다	
형 무선의	
동 정복하다	

Workbook

Day 28 | 월 일 |

영어 단어에 해당하는 한국어 뜻을 함께 적으세요.

performance	공연	performance	공연
victim	피해자, 희생자		
detective	형사, 탐정		
charm	매력		
strengthen	강화되다, 강력해지다		
bacon	베이컨		
climb	오르다, 올라가다		
slave	노예		
norm	규범, 표준		
adopt	입양하다, 채택하다		
apply	지원하다		
look down on	~을 내려다보다, 얕보다		
complex	복잡한		
encounter	~와 우연히 마주치다		
destiny	운명		
laboratory	실험실, 연구소		
intention	의도, 목적		
expert	전문가		
nutrient	영양소, 영양분		
satisfied	만족하는, 만족스러워하는		
nuclear	핵의, 원자력의		
put into practice	~을 실행하다		
inspect	조사하다, 검사하다		
genetic	유전의, 유전학의		
switch	전환되다, 바꾸다; 스위치		
realize	깨닫다, 실현하다		
arrow	화살		
mechanic	정비사		
in spite of	~에도 불구하고		
stool	(등받이가 없는) 의자, 스툴		

다음 단어에 해당하는 영어 단어 또는 우리말을 쓰세요.

O____개 X____개

영어	한국어
adopt	
apply	
arrow	
bacon	
charm	
climb	
complex	
destiny	
detective	
encounter	
expert	
genetic	
in spite of	
inspect (v)	
intention	
laboratory	
look down on	
mechanic	
norm	
nuclear	
nutrient	
put into practice	
realize	
satisfied	
slave	
stool	
strengthen	
switch	
victim	
performance	

한국어	영어
명 영양소, 영양분	
형 복잡한	
명 규범, 표준	
명 실험실, 연구소	
동 오르다, 올라가다	
명 화살	
명 피해자, 희생자	
동 조사하다, 검사하다	
명 형사, 탐정	
~을 실행하다	
동 깨닫다, 실현하다	
~을 내려다보다, 얕보다	
명 매력	
형 핵의, 원자력의	
동 강화되다, 강력해지다	
명 의도, 목적	
동 전환되다, 바꾸다 명 스위치	
동 ~와 우연히 마주치다	
명 노예	
~에도 불구하고	
명 베이컨	
명 전문가	
동 입양하다, 채택하다	
명 (등받이가 없는) 의자, 스툴	
명 정비사	
명 공연	
형 유전의, 유전학의	
동 지원하다	
명 운명	
형 만족하는, 만족스러워하는	

Workbook

Day 29

| 월 일 |

영어 단어에 해당하는 한국어 뜻을 함께 적으세요.

cabbage	양배추	cabbage	양배추
utilize	이용하다, 활용하다		
saw	톱질하다, 톱으로 자르다		
turn out	~인 것으로 드러나다, ~인 것으로 밝혀지다		
foundation	기초, 근거, 토대		
wag	흔들다		
commonly	흔히, 보통		
be worried about	~에 대해 걱정하다		
fold	접다		
beard	턱수염		
infant	유아, 아기; 유아의		
latest	(가장) 최근의, 최신의		
dedication	헌신, 전념		
pioneer	선구자, 개척자		
once in a while	가끔, 때때로		
compare	비교하다		
touch	감동시키다		
beast	짐승, 야수		
illegal	불법적인		
hopeless	희망이 없는		
preview	시사(회)		
growth	성장		
retire	은퇴하다		
dumb	어리석은, 말문이 막힌		
eyelid	눈꺼풀		
adapt	맞추다, 적응하다		
kneel	무릎을 꿇다		
litter	쓰레기		
long for	열망하다, 갈망하다		
marginal	미미한, 중요하지 않은		

다음 단어에 해당하는 영어 단어 또는 우리말을 쓰세요. O____개 X____개

영어	한국어
adapt	
be worried about	
beard	
beast	
cabbage	
commonly	
compare	
dedication	
dumb	
eyelid	
fold	
foundation	
growth	
hopeless	
illegal	
infant	
kneel	
latest	
litter	
long for	
marginal	
once in a while	
retire	
pioneer	
preview	
saw	
touch	
turn out	
utilize	
wag	

한국어	영어
~에 대해 걱정하다	
형 불법적인	
명 눈꺼풀	
동 열망하다, 갈망하다	
명 선구자, 개척자	
형 어리석은, 말문이 막힌	
~인 것으로 드러나다, ~인 것으로 밝혀지다	
부 흔히, 보통	
동 감동시키다	
명 턱수염	
동 이용하다, 활용하다	
명 짐승, 야수	
동 은퇴하다	
형 (가장) 최근의, 최신의	
명 양배추	
가끔, 때때로	
동 접다	
동 맞추다, 적응하다	
형 미미한, 중요하지 않은	
동 톱질하다, 톱으로 자르다	
형 희망이 없는	
동 비교하다	
명 유아, 아기 형 유아의	
명 기초, 근거, 토대	
명 시사(회)	
동 무릎을 꿇다	
동 흔들다	
명 쓰레기	
명 성장	
명 헌신, 전념	

Workbook

Day 30

| 월 일 |

영어 단어에 해당하는 한국어 뜻을 함께 적으세요.

critical	비판적인, 비난하는	critical	비판적인, 비난하는
evolve	전개시키다, 진화하다		
merchant	상인		
financial	재정적인		
imitate	모방하다, 흉내를 내다		
penalty	처벌, 형벌, 벌금		
poster	벽보, 포스터		
prevention	예방, 방지		
constant	끊임없는, 일정한		
alter	변경하다, 바꾸다		
cultural	문화의, 문화적인		
conclusion	결론		
atmosphere	대기, 공기		
policy	정책, 방침		
fame	명성		
electronic	전자의		
distinguish	구별하다		
establish	설립하다		
specific	특수한, 명백한		
informal	비공식의		
consume	쓰다, 소비하다		
potential	잠재적인; 가능성, 잠재력		
standard	기준, 수준		
greedy	탐욕스러운		
trial	시도		
receipt	영수증		
obvious	분명한, 명백한		
primary	주된, 주요한		
keep ~ing	계속해서 ~하다		
certainly	틀림없이, 분명히		

다음 단어에 해당하는 영어 단어 또는 우리말을 쓰세요. O___개 X___개

영어	한국어
alter	
atmosphere	
certainly	
conclusion	
constant	
consume	
critical	
cultural	
distinguish	
electronic	
establish	
evolve	
fame	
financial	
greedy	
imitate	
informal	
keep ~ing	
merchant	
obvious	
penalty	
policy	
poster	
potential	
prevention	
primary	
receipt	
specific	
standard	
trial	

한국어	영어
동 구별하다	
명 처벌, 형벌, 벌금	
형 탐욕스러운	
명 결론	
동 전개시키다, 진화하다	
부 틀림없이, 분명히	
형 비공식의	
형 재정적인	
형 문화의, 문화적인	
형 특수한, 명백한	
명 기준, 수준	
형 전자의	
형 끊임없는, 일정한	
형 비판적인, 비난하는	
명 영수증	
명 대기, 공기	
명 시도	
명 벽보, 포스터	
동 설립하다	
동 모방하다, 흉내를 내다	
형 주된, 주요한	
명 정책, 방침	
형 분명한, 명백한	
명 상인	
동 쓰다, 소비하다	
명 예방, 방지	
계속해서 ~하다	
명 명성	
형 잠재적인 명 가능성, 잠재력	
동 변경하다, 바꾸다	

memo

memo